HATED AND PROUD

— MARK DYAL —

HATED & PROUD

— ULTRAS CONTRA MODERNITY —

ARKTOS
LONDON 2018

Printed in the United Kingdom.

ISBN	978-1-912079-23-0 (Softcover)
	978-1-912079-24-7 (Hardback)
	978-1-912079-25-4 (Ebook)

| **EDITING** | Martin Locker |
| **COVER AND LAYOUT** | Tor Westman |

🌐 Arktos.com　　📘 fb.com/Arktos　　🐦 @arktosmedia　　📷 arktosmedia

CHAPTER SIX

Romanità and the Ultras   163

CHAPTER SEVEN

Globalization and Local Particularity   197

CHAPTER EIGHT

Circo Massimo and the Ultra War Against *Calcio Moderno* 232

CHAPTER NINE

Conclusion 268

AFTERWORD

Hated and Proud 289

Bibliography 316

Index 332

Acknowledgment and Dedication

This is a book that is still perhaps too close to my heart to be published, and it is certainly one that carries a unique burden. The Ultras, both those who are mentioned in this book and those who are not, do not take kindly to being represented or defined by those who do not inhabit their world. I did so once, and did everything I could to learn from them, and to respect their form of life. But even with that, the limitations of research and, in truth, my own Roman transformation made it impossible to include the vast multitude of unique and politically contrary viewpoints in *Curva Sud Roma*. All will admit that the Far Right was the dominant political force in the *Curva*, but it was never the only one. I could have just as easily focused on the radical Left, anarchists, socialists, or the various modernist-aesthetic groups that have carved out their own "derelict space" in the *Curva*. In other words, there is not one *Curva Sud Roma* but many. I merely chose the *Curva* that could be lived and studied on my own terms.

Furthermore, the Ultras absolutely despise anyone who seeks to profit from their actions, and while I do not expect a substantial profit from this book, I must assume that Arktos Media does. For my part, it fills me with dread that publishing this book would taint my time as a part of *Curva Sud Roma*. I only do so now because enough time has passed to make the information it contains rather useless to the State in its war of capture against free spaces like *Curva Sud Roma*, and because I feel that it can contribute on many other front lines to the Ultras' war against the homogenization and standardization that the liberal and neo-liberal State imposes upon its deracinated subjects.

I would like to thank Arktos Media for giving me the chance to share this story with the few radical souls who are able to embrace its message. The journey to publication was long, painful, confounding, and disappointing, but ultimately triumphant; and I sincerely and respectfully thank Daniel Friberg, Martin Locker, Tor Westman, and last but not least John Morgan for helping to bring this to fruition. None of us can create the noble life we envision alone; every triumph and defeat is collective and I am happy to share mine with you.

To have earned a Ph.D. and then, in the eyes of most (who have never read 'Schopenhauer as Educator'), to have thrown it away running around with a bunch of crazy extremists, is something about which I am at once regretful and prideful. I regret that the members of my Ph.D. committee didn't get the chance to welcome me into their fraternity after working so hard to help me become a scholar. Michael Blim, Jane Schneider, and Gerald Creed deserve all of the credit for my credentials and none of the blame for what I have done with them. That being said, I am proud that I as continue to negotiate the terrain that both conjoins and separates the American radical Left and extreme Right, I have encountered so many amazing people; none more so than Hugh Maguire, who's intelligence, comradery, and friendship justifies whatever price I end up paying for rejecting my inheritance.

To Lorenzo Contucci, Federico Esposito, my Ultra brothers and sisters who I continue to hold as deeply as possible in my heart, and to the other 'keepers of the faith,' I only ask your forgiveness for mythologizing or perhaps immortalizing *my Curva Sud*. I do so just as I lived amongst you: not to represent, but to experience and understand. As such, the *Curva* will forever be yours, but this story is mine: it couldn't have been written by anyone else. I admit to changing names of both individuals and groups when merited, and to committing the common anthropological sin of making the implicit perhaps a little bit too explicit, and to being astonished every day by the potential richness of the Ultras' critique of the contemporary world. In my defense, I will only ever say that; and that it was the Ultras themselves who taught me to love Nietzsche.

To the present generation of Ultras, I ask you to work together to protect the *Curva* from the influence of *il calcio moderno*; to continue to oppose the foreign regime that seeks absolutely nothing but the most vulgar of financial profits from both AS Roma and a thoroughly emasculated *Curva Sud Roma*; and above all, to protect and adore the city, people, and history of Rome.

This book is dedicated to my wife, without whom Rome would have been just a dream, to my son, in whose body flows the instincts and inspirations of the greatest heroes ever to fight for the Eternal City, and to *Curva Sud Roma: nessun mai t'amerà più di me.*

CHAPTER ONE

Ultras Contra Modernity

This is a book about war; the war that has been raging in the West since the first of us gave control, power, and sovereignty over life to someone else in order to live more comfortably and securely. Better yet, it is the war that has been raging since one of us learned about this inequitable exchange while watching his children suffer its consequences, and yet hadn't the courage to do anything about it. With brutal clarity and simplicity, Nietzsche called this war *Roma contra Judea*: the battle of a warring and violently noble form of life against the ideas *cum* forces that disarmed and recreated it as fodder for a marketplace of pious merchants and good citizens.[1] This book is a study of a small group of men and women in Rome, Italy, that are engaged in re-establishing something 'noble' about life. These men and women have stopped being pious, good, or anything else that their enemies demand of them. Sure, like all of us who speak about destroying what keeps us docile, they have an ambiguous relationship with their enemy: they despise their mother, as it were, but still snuggle up close to her and fall asleep every night.

---

1 Throughout the text I use form of life as an explicit reference to Nietzsche's use of the concept as inter-cultural and intra-cultural differences that are always at odds with one another; such as his understandings of noble and slave morality. See Chapter Five for greater explanation.

1

And yet they fight: with words, counter-ideas and concepts, with fists, bats, and sheer will. This is a book about how they have turned life into a fight against what so very many of us begrudgingly or fearfully accept. It is a book about Ultras; the extreme. Ultras are fanatical soccer fans, at least, that is how the media knows them. But what makes them extreme is neither the soccer nor the fandom, and that is what this book seeks to explain. As such, one may be disappointed that it is less forthcoming about certain fan-based Ultra behaviors, and certainly that it is grounded in radical political theory. Likewise, the distance between the years of study and the book's subsequent publication might seem a limitation, especially as so much has changed in the meantime — most notably the 2011 purchase of AS Roma by an American investment banker, and subsequent attempts to rid AS Roma fandom of the Ultras. But life is always in the meantime, in the middle, and if things have changed with Rome, the Ultras, soccer, political violence, and even the cuisine described herein, it is only thanks to the forces brought into the world by all that this book explains.

This book began its life as a thesis written in order to obtain a Ph.D. in Anthropology, but even in that form it was far from what the American Academy has come to demand of its best and brightest students. Instead of an objective study that could innocently claim to be compliant with contemporary moral standards and political subjectivities, it was a defiant defense of men and women who have been deemed indefensible by those very standards and subjectivities; and it was a document of my own 'becoming-Ultra.' 'Going native' is a relatively accepted process within Cultural Anthropology: firstly, because it takes a certain amount of empathy to live amongst a different people, dig into their dirt, and ultimately champion whatever it is that one might find therein; and secondly, because who in their right mind would spend thirty-something years being molded, organized, conditioned, nay *created* in academia, only to find something beautiful, exhilarating, majestically critical, and even festive in such horrible things as Fascism, Futurism, ethnocentrism, and violence?

That I did so, and did so without abandoning the margins of a still acceptable type of philosophy, political theory, and anthropology, still leaves me with a sense of wonder. Who knew that reading and *living* Nietzsche and Sorel in the shadow of an empire that had fallen to the power of *ideas* would be so transformative? Who knew what would happen when radically critical ideas were lived and embodied by violently unapologetic men and women? Who knew that standing together in defiance of the very core values and behaviors demanded of us by the State and its economically defined form of life would make every subsequent compromise with that form of life an act of degradation? And who knew that it was all there in 'Schopenhauer as Educator'; the path of my own becoming-useless to the world I inherited?

Of course, that I had so much fun and learned so many things while becoming indefensible, didn't make the Academy that I (reluctantly) rejoined after leaving Rome any more susceptible to accepting either my own thunderous process of self-overcoming and birthright ruination, or embarking on one of its own. However, at least it had an inkling of what I would and wouldn't do in the name of a career spent molding, organizing, conditioning, nay *creating* the next few generations of 'good' Western people.

And so, it is with this in mind that an occasional academic tone of voice and flourish of theoretical explanation still remains in this book; for it is as much a study of the mind breaking free from the functions of disciplinary words, ideas, and concepts, as it is an examination of Rome, Ultras, contemporary Fascism, morality, and belonging. Thus, it is still my intention that young scholars and thinkers who have been unthinkingly and enthusiastically herded into the Academy might find something useful herein. More so, however, it is hoped that they will read this book, be inspired to read thinkers far more valuable than myself, and then take to the streets prepared to overcome their own weakness in the face of tyranny. Or perhaps they will take to a stadium, for that is where I first met the Ultras.

My first encounter with Ultras happened on Saturday, 22 April 2006, at Rome's Olympic Stadium. My family and I were finally on a Roman holiday during the soccer season, and I forced our group to attend the

day's match between AS Roma and UC Sampdoria. As a proper, but necessarily deterritorialized,[2] fan of AS Roma, I was absolutely giddy with
the possibility of seeing the team play in Rome (pre-season games in New
York City, I would soon learn, were mere simulacra of the real thing).
Back in New York I had been active on message boards and did everything I could to watch or follow games. One of my undying memories of
September 11, 2001 is that Roma were to play Real Madrid in the UEFA
Champions League, a game to be shown live on ESPN; although the game
was played, ESPN's sportscasters were too busy discussing the day's events
to air it. I bought countless jerseys, shirts, sweatshirts, and anything else
I could find emblazoned with AS Roma's shield. I was, in the parlance of
both capitalism and Italian soccer, a 'good fan.'

Figure 1. *Curva Sud* wishing Rome a happy birthday, April 22, 2006.

2   Cornel Sandvoss (2003) uses deterritorialization to denote a detachment of social,
     cultural, political, and economic life from specific locales. It is this meaning, rather
     than the Deleuzian opening up of existing relations to new potentialities, that I have
     in mind here.

So, one can imagine my pride as I settled into my swanky chair-backed seat in the *Monte Mario* grand stand, surrounded by the well dressed and well-mannered elite of good soccer fandom in Rome; and then … and then it all turned upside down. The Ultras began their festival, April 22, 2006, one day removed from the 2,759th birthday of Rome, and suddenly I was no longer in America, or Italy, but instead within two sections partitioned by eight-foot Plexiglas walls of the *Curva Sud,* the southern end of the stadium that is home to AS Roma's Ultras. Looking back, it's hard to believe I was only a few short months away from discovering just how *far,* in fact, I remained from the *Curva,* from knowing that the distance between *Curva Sud* and *Monte Mario* was equivalent to the distance between Achilles and the guy taking orders at Popeye's Fried Chicken. But that Sunday, I felt only that I had made it; that I was home.

During the game, as the good fans surrounding me clapped and cheered politely, the Ultras sang defiant and devotional offerings to Rome and AS Roma, waved flags in the shared *giallorosso* (red and yellow) colors of both, and held aloft emergency flares and smoke bombs that burned in the same colors as their flags. At various points, they displayed homemade banners throughout the *Curva.* None of this related very much to the on-field action of the day. That no one scored for AS Roma seemed not to dampen the Ultras' enthusiasm. Nor did it matter that no one else in the stadium joined in their songs, flag waving, or any other exhibited behaviors. They stood and cheered on their team from the opening to closing whistle, resting only during the twenty-minute halftime break.

All of this action took place behind a fortress of long banners, each of which displayed the name of a particular group. More than a *curva* of thousands acting in unison, what was happening instead was several groups of approximately one hundred persons each singing as a group — their group. It was evident that each person holding an emergency flare did so as a member of his or her unique group, as these were not universal in the *Curva,* but only in front of or near a group banner. Similarly, the songs were begun by one group and then spread through the *Curva,* becoming more widely audible. And, as one looked more closely, the flags being waved, while sharing the colors of AS Roma and the city of Rome, more often than not glorified the group over which it was being waved.

This encounter with the Ultras mirrors that of most persons, whether as soccer fans (rival or compatriot), journalists, or academics. It notes the most obvious aspects of their behavior: aesthetics, performance, and organization. I had known of the Ultras for some time before encountering them in person: I had heard them on game broadcasts and read about their exploits in newspapers — most of which painted a picture of violent thuggery, hatred for the police, and of soccer games being reduced to general mayhem. Interestingly, it was largely along these lines that the other good fans on the message boards discussed the Ultras, when they mentioned them at all. But even as a good academic American, with credentials including an advanced degree in African-American and African Studies, who was in the process of joining one of the most influential Marxist-based Anthropology programs in the country, there was always something about the Ultras, specifically *Curva Sud Roma*, that enchanted me; that perhaps gave me a premonition of the possibility of *another form of life* — and I wanted to know why and how they did what they did.

But it wasn't until an innocent conversation with Professor Jane Schneider — several years after their behaviors caught my attention — in which I explained that a soccer game had been stopped by Ultras in Rome, that it dawned on me that I could actually go to Rome and find out.[3] And what I discovered, explained in the pages that follow, is that there exists in this world men and women of a certain type that instinctually and willfully fail to conform to the norms, subjectivities, and moralities of the bourgeois form of life; and that, in their freedom — or dereliction — they are no longer affected by prohibitions against violence, moralities of altruistic inclusiveness, or the reduction of life to an economic rationality.

What is more, I discovered that in order to explain these men to the world — in ethnographic terms — I would have to abandon the very same norms, subjectivities, and moralities of the bourgeois form of life. These

---

3   Beyond meeting my eventual wife and partner in crime, that brief discussion with
     Professor Schneider is perhaps the most important few minutes of my life.

two currents intersect to form the ferocious spirit of this book — a spirit that could be called ontological and epistemological, if both of these terms could in fact be separated. For indeed, the ethnographic story that follows seeks to demonstrate above all else the impossibility of the one without the other. Before we get to that, however (and in order to make this clearer), we must meet the Ultras and some of the concepts they use to create their festive, violent, and derelict form of life.

The most visible aspect of the Ultras is their various ritualized behaviors relating to the attendance of soccer matches: the singing of songs for their city and team and against those of their opponents, waving of flags of city and team, performing large choreographed displays of sometimes remarkable complexity and beauty, lighting of emergency flares and powerful bombs, and displaying homemade banners with various messages intended for opponents, contiguous fans, and the broader public.

If the aesthetic elements of the Ultras are their most visible and superficial, given that most who experience the Ultras from afar delve no deeper than their in-stadium performances, then my search for the 'how and why' of the Ultras' behaviors demanded another approach. Understanding the Ultra phenomenon in aesthetic terms of carnival, ritual, performance, and fandom is at best partial, and leaves us wondering how to explain the full set of behaviors witnessed on the evening of February 2, 2007, when police officer Fillipo Raciti was killed during rioting after a game between Catania and Palermo. That evening the Catania Ultras targeted the forces of the State's law and order and engaged them in a relatively contained but deadly guerilla skirmish.

Nor do the Ultra aesthetics, as symbolically violent as they may be, allow one to expect the larger, but less deadly, war against the State, law and order, and the business of soccer, witnessed in Rome, Milan, and Bergamo following the police killing of Gabriele Sandri on November 11, 2007. Both of these killings brought to light the relationships between the Roman Ultras and the hegemony of the State and media, and between the Ultras and a political-philosophical discourse of radical and Counter-Enlightenment ideas.

In essence, I had to move from fandom and the carnivalesque aesthetics to deadly guerilla attacks on armed representatives of the liberal State. The trail that connects these two phenomena is clearly marked, however, assuming that one can read the signs that the Ultras leave throughout their cities. For instance, in Rome the Ultras marked a wall with graffiti reading, 'Enough immigrants, homes and work for Italians,' and signed the message *AS Roma Ultras* (thus taking credit for the sentiment *as Ultras*).

Figure 2. *AS Roma Ultras* graffiti: 'Enough immigrants, homes and work for Italians.' Vicolo del Lupo, Rome, 2007.

Taking up Giulianotti's challenge to study soccer in host communities and in the subjective terms through which it is locally known, during fifteen months of anthropological fieldwork I came to understand the Ultras who support AS Roma not as impassioned fans who occasionally take part in the political process as members of a politically liberal society, but rather as an extremely political counter-modern cultural movement which aims to restore communal, spiritual, and ritual dimensions to modern life. They seek to do so by challenging the political, ideological, and aesthetic processes of global-market capitalism, which — through global consumerism, cultural and political pluralism, and individualism — threatens to destroy the particularity of Roman cultural forms.

After the death of Raciti in February 2007, many commentators were quick to label the perpetrators of violence as delinquents out only to cause trouble and commit anti-social behavior. Even those who tried to defend the Ultras were unwilling or unable to see what happened as part of a larger project, or as part of a counter-modern conceptual system. Professor Vincenzo Abbantanuono likened the Ultras to the 'disaffected' French youth who burned the Parisian suburbs in the autumn of 2005. These were people, he said, who acted without a 'political conscience.'[4]

We are left to wonder at his reaction to the news that the young man accused of killing Officer Raciti was a middle-class member of the Fascist party *Forza Nuova*, who had worked hard the previous summer to have a Gay Pride parade cancelled in Catania. Elsewhere, in Civitavecchia, an interesting piece of Ultra graffiti relating to the Catania violence was found. '2-2-2007 Vendetta for Carlo Giuliani,' it read, referring to the protestor killed at the 27th G8 Summit in Genova in 2001.[5]

The details of the Raciti killing reveal that the Ultras' violence, in this case against the State, is not perpetrated without a political conscience. Roversi and Balestri (2002) have shown that the Ultras were politicized in the 1990s, even beyond their original class-based political forms. Actual mob-and-political violence aside, what this book seeks to understand is how these politicized Ultras use their respective ideologies to create, maintain, and elevate their rivalries, understandings of Italian soccer and social life. In other words, my work understands, like Antonio Gramsci, that all aspects of human experience are political and involve the creation of knowledges (narratives) and counter-knowledges.

The political concerns of AS Roma's Ultras *as Ultras* are ambivalently related to contemporary Fascism's most popular parties, *CasaPound Italia*, *Fiamma Tricolore* and *Forza Nuova*. While the issues that concern these

---

4   Quoted on RAI News, February 3, 2007.

5   *La Repubblica*, Friday, February 9, 2007. Sec. B, p. 2.

Ultras are certainly important to these parties, my research demonstrates that the large majority of Ultras have become devoted to these concerns without the intervention of organized Fascism. The issues I have in mind range from the political (such as immigration and international trade) to the metapolitical (such as rights-based movements, cultural protection, and sovereignty). The link to Fascism is clouded further by the highly philosophical nature of their own political agenda against the business of soccer and its links to the neoliberal State. Thus, the ambivalence of the relationship between organized party-based Fascism and the Ultras is such that the latter can be considered more of a cultural than a political movement. As such, it has more in common with New Right political philosophy than with political Fascism.[6] In other words, the politics of the Ultras is ultimately less concerned with the political *qua politics* than with how fascist-inspired political ideas shape their vision of Rome, the AS Roma soccer team, and themselves.

Because of this, in no way can the influence of the Right on AS Roma's Ultras be seen as deriving from an invasion by the Far Right parties, as others have argued.[7] Instead, fieldwork demonstrated that the Ultras harbor and utilize a moral and ethical system that generates its own political orientation. If some are Fascists it is because of the common elements that exist between the Ultras and Fascism — most notably *squadrismo* (organization and activities in the form of paramilitary groups): an ethic of violence that celebrates engagement and aggression, pageantry as a form of political action, and a harsh critique of modernity.[8]

Griffin's *Modernism and Fascism* continues the earlier analysis of Emilio Gentile that showed that, while Fascism was a Modernist force due to its modernizing, it was informed by an attack on modernity itself. The question for Fascism was, then, what form of modernity was it to create? While modernizing and attaching itself to Futurism and its vision of speed, industry, efficiency, and power, Fascism also promoted agrarianism,

---

6   Bar-On, 2007, pp. 6–25.

7   Dal Lago and De Biasi, 2002; De Biasi and Lanfranchi, 1997; Podaliri and Balestri, 1998.

8   Griffin, 2007, p. 181.

autarchy, and the celebration of Italian folkways. It was devoted on the one hand to increasing industrial output, and to using international warfare as a means of masculinizing populations, but on the other hand to a philosophical anti-materialism and hostility to political liberalism. Furthermore, Sternhell argues that while Fascism maintained capitalism as an economic model it was horrified, via Nietzsche, of modern bourgeois values such as universalism, individualism, progress, natural rights, and equality.[9]

According to Griffin, Gentile, and Sternhell, this contradiction was born not only from the material limitations of early-20th century Italy but also from the ideological and philosophical influences of Fascism. These influences, in the persons of Nietzsche, Ernst Junger, Ezra Pound, Gabriele d'Annunzio (and, for Hitler, Benito Mussolini), are now termed as part of the Counter-Enlightenment tradition.[10] These thinkers, amongst others, similarly influence today's Ultras of AS Roma, who are themselves committed to challenging the hegemony of the current state of modernity — be it understood as post-modernity, hyper-modernity, or globalized-market capitalism. Thus, I argue that they, like Fascism itself, are counter-to-modern, even if neither is pastoral in outlook.

Franco Ferraresi has studied the post-war Right in Italy and concluded that, although the Far Right is often in organizational disarray, Counter-Enlightenment thought is still popular there, as are the Counter-Enlightenment philosophical traditions of Friedrich Nietzsche and Julius Evola. This thought carries with it, in his words, 'nationalism, chauvinism, ethnocentrism, and xenophobia ... frequently couched in the terms of rescuing original identities [that are] threatened by the encroachment of ... globalization [and] the Americanization of culture.'[11]

Within the political activities and ideas of the Ultras we find precisely these elements of Counter-Enlightenment thought. It was Ferraresi's work that prompted me to focus on the ideological elements of Ultra behavior.

---

9   Sternhell, 1994, pp. 7–8.

10   Wolin, 2004.

11   Ferraresi, 1996, p. 56.

Knowing from scholarship on the Ultras that the political Right became popular amongst them during the same late-1990s period in which Ferraresi was studying the Italian Far Right, I immediately began searching for intersections between the ideology of the one within the other. The most obvious common links between the Ultras and the Far Right, as well as between Ferraresi's and my analysis, are Nietzsche and Evola, both of which feature prominently in this book. However, where Ferraresi and I diverge is in his assumption that the only youth manifestation of Rightist ideology is the skinheads, of which Italy is largely bereft.[12]

Ultras Defined, Including Key Concepts

As I have already demonstrated, the Ultras are misunderstood if seen as merely impassioned fans that occasionally, as members of a politically liberal society, take part in the political process. When defining the phenomenon, then, one cannot overlook the political nature of how they conceive and perceive themselves, nor the pageantry and beauty of their public displays in and around Italian (and European) stadiums. The problems others encounter when attempting to understand the Ultras occur largely because they tend to separate the aesthetic from the political. When one combines them, however, and refuses to see them as distinct parts of the Ultras' conception and behavior, who they are and why they do what they do becomes clearer.

In realigning aesthetics and the political, this book seeks to understand the relations among mental images, philosophical/historical ideas, and aesthetic principles that express themselves in public rituals and representations.[13] Thus it will at once collapse the division between spiritual and material, being inclined to search for the micro-historical and micro-political relations between thought and language. The relations between class, status, and political participation — while also relevant to

---

12   Ferraresi, 1996, p. 201.

13   Fugo, 2003, p. 19.

the material consequences of the spiritual thrust of the Ultra 'form of life,' — will be a secondary focus.

Although I am very comfortable with this kind of approach, I feel that the Ultras themselves prompted the methodology I used. The Ultras live as what Victor Turner called 'social anti-structures', because they have withdrawn symbolically and actually from the larger community in order to fully embrace their 'signal mark of identity.'[14] While they are aware of who they are and what is their historical and cultural mission — the terms of which, as will be explained, come largely from Fascism, Futurism, and political philosophers like Nietzsche, Sorel, and Le Bon, who were all highly critical of modernity — their political focus is largely 'ritual and cultish.' Politics of this kind are not only interested in transforming society, but in doing so strictly within the terms of the cosmological myths that buttress the phenomenon in question. This focus on the political from the perspective of the symbolic challenges the division between real (material, power-oriented) elements and symbolic (a sign-driven 'language' constructive of identities) elements, seeing instead a continuum of change and action that simultaneously engages our emotional and instinctual centers.[15]

Therefore the focus of inquiry duly shifts, from the actual workings of liberal politics, per se, to an understanding of the intellectual and ideational background of a system of politics and its 'reality making' function, not in a neo-Marxist way to connote a mode of deception whereby the ruling class stays in power, but as a system of knowledge (or controlling concepts and theories) that does not merely describe but creates reality.[16] The distinction between politics and political ideology, then, is rendered artificial. The categories 'overlap, interpenetrate, and feed from each other, exchange, transform into one another.'[17] This is especially important in Italy, where politics becomes a marker of identity in highly personal

---

14   Turner, 1979, p. 48.

15   Kertzer, 1988, p. 4; Kertzer, 1996.

16   Pronger, 2002.

17   Schechner, 1988, p. 197.

ways, bleeding into other areas of life seemingly unrelated to the political system.[18]

Having provided the reader with explanation of the methodological assumptions I hold about politics, narrative, and human behavior, I will now turn to defining four of the major concepts of this project: *Calcio Moderno*; *mentalità*; Ultras; and agonistic, or oppositional form of life.

Calcio Moderno, A Brief Overview

Calcio Moderno (Modern Soccer) is perhaps the most important concept used by the Ultras at this particular time — not only because it ties their self-interests to international manifestations of resistance to globalization, but because it incorporates the other important concepts identified above. It is used throughout the book to denote the postmodernization of fandom and the sports experience, the focus of which has shifted toward the cultivation of global markets at the expense of local communities. It also refers to the business of soccer, including the clubs, international federations (such as FIFA and UEFA), the media, and the system of club owners and player transfers (trades). Thus, *Calcio Moderno* provides the view of globalization held by the Ultras, through which they come to equate anything harmful to themselves, the Ultras phenomenon, or AS Roma, as being equally harmful to Rome and its local culture and traditions.

Mentalità: A Poetic Ideology

I will use a particular (maybe peculiar) vocabulary to discuss the ways in which the Ultras understand, and interact with, their environment. Anthropology has developed a number of strategies for explaining this problem. The term 'ideology' is still the most popular way of denoting a system of logic that impacts in some way upon reality. Already, in 1973, Clifford Geertz saw fit to perform a genealogy of ideology; such was the term's overuse. Marx popularized the concept in negative terms, as a bourgeois 'discursive sheet' laid atop the reality of proletarian suffering

---

18   Kertzer, 1996.

and need for unity.[19] Biologist James Danielli uses 'ideology' but to denote 'the discursive practices which institute each human society's field of consciousness.'[20] The idea of an order of consciousness as part of a cultural system is perhaps still best explained by Evans-Pritchard, for he shows that the Azande[21] exist within a symbolically coded system of representation by which consciousness is inscribed. This system, as he says, is 'the very texture of ... thought.'[22] The idea of 'texture of thought' moves us closer to how 'ideology' will be used in this study. Geertz correctly critiqued the term as inexact and suffering from a lack of value. However, his idea of a cultural system as a 'web of meaning' seems closer to how recent scholarship uses 'ideology.'[23]

A critical thinker in 2016 experiences 'ideology' differently than did previous generations. Verily, we do so not even as 'ideology.' This is because of the success and popularity of Bourdieu's 'habitus' and Foucault's 'episteme' as variations on 'ideology.' Habitus names the categories through which we interact with the world. It is 'a system of acquired dispositions functioning ... as categories of perception and assessment.'[24] Foucault's 'episteme,' in contrast to 'habitus,' is less focused on the body and the material conditions of existence. Instead, it is explained succinctly as an 'order of knowledge' and a 'general grammar', consisting of language and structures of power (both political and discursive) that create the very 'conditions of possibility of existence.'[25]

Even where ideology is used, it is understood as a system through which power and ideas collide. Eric Wolf offers a rich critique of our 'metaphysical' tendency to, on the one hand, acknowledge the cultural

---

19   Hoberman, 1984, p. 17.

20   1980, pp. 87–94.

21   Editor's note: The Azande are an ethnic group living primarily in the northeast Congo, southwest/south central Sudan, and the southeast Central African Republic.

22   Evans-Pritchard, 1976, p. 222.

23   Geertz, 1973, p. 124.

24   Brownell, 1995, p. 17.

25   Foucault, 1970, p. xxiv.

nature of conception, without, on the other hand, seeking to understand the consequences of conception upon culture.[26] Culture-specific ideologies, he explains, may share a function — to 'orient society to act within the field of its [society's] operations,' but they are unique in form, logic, rationale, and effect. Thus, we must seek to pull back our gaze and incorporate into ideology's purposes the 'material resources and organizational arrangements' of the world being affected.[27]

Similarly, Antonio Gramsci accentuated the active nature of thought in his understanding of ideology. He understood ideas to be the moving force of culture, but not at the expense of the material or oppositional forces also at play within a society. The class impact on ideas and ideology, he explains, is so pervasive that the lower, or 'subaltern' classes, only come to self-consciousness by way of a series of negations of the class power and identity of their ruling class enemies.[28] In this way, Gramsci left no distance between the availability of self-consciousness and the possibility of class warfare, as well as theorizing the power central to all workings of culture.

Later scholars also sought a liberatory model of idea formation. Sylvia Wynter uses 'episteme' as an alternative to 'ideology' because it lends itself to an understanding of each culture's specific 'system of symbolic representation,' or 'mode of subjective understanding.' However, even as she searches for clarity and power from concepts, she also uses Fanon's 'sociogeny' or 'sociogenic principle' to explain culture-specific behavior-orienting criteria.[29] Both Wynter and Fanon stress the creation of knowledge inherent in ideology and central to all cultures. They do so not to understand this process on its terms but to connect it with the failings of modernity to provide an ecumenical basis of knowing the human species. As such, they point to a deeper understanding of the role of concepts and ethics in cultural processes.

---

26   Eric Wolf, 1999, pp. 279–283.

27   Wolf, 1999, p. 280.

28   Crehan, 2002, pp. 99–104.

29   Fanon, 1967, pp. 2–14; Wynter, 1995, pp. 5–57.

Similarly, Allan Young maintains the discursive theme in describing the 'practices, technologies, and narratives ... of various interests, institutions, and moral arguments' constitutive of reality.[30] Paul Kroskrity goes further, but also resorts to using 'ideology' in explaining the 'language ideologies' that 'represent the perception of language and discourse that is constructed in the interest of a specific social or cultural group.' This includes 'notions of what is 'true,' 'morally good,' or 'aesthetically pleasing.'[31] What these scholars point to is a methodology that accounts for the reality-producing power of knowledge. But, as I hope to make clear, so do the subjects of this study.

Fascism and the Problem of Morality in Social Science

The Ultras of AS Roma not only speak about a *mentalità* and a form of life disconnected from, and at odds with, the modernity of the liberal global-market, but they act upon this disconnection. In acting, they express a deep and conscious commitment to the ideas and ideals around which they cohere.

For instance, I passed an evening with a small group of Ultras discussing the *arditi* and their relation to the *Brigate Nere* (Black Brigades — Special Forces of the Italian Social Republic [RSI] at the end of WWII). Aside from the oddity (from the perspective of an American) of a group of young men (each younger than thirty) casually discussing an obscure history, the scene was valuable because they spoke both with reverence and an understanding that in these soldiers there was a model of proper contemporary behavior.

This was furthered by their attempts to equate themselves with the *arditi* and *Brigate Nere*. 'The Ultras,' said Massimiliano, 'are today scorned like the *arditi* after the First World War — and demonized like the fighters of *Salò* [alternate name for the RSI]. It is only right, though, because we all

---

30   Allan Young, 1995, p. 5.

31   Kroskrity, 2000, p. 8.

wanted the same things.' Among the romantic list of common desires was 'to live according to values — bravery, strength in the face of any opposition, and brotherhood.' Eventually, the conversation became less solemn and concluded with the participants celebrating their identity as '*bastardi neri*' (black bastards, or hard men).

After leaving the bar, I witnessed these Ultras holler mild insults at African purse sellers packing away their sack of merchandise for the evening. If I witnessed, or more importantly, noted and described, only the insults — which asked the Africans to do something more substantial (*significativo*) with their lives (and to do so away from Rome) — or worse, chose to disconnect them from the evening's discussion, it would be a lot easier to dismiss them as racists and xenophobes. While using terms and concepts that encapsulate a wide variety of behaviors, like *mentalità* and agonistic culture, I also tried to move away from terms like racism or xenophobia, because these tend to mask the motivation and even humanity of those so labeled.

Instead, as is apparent from this vignette, the subjects of this study forced me to understand the moral aspect of creating social science. Most of the respondents to my questionnaires consider themselves to be Fascists. Indeed, the 'air one breathes' amongst the Ultras is thick with the memory, examples, and folklore of the Fascist period. Recent scholarship on Fascism has rehabilitated the phenomenon as a valuable subject of study, but there are still consequences of the moral and political aversions to the phenomenon, including misleading accounts of policy and personalities. RJB Bosworth is praised for his biography of Mussolini and his history of Mussolini's Italy, yet the latter text is littered with words like 'wicked,' 'evil,' 'intrusive,' 'racist,' 'henchmen,' 'corrupt,' 'lies,' 'neurotic,' and 'gullible.'[32]

Carlo Ginzburg has shown that micro-histories, with a greatly reduced scale of observation, allow one to challenge the 'polarizations between social and cultural history, [and] analysis and narrative.' Micro-histories focus on individual cultural acts, events, or reproductions,

---

32   Bosworth, 2005, pp. 4–5.

thereby repositioning macro-historical studies and, in the case of Fascism, their moralizing tendencies. Though I do not resort to micro-history, the method does lend itself to understanding the relationship between words and grammar — or experience and its narrative structures.[33]

Like Ginzburg, I use the sources that my subjects use to describe and explain themselves. Alas, these sources, like Fascism, are all morally and politically tainted. Though Nietzsche, Sorel, Le Bon, and Evola are attacked for lacking a commitment to a liberal democratic or egalitarian social order, they are popular in Ultra circles. It is fitting, then, that Ultra ideas and vocabulary be used to explain aspects of Ultra behavior and thought.

Mentalità and Myth

Having presented the need for a 'poetic' usage of ideology, we may now turn to the reason for the previous diversion: the *mentalità* of the Ultras. Like ideology, *mentalità* connotes many things. *Mentalità* translates normally as mentality, but it can also denote a cultural worldview, so as to extend beyond the individual mind-set that it denotes in English. The Ultras — who use the word perhaps more consistently than any other when discussing the world and themselves — mean it in this broader sense. Hence, the way it is defined here is important. Before doing so, I want to briefly discuss how the Ultras use *mentalità*. I will then turn to the basis of my thinking of a definition. This comes not only from those who study Weltanschauung but also consciousness, narrative, and myth

Mentalità is most commonly used by the Ultras as an explanation of what makes them different from others. Usually, the 'others' in question are the bourgeois fans glorified by the Italian media as 'real' or 'true' soccer fans, or the bourgeoisie in general. The distance between the Ultras and the bourgeoisie is guaranteed by behavior — violence, aggression, and extreme commitment to rivalry and hostility; but also, according to Pasquale, a longtime Ultra, honor, commitment, and 'unfailing

---

33   Ginzburg and Poni, 1991, p. 8.

steadfastness' (*fermezza*). However, the Ultras explain their own commitment to these behaviors as a product of *mentalità*. This is an important
element of the Ultras phenomenon because the majority of Ultras could
be classified economically as bourgeois; yet they speak of the bourgeoisie
as living a life that is empty and fatuous. That they do not live such a life
is, again, a product of their *mentalità*.

Figure 3. *Curva Sud* greets the world at large, 2007.

It is also interesting that the Ultras use *mentalità* as an explanation of their
difference from others, as the concept is common amongst Italians as a
way to understand, not only individual personalities, but also social and
political aggregates as well. For instance, while one may possess a *mentalità infantile* (childish outlook) or *mentalità chiusa* (closed-mind), there is
also the possibility of a *mentalità dei popoli latini* (Latin worldview). It is
commonly said, pejoratively, that a *mentalità del Sud* (Southern personal-
ity/form of life/culture/mentality) may explain the underdevelopment of
the southern Italian regions.

When used to discuss social and political aggregates, it seems the larger the aggregate, the more negative becomes the *mentalità* said to be in use. For example, both Barzini (1996) and De Martino (2005) posit the existence of something peculiar to Italy, Italians, or certain Italians. Barzini's text is, in essence, a list of features of the Italian *mentalità* — almost all of them negative and parochial. Moe (2002) studied the creation of the Southern Question — the idea that the south is somehow culturally and morally different from the rest of Italy — and, in the end, explains that foreign authors discerned a spiritual difference between Italians and other Europeans (of the north and west).

Conversely, the *mentalità* of townspeople, political parties, or phenomena like the Ultras, is usually discussed as the basis of extremely positive co-identification. In Rome, the Roman *mentalità* was given as rationale for a refusal to eat peanut butter. When presented with the decidedly American sandwich spread, a friend in Monteverde, the neighborhood in which I lived, declined a taste on the grounds that, 'it is not part of our *mentalità* to eat something like that.' Returning to the Ultras, *mentalità* was most commonly invoked during games away from Rome — or in discussing these games — when engaging with opposing Ultras. 'The thirst for feelings of raw electricity,' I was told by Stefano, a forty-one-year-old Ultra of the group *Monteverde*, 'is something particular to the Ultras. You either have it or you do not; and those who do not would never do what we do. Our *mentalità* seeks these encounters.'

It is important to understand how diffused amongst AS Roma's Ultras is this idea of *mentalità* as something that promotes aggression, violence, and a defensive posture toward a variety of foes. Every Ultra I encountered in Rome spoke of the Ultras as, if nothing else, completely and utterly different from others. On the occasions when *mentalità* was invoked, it was consistently presented as the basis of that difference. Often it seemed that what the Ultras meant was an earned credibility, or honor, in the sense of Campbell's (1964) understanding of how threats confer manliness in honor-based societies. We might think of it thus as a spirit — as a common indicator of responsibility and expectation. However, *mentalità* was also given as an indescribable sensation of connectedness to other *AS Roma Ultras* created during important AS Roma games, as if one could sense *mentalità* in the air. In this way, the *mentalità* could incorporate the tension and hostility with the elation and camaraderie — sensations of the heart — felt during and after games.

One can see that their usage of the concept leaves us unable to codify it in any meaningful sense. To the American reader, it might seem that culture is a good translation and way towards understanding *mentalità*. However, it too becomes just a metaphor when faced with the wide range of usages of *mentalità*. This confusion is compounded by the fact that many of these same Ultras only use culture to connote physical/material goods and cuisines. Otherwise, *mentalità* was used. Therefore, I created my own definition of *mentalità* drawn from its usages and features. I will begin the discussion of that definition with myth.

Augustine described consciousness as a process of 'expectation, attention, and memory:' 'the future, which [the mind] expects, passes through the present, to which it attends, into the past, which it remembers.'[34] As Kirsten Hastrup explains, through memory of the past and anticipation of the future we use cultural symbols and institutions to create a bridge between these two and the present. In the present, action and experience meet.[35]

This connection of past, present, and future is critical to the way the in which Ultras engage the life experience. Like others, they use narrative to weave a 'conscious self,' but they do so with great emphasis on myth, martyrs/heroes, brotherhood, and place.[36] Therefore the construction of personal meaning is an especially conscious process amongst the Ultras, particularly given the collective and public nature of the 'language,' myths, or narratives used.[37]

---

34   Saint Augustine, 1961, p. 277.

35   Hastrup, 1995.

36   Rose, 1997, pp. 224–248.

37   Rapport, 1998, pp. 81–101.

Myth is central to the Ultras' *mentalità*. How it is used lends itself to being studied from the perspectives of the anthropological pillars on myth: Durkheim, Malinowski, and Levi-Strauss. Myth, according to Durkheim, strengthens social cohesion and unity by inscribing norms of social order, via ritual and ritualized institutional behavior. Malinowski focused instead on the value of myth, especially as a tool in the legitimation of a particular social structure, thus connecting myth with power, morality, and social mores. Levi-Strauss searched for meaning not in the narratives of myth but in their subconscious structure, thus understanding myth as an objective, universal mode of thought. Together, these three approaches all offer insights into the purpose and functioning of myth in the Ultra *mentalità*.[38] That it is cohesive and constructive of distinction between groups, that it is connected to morality and has value in justifying social structure, and that it operates as a self-standing phenomenon will all become clear in the chapters that follow.

The Ultra *mentalità* operates as an ideal against modern liberal market-driven understandings and expectations of the human. The myths that the Ultras are the only bastion of purity left in Italian soccer, and that they are the 'keepers of the faith,' on guard against the victory of *Calcio Moderno*, motivate them to critique consumerism as a goal and, more importantly, to seek to establish or maintain structures, in the form of both Ultra groups and political organizations, that undermine the democratic and egalitarian foundations of the liberal State. Nietzsche urged the pursuit of a life in which myth acted to offset modernity's 'common-currency humans' and absence of mystery.[39] He attacked the modern life in which the utilitarian pursuit of money and career had defeated the heroic life spent in creative and dangerous pursuits of nobility and honor. Likewise, Sorel understood myth as a 'supra-ordinate goal,' the foundation of motivation and action.[40] He explains that the collapse of myth (as motivator of behavior) in the modern world has contributed to the victory of a limited

---

38 Durkheim, 2001; Malinowski, 1992; Levi-Strauss, 1990.

39 Nietzsche, 2004, p. 36.

40 Sorel, 1999, p. 20.

historical outlook (with no belief in glory) and atomistic individualism (with no understanding of or desire for collective greatness).[41] The Ultras understand myth, as do Nietzsche and Sorel, as a goal and a motivating force to a very particular form of life that is aggressive, violent, and martial.

Mentalità Defined

Moving beyond an understanding of *mentalità* that is limited to an individual's outlook, I stress its connections with consciousness or *Weltanschauung*. I do so because *mentalità* provides not only an impetus to behavior but also an orientation toward behavior. Geertz differentiates *Weltanschauung* from ethos in order to distinguish cognition from evaluation.[42]

Weltanschauung refers to the picture of the actual social conditions of a group — 'their concept of nature, self, and society' — while ethos is the group's moral-ethical, aesthetic, and evaluative structures.[43] This division occurs at the level of culture and it ensures cultural stability, assuming the *Weltanschauung* is an accurate representation of the culture's ethos. If one takes the division of *Weltanschauung* and ethos as a given, then I am proposing, based on the strong ethical content in much Ultra behavior, that through *mentalità* they are rejoined.

The ethical component of *mentalità* must be stressed. As the Ultras construct what I call an agonistic form of life, in which all social relations reflect a will to opposition and rivalry, they also develop an emic personality that revels in the distance between themselves and others. Thus, their character clearly reflects the milieu in which it is formed. The tension between the Ultras and the larger social context with which they must interact in order to attend soccer games, and crucially, in which they are judged, impacts the ethical content of their *mentalità*. In other

---

41   Sorel, 1999, p. 27.

42   Geertz, 1973, pp. 126–127.

43   Geertz, 1973, p. 127.

words, there is reciprocity between State and media power and the Ultras' *mentalità*.[44]

Seeing themselves as largely outside the State, or as a pure critique of the Italian State, the Ultras often seem a contained universe where the discourse of strength and honor interact with a will to violence and rivalry. Upon closer inspection, however, it becomes clear that the content of the *mentalità* is a response, or counter, to the power of the State to impact upon the freedoms of the Ultras. With the advent of new bureaucratic means of excluding the Ultras from soccer games, their feelings of repression have never been more pronounced. Thus, they possess a seething bitterness toward the State and the forces of law and order. Additionally, however, the State and media have the power to morally condemn the Ultras and, until the wide availability of Internet access and cell phones, to control information and public discourse about them.

When the State prohibits the Ultras from attending games they find other spaces to watch or participate, be they spaces of consumption or of protest. In some cases, Ultras would watch AS Roma play in bars or in homes. Following the prohibition against fans in certain stadiums enacted after the death of Raciti, Ultras traveled to these same stadiums to protest against the restriction of personal freedom in Italy, but from the outside. The tendency amongst the Ultras of AS Roma is to subvert State repression by restricting their in-stadium performances and at the same time aggregating in smaller numbers in alternative spaces.

When the hegemony of the State is displayed through the creation and dissemination of a moralist discourse of Ultra criminality, the Ultras incorporate such discourses into the content of their *mentalità*.[45] This makes the relationship between the Ultras and the media complex and dynamic. Although the Ultras embrace an agonistic form of life, the terms of their 'agon' — conceptual and violent oppositions and a sense of worth correlated to how deeply one is aggressive and oppositional — are brought home only by how thoroughly they are condemned by the media. Thus, as

---

44 Wolf, 1999, pp. 252–257.

45 Wolf, 1999, pp. 44–45.

the media attacks the Ultras for being too violent and focused on rivalry, the Ultras respond with even higher levels of hostility. Similarly, the media uses a highly moralistic language to condemn the Ultras. This language in turn is central to the Ultra *mentalità*. Because of this fluidity, the media's discourse often matches that of the Ultras week-to-week. Further, this keeps the *mentalità* relevant and active for the Ultras because the world condemns them on the same terms in which they condemn the world.

Thus, I define *mentalità* as a systemic narrative of beliefs, attitudes, and values that motivates behavior and provides a particular moral-ethical orientation to behavior. It links the present to past and future through myths and cultural symbols that enable groups to cohere and construct distinctions between them and others.

Much of what constitutes the *mentalità* of today's Ultras comes from Italian political history: namely, Fascism, and the other counter-modern movements that either contributed to, or coexisted with, Fascism. Thus, it has taken as its own the intellectual components of these prior movements. Like the Fascists, the Ultras maintain a desire toward strength, honor, discipline, order, valor, heroism, memory, and tradition. Like Fascism and Futurism, they also celebrate war and a militarism that consists of warrior attributes. At the level of their *mentalità* and political motivations, the Ultras harbor a vision of the future and a strong critique of modernity. At the level of their culture there is a desire to embrace the mythic and spiritual dimension of life — a life built on communal and spiritual principles: a life with a clear *nonos*.

Like *mentalità*, which is used by all strata of Italian society, the Ultras' use of honor connects them to other Italian and Mediterranean forms of life. Despite the fact that honor is as varied in its uses throughout the Mediterranean as is *mentalità* in Italy, anthropology made it the basis of the creation of the Mediterranean cultural area. Peristiany identified an ideal of honor operating in the majority of Mediterranean cultures that is pursued at the expense of material advantage. At a civilizational level, this contributed to economic underdevelopment and material backwardness. On a personal level, honor is a virtue — *the virtue* even — but one that is functional only within an environment of competition and competitive-ness. Individuals assert themselves against others, co-identified as equal protagonists, in a system of honor and dishonor. Peristiany understands honor as a moral sentiment but also as a 'fact of repute and precedence,' attesting to its systemic nature.[46]

Although I assert below that the Ultras possess an agonistic form of life, which also connects them with a concept central to the creation of a southern or Mediterranean anthropology, I do so only as a metaphor for a life defined by rivalry and hostility, which puts them at odds with the prevailing form of modern life in contemporary Italy. I have taken the concept from Friedrich Nietzsche and intend it to be used as a point of distinction from what Gianni Vattimo calls the contemporary 'neutraliza-tion of culture and politics.'[47]

Likewise, here, I discuss honor not as a characteristic given the Ultras by a metaphysical Mediterraneanism, but as part of a set of behaviors they have taken from Fascism and Counter-Enlightenment philosophy. Indeed, while honor as I have just presented it fits perfectly within the Ultras' rejection of capitalism and *Calcio Moderno* (the business of soccer) for the sake of something more primordial, it is possible that the Fascists were also influenced by honor in a Mediterranean context. However, if, as Herzfeld explains, poetics must be locally contextual, I have relied upon the Ultras' own discussions of honor (within a system of other traits dis-cussed at length below) in placing it so prominently in this study. In other words, while it may be demonstrable as a Mediterranean character trait, it is unquestionably central to Fascism and its critique of modernity.

For the Ultras, *mentalità* is their proof of having a deeper agenda than just being 'delinquents' or 'fans.' It is used as a guiding structural principle, much as anthropologists use 'culture.' And, like culture itself, *mentalità* is the ground of reality — as I said above, both ethos and Weltanschauung. It is not only the 'why' that drives their behavior in a grand scale but a set of ethical values that also acts as a break on behavior. It is, in effect, the

---

46 Peristiany, 1965, pp. 1–11.

47 Vattimo, 2011, p. 174.

'content of their character.' Through *mentalità,* an Ultra can be shown to act in accordance with 'being Ultra' or not. Thus, without a commitment to the *mentalità,* according to the Ultras, one is simply not an Ultra.

Ultras Defined

Taking all of this into consideration, the political and ethical components of the Ultra phenomenon, the depth of the symbolic field that animates their public spectacles, and even the particular elements of their general history, I define the Ultras as a type of fan organization originating in the late-1960s that brings, along with carnivalesque behaviors with flags, banners, choreographed displays, flares, bombs, and a catalogue of songs of various levels of devotion and scorn: a high level of social and political thought and action is put into the act of fandom.

The Ultras often understand themselves, as do I, as a movement, an ideology, and/or a culture that seeks to restore communal, spiritual, and ritual dimensions to modern life. They seek to do so by challenging the political, ideological, and aesthetic processes of modern industrial culture, which, through global consumerism, cultural and political pluralism, and individualism, threaten to destroy the particularity and uniqueness of Italian (and in the case of AS Roma's Ultras, Roman) cultural forms.

The Ultras are a social phenomenon. They aggregate in groups ranging from three to five people to as many as 2,000. Despite the myriad divisions between the groups, which often lead to conflict and strife within the Ultras, there is no impetus to enter the *Curva* or go to away games alone. Soccer provides the context for the Ultra phenomenon for reasons that are unclear. According to Roversi, the leading scholar of Ultra origins, the Ultras began in the *curvas* because those who formed the original groups were already there.[48] That the *AS Roma Ultra* groups have maintained their connections to *Curva Sud* is mainly because of the bleeding of the AS Roma soccer team into an idealization of the city and its history.

---

48   Roversi, 1994, p. 360.

Of course, each generation of Ultras has been fans of the game and the team. However, just being fans opens them to other avenues of consuming the game and team that do not involve the sacrifices, dangers, and discipline of the Ultras. Hence, there must be another seduction of the Ultras beyond the game itself. I understand that other seduction to be the *mentalità* and the ethical opposition to the modern bourgeois form of life. To wit, as the State has become more hostile to Ultra in-stadium behaviors we are finding groups — *Padroni di Casa* is one — that are willing to aggregate as Ultras but to operate primarily beyond the in-stadium milieu that has defined the Ultras up-to-now.

The Ultras can be categorized as a movement form of what Roger Griffin calls 'political modernism,' in as much as they seek an 'alternative modernity and temporality' (a limited social order in open revolt against the values of modern liberalism) that is incompatible with liberal conceptions of the human and society.[49]

Agonistic Form of Life

In the aftermath of the February 2007 game and riot in Catania, Palermo manager Francesco Guidolin complained that the Catania fans had created the atmosphere of a 'war zone.' Dal Lago and De Biasi identified 'war' as the most dominant metaphor in the Ultras *mentalità*.[50] The Ultras' self-understanding is produced by an ever-present system of antagonisms. Rivalries between and within town, region, geopolitical boundary, political affiliation or ideology, and historical rivalry form the basis of the Ultra involvement with soccer, so much so that it is nearly impossible for them to engage with the game without the presence of one of these forms of opposition. I conceptualize these as 'natural oppositions' because they are components of Ultra interaction with soccer that can potentially only involve other Ultras. The Ultra oppositions to the media and the State I

---

49 Griffin, 2007, pp. 181 and 201.

50 Dal Lago and De Biasi, 1994, p. 85.

think of as 'meta-natural', because they address the larger political issues of the Ultra war against *Calcio Moderno*.

In his essay 'Homer's Contest,' Friedrich Nietzsche explains that the Greeks lived a life of 'combat and victory' in which warring competition, and pleasure in victory, was acknowledged; they even colored their ethical concepts like *eris*. To battle was a means of salvation, not just for one's people or city but also against the very chaos of the natural world.

However, for contemporary scholars of 'agonistic pluralism,' a deconstructionist theoretical movement that seeks to explain the irreducibility of difference in democratic societies, the enemy is largely we ourselves. Agonism for these scholars, such as Samuel Chambers, Bonnie Honig, and Chantal Mouffe, does not apply to the foundations or possibilities of greatness of a cultural system, as posited Nietzsche, but instead to the nature of democracy which is pluralist and designed to maximize debate.[51]

Where agonistic pluralism seeks a mutually affirming, largely discursive struggle between multicultural or political combatants, Nietzsche understands the agonist to actually compete or fight in order to elevate his self-status, and the status of the protagonist's city at the expense of others. For AS Roma's Ultras, pluralism is impossibility. Their commitment to agon is so deep that there is scant possibility of unity within their own *curva*, let alone amongst Ultras representing other teams and cities.

While the agonism of the Ultras contains elements of both the Nietzschean and pluralist understandings of agon, the Nietzschean is central to the Ultra phenomenon. They understand themselves as agonists who fight for the honor of their city, their team, their *curva*, and their group. They compete during games through songs, banners, and choreographed displays for a sense of pride and victory that is felt just as strongly as the victories gained on the soccer field or in the streets through fighting.

However, as *Calcio Moderno*, the idea and system of an industry of soccer that places the utmost importance on profits and revenues, has begun to be the hegemonic conception of the game in Italy, the Ultras have been forced to limit themselves to a form of agon which is closer to

---

51   Chambers, 2001; Honig, 1993; Mouffe, 2005.

the 'moralistic' option offered by pluralism. In the post-Raciti world of soccer, insulting banners or songs now lead to games being played behind closed doors. Game-related violence, which was virtually non-policed until Raciti's death, now leads to time in jail.

The new social barriers to Ultra agonism have done nothing to limit the oppositional nature of their mentality and self-understanding, however. 'Being an Ultra,' I was told by Massimo, a former member of the fascist group *Monteverde*, 'is embracing rivalry, hostility, and *Romanità* (extreme attachment to Rome and things Roman). Without these, one is not an Ultra [of AS Roma].'

Agon and Altruism

Agon is an important way to begin to understand the Ultras because of the way it connects with their extremely limited modes of altruism. It was often put to me that 'Roman culture was the most beautiful in Italy,' but that foreigners and foreign influence were diluting the culture. This understanding of political and social forces working to promote the degradation of Roman 'traditional life' was uncovered as well by Michael Herzfeld as he studied the impact of gentrification on the Monti neighborhood of Rome.[52] I was repeatedly told that the Romans must do something to protect themselves from dilution. Given statements like this, I was pressed to understand the implications of having such a narrow, protected, and antagonistic sense of self or inclusion.

If, as Sunic and others have argued, the altruism of liberal globalization is driven by a morality of total inclusion, wherein the universalization of man is made complete in a global marketplace, then the altruism of the Ultras can be described as one of exclusion, exclusivity, and local particularity.[53] Their inter-altruistic co-identification is exaggeratedly restricted. And, I am suggesting, their narrow boundaries between 'us and them'

---

52   Herzfeld, 2009.

53   de Benoist and Champetier, 2000, pp. 40–41; Sedgwick, 2004, p. 100; Sunic, 2007, pp. 5–8.

are related to their aggressive and militarist morality. The Ultras not only utilize a highly-moralized critique of modernity but one that is rich with the words of Counter-Enlightenment thinkers like Nietzsche and Evola. They blame cultural degeneration on the values celebrated by liberalism. As Evola explained, 'what is needed is a new radical front with clear boundaries between friend and foe. The future does not belong to those of crumbling and hybrid ideas but those of radicalism — the radicalism of absolute negations and majestic affirmations.'[54]

Natural Oppositions

AS Roma's Ultras utilize history, geography, and politics to create an ever-evolving system of rivalries. Their closest rival is SS Lazio, the second team of Rome. Only three other Italian cities (Turin, Milan, and Genova) are home to more than one high-level soccer club. The clubs in each of these share one another as their central rivals. However, the more interesting aspects of hostility formation occur beyond intra-city rivalry.

AC Milan is the most hated enemy of AS Roma's Ultras, SS Lazio aside. This is because of the killing of Roman Ultra Antonio De Falchi by his AC Milan counterparts outside Milan's San Siro stadium in 1989. Since his death, AS Roma's Ultras dedicate their fandom and aggression to De Falchi each time the two teams meet.

Somewhat more abstractly than killings between *curvas*, AS Roma's Ultras maintain rivalries based on Roman and Italian history. One of the most bitter, if rarely contested, given the small stature of the team involved, was with AC Perugia. The rivalry with the small (now defunct) Umbrian team stemmed from a centuries old rivalry between the two cities, as Perugia stood on the fringes of Roman dominion for most of its early history. Similarly, the Ultras share a common hatred with AC Fiorentina of Florence because of that city's status as a Guelph stronghold during the late-Middle Ages, when the rival Ghibellines led the Pope's enemies in Rome. For the same reason, there is rivalry with Genoa FC

---

54   Evola, 2002, p. 113.

of Genova. Modern political history has given a deeply felt hatred to the games contested between AS Roma and both Atalanta BC of Bergamo and Brescia Calcio of Brescia. These rivalries are based on the rise of the *Lega* phenomenon and its opposition to Rome as capital and symbol of Italian corruption. Meanwhile, AS Roma's Ultras share a special rivalry with the South's other large club, SSC Napoli of Naples, as discussed in later chapters. To AS Roma's Ultras, SSC Napoli is the 'team of the South,' a region stereotyped for poverty, underdevelopment, and organized crime (see Schneider, 1998).

Finally, politics proper is a common motivator of Ultra rivalry. AS Roma's Ultras tend toward the Far Right politically and thus are aggressively opposed to *curvas* that gravitate in the opposite direction. The main example of a Leftist *curva* in Italy is the *Curva Nord* of AC Livorno's Ultras. Like the rivalry with SSC Napoli (and with Naples in general), this one will be discussed at length below, but it is notable here as a rivalry which is felt only by the Ultras. There is no rivalry between the teams, as AC Livorno only rarely plays in *Serie A*, out of which AS Roma has only spent one season. When the two teams do play, the opposing *curvas* more closely resemble extreme political rallies than groups of soccer fans. Before the post-Raciti crackdown, AS Roma's Ultras would display numerous Nazi flags, neo-Fascist celtic cross banners, and banners with various anti-communist messages. Lately, Roman Salutes and chants of *Duce* have replaced these.

Meta-Natural Oppositions

The Ultras' soccer rivalries I have labeled 'natural' because they 'make sense' within the world of soccer. One could argue — as do many of the Leftists within *Curva Sud Roma* — that political rivalries are unnatural to the Ultras; but it is difficult to examine the history of the Ultras and not conclude that political affiliations have played a role from the beginning. Furthermore, while the political warfare between the Far Left and Far Right can explode into violence in any Italian city at any moment, I found it unlikely that AS Roma's Fascist Ultras would travel to Livorno to engage its communist Ultras unless a game was also taking place.

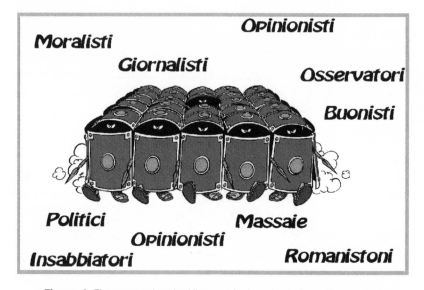

Figure 4. Flyer portraying the Ultras as legionaries in formation against their enemies, 2008.

In contrast to these oppositions we must also be aware of the hostility that exists between the State, the press, and the Ultras. These oppositions I have labeled meta-natural because they exist beyond the natural soccer related rivalries, but also because they offer a commentary on the natural rivalries as well. As I explained above, the Ultras' *mentalità* contains an ethical critique of modern bourgeois life. It presents itself, and the Ultras' form of life, as an oppositional cultural model guided by commitments to strength, honor, aggression, brotherhood, and spiritualism. But it also presents itself as an opposing model of virtue that is created by action, occasional violence, shared exhilarating/traumatic experiences, and courage. I found these characteristics to have been imported into the Ultras by group leaders influenced by Fascism, Roman history, and the political philosophy of Nietzsche, Evola, and Sorel. However, I also found that the

Ultras celebrated these characteristics most often after the media and the State had attacked them for having them.

There is a correlation of power between the Ultras and the State and media. This power is not only political but also moral, as the hegemonic media is — for all but the Ultras themselves — able to control the discourse and the terms of debate on the Ultras. Apart from bemoaning the criminality of the Ultras, the media uses a moralistic language to condemn the Ultras as 'delinquent animals' who engage in barbaric behavior attached to a misguided and misplaced sense of rivalry. The media is helped in this by spectacular newsreel footage of the Ultras violently engaging one another and the police. Before returning to the criminalization of the Ultra phenomenon, I must turn to the hostilities between the State and the Ultras.

From the perspective of AS Roma's Ultras, the State is ambiguous. Even for the fascists, the State is not the goal of Fascism's redemptive powers but only the city of Rome. The Ultras with whom I conversed for hours about Nietzsche's critique of liberalism, Evola's reconceptualization of *Romanità*, and Sorel's understanding of the role of political violence never moved their arguments to the Italian State. However, if one was asked who or what is the greatest threat to the Ultras and their form of life, the answer would be quick and consistent: the police (usually referred to as *la guardia*, the guard, or *l'infame*, the infamous) or *Calcio Moderno*. Demonstrating a shrewd understanding of the subservience of the liberal State to economic interests, the Ultras understood the police principally as the guardians of the business interests of soccer, and of the State only by extension. Similarly, the Ultras seek to make life difficult for global capitalism, in the form of advertising, foreign investment, and commoditization, associated with soccer. By extension, though, they understand the State to represent the same interests, so that the State is subsumed as well into *Calcio Moderno*.

That being said, there is true hostility between the Ultras and the forces of law and order. This hostility pre-exists the killings of 2007, reaching back to the mid-1990s and the turn to the Right of many of Italy's *curvas*.[55] Giorgio Agamben has provided an enlightening way to understand this hostility and the relations between the Ultras and the State, arguing that liberal States are able to utilize what he calls a 'state of exception' or state of emergency to diminish individual rights in order to strengthen the security of the State. I argue that such a state of exception is the normal context of interaction between the Ultras and the State. Each Ultra is under suspicion and surveillance (as CCTV systems are required in Italy's stadiums) and each game is militarized with hundreds of riot police in highly visible formation. One of my most vivid fieldwork memories is of State Police officers sitting atop a mini-tank complete with machine-gun turret outside the guest section of Florence's *Artemio Franchi* stadium. I was forced to wonder what the Ultras would have had to do for them to open fire.

For most citizens of liberal states, the State's power is largely internalized. Policing is not simply an act of repression but one of complementary exchange. The goals of the State are merged with those of the (bourgeois) citizen. Thus, the prosperity of one is grounded in adherence to the ideals and, in the words of Schmitt, friend-enemy relations of the other.[56] The night of Sandri's murder saw Ultras in Rome attack police stations in addition to the offices of the Italian Olympic Committee. In response, members of Romano Prodi's government labeled the Ultras 'terrorists' who were seeking to wrest control of the State. This language was buttressed by the condemnations of journalists and, in turn, by non-Ultra Italians with whom I interacted daily. The highly moral language used by the media, when analyzed in this light, is perfectly suited not only to demonize the Ultras, but also to present them as beyond the moral and political responsibility of the State.

---

55   Podaliri and Balestri, 1998, p. 89.

56   Crehan, 2002, p. 100.

Calcio Moderno Revisited

Earlier I spoke of *Calcio Moderno* as the idea and system of an industry of soccer. It is better understood as the postmodernization of fandom and commoditization of soccer. *Calcio Moderno* acts as one of the most important signposts in the world of the Ultras. It is an organizing principle that has no peer in their worldview, and as such it interacts with their world in a variety of ways.[57] Most importantly for the scope of this book is its relationship with the rise amongst the Ultras of a discourse of counter-globalization.

The concept itself began as a critique of the industrialization of soccer in the late-1990s, as the Ultras feared that the game was becoming a malleable form of entertainment rather than a deeply ingrained manifestation of local cultures. Similarly, they feared that the game was becoming a nexus of multinational corporations that would reduce it to a vehicle for selling advertising.[58]

As their fears began to be realized, opposition to *Calcio Moderno* became a counter-ideology to globalization. The Ultras believe that television audiences and the revenues generated by advertising are more highly valued by clubs than local fan support; and that fans are now understood merely as consumers. Indeed, American-style merchandising is openly touted by FIFA and UEFA as a progressive generator of income for the clubs under their jurisdiction. While the sporting aspects of *Calcio Moderno* are worrying enough for the Ultras — including the creation of worldwide fan bases and the power of television executives to determine game times — it is more so the sterilization and standardization promoted by *Calcio Moderno* on which the Ultras have declared war.[59]

This aspect of the discourse of *Calcio Moderno*, and even globalization, is perhaps the most active but also most elusive. The Ultras declare themselves *non omologati* (non-standardized) and seek to negate what they see as the encroachment of a foreign, corporate friendly morality of

---

57 Podaliri and Balestri, 1998, p. 98.

58 McGill, 2001, p. 29.

59 Sandvoss, 2003.

inclusion, tolerance (of racial, sexual, ethnic difference), and multiculturalism. While the Italian media attacks the Ultras for existing beyond the
bounds of this morality, the Ultras counter-attack by accusing the media
of attacking them *only* because they are beyond bourgeois liberal morality.

Figure 5. 'No to Modern Soccer,' the basis of an ethical life, 2007.

The idea of protecting the game and those with whom it is entwined (the
Ultras themselves) from processes of globalization and liberalization is an
important aspect of Ultra life. *Calcio Moderno* motivates behaviors that
center on protecting the sport from forces that would divorce it from its
local particularities. And, because the sport, clubs, and cities in which they
take place are conflated within Ultra thought, I argue that their behaviors,
by extension, are designed to protect their cities from the destructive
standardization of globalization.

Conclusion

Even from this introduction to the theoretical and philosophical assumptions at the heart of this book, it should be clear that the Ultras are far more than mere soccer fans or hooligans, and that they offer men and women on the extreme edges of liberal modernity an example of the great potentials for a non-bourgeois life open to each of us. Thus, this book will ultimately have more in common with surveys of political extremism, extreme political ideologies and counter-modernity, the imposition of globalization upon indigenous populations, and the rise of a Western television-based monoculture, than with studies of sports spectators. That being said, however, it is hoped that men and women who only wish to support their soccer team of choice will take some of the extremism herein to heart, and make something beautiful, violent, and derelict of their fandom.

CHAPTER TWO

The Everyday Life of the Ultras

In the coming chapters, the most important elements of the Ultras will come into focus, including their relationships with violence, Fascism, and Counter-Enlightenment political philosophy. This chapter will instead present the more mundane aspects of the Ultra experience: namely, the game-attending experiences. Based on what we already know of the Ultras and their in-stadium behaviors, it might seem incongruous to describe game attendance as mundane. But, given the unpredictability of so much of the beyond-the-stadium life of the Ultras — the involvement of soccer-and-State-related authorities in their activities and the extreme nature of their political activities — going to a game often appears as the most normal activity in their lives.

The chapter will be divided between Ultra experiences before, during, and after games away from Rome, and in their home stadium. I will present a detailed account of an away game to Palermo so that one may know exactly what goes on when Ultras travel for hours to see AS Roma play, and in order to explain why doing so is important to the Ultras. Then, I will present the reader with game experiences in Rome's Olympic Stadium.

Even a writer as quantitatively focused as Antonio Roversi has acknowledged that 'war' is the principle metaphor in the Ultras' self-understanding.[1] Dal Lago agreed with this idea and applied it to the in-game theatrics of the Ultras. His study, *Descrizione di Una Battaglia*, treats these theatrics as part of a larger cultural milieu in which symbolic plasticity and the movability of signs (such as the decontextualized political symbols adopted by the Ultras) bring the Ultras closer to the 'festival' described by Georges Bataille.[2]

Simply put, Bataille's 'festival' is an event in which prohibitions are transgressed and servility is contested, thereby limiting the distance between the profane and the sacred or forbidden aspects of human life. The festival is often violent, and transgressions seemingly verge on the animalistic. When the festival, or moment of transgression, is completed, the boundary between the profane and sacred is shattered, thus giving life a deeper and richer course.[3]

According to Dal Lago, the Ultras understand soccer as a world strictly divided between friend and foe, and matches as a series of ritualized, and symbolic, confrontations between foes. The stadium, it follows, is transformed into a setting for these 'festive' confrontations. I say 'festive' because Dal Lago implies that this takes place in a 'liminal zone' in which the overweening order of profane life is momentarily cast off, allowing the Ultras to discharge the frustrations inherent in that life.[4]

While maintaining the central thrust of Bataille's understanding of the festival as a moment in which the forbidden is achieved and thereby enriches the experience of life, I question Dal Lago's assumptions that this moment takes place in a location wherein Ultras leave behind, or unchain themselves from, their 'daily' or profane lives.

Instead, my research shows that the Ultras are Ultras because of an exaggeration, rather than a transcendence, of the cultural systems that

---

1   Roversi, 1990, p. 70.

2   Dal Lago, *Battaglia*.

3   Bataille, 1997, p. 251.

4   Dal Lago, 1990, p. 143.

make up 'profane existence.' In other words, the rivalries and oppositions that fill soccer with meaning for the Ultras are brought into the stadium from other arenas, be they political, mythical, geographical, or historical. It is their willingness to live every day according to these rivalries that ultimately makes them Ultras and not just highly interested fans. Thus, we should not be surprised, as was John Foot, that two of the *AS Roma Ultras* arrested for getting the 2003–4 SS Lazio-AS Roma game suspended at halftime worked as a 'cameraman and a financial consultant.'[5]

Nevertheless, there is value in using Victor Turner's theoretical con-structions of 'the liminal' to explain Ultra behavior. Certainly, the away game experience acts as a rite of passage through which an Ultra comes to be ultra. More than liminality, though, it is the idea of *communitas* made popular by Victor Turner that best explains something about the Ultras. *Communitas* is a form of 'social anti-structure' through which persons who share biology, culture, or even extreme personal experience unite in opposition to the larger social structure to which they, nominally at least, belong.[6] The Ultras' use of war, as an example of what I am calling their agonistic culture (as I will demonstrate below and in Chapter Five), is the basis of their *communitas*. The extreme behaviors they share give them a rationale for severely limiting the scope of their altruistic horizons.

It is with this in mind that we now move to a description of Ultra behaviors before, during, and after away games. It is away from Rome that AS Roma's Ultras are best able to play-out one of the central tropes of war, and the Ultra phenomenon: redemption through struggle and sacrifice.

The *Trasferta* (away game)

One of the simplest but most common areas of Ultra behavior in which sacrifice is a guiding principle is their devotion to traveling long distances and to overcoming all obstacles to witness and participate in AS Roma's games. One accrues special status among the Ultras if seen in the guest

5   Foot, 2006, p. 307.

6   Turner, 1979, pp. 237–238.

sections of stadiums far from Rome. For example, at the end of the 2006–2007 season, AS Roma played a practically meaningless game at Palermo. Because the team's final standing in the championship was essentially already determined, there was no 'sporting' reason to go to the game. However, for the Ultras it was an important opportunity to sacrifice and, more importantly, to suffer for the colors of the team and city.

After years of following AS Roma away from Rome, the experience of doing so acquires a certain rhythm. The following sections describe some of the most important or meaningful aspects of the away game experience. Rightly, it begins the week before a game and the search for tickets. It continues through the travel to and arrival at the stadium and concludes with the game and return to Rome.

Buying Tickets

Every away game begins the week prior with a hunt for tickets. Before the Amato Decree, a set of laws passed in the days following the February 2007 death of Officer Raciti which severely restrict the actions of the Ultras, those in the groups that received tickets directly from AS Roma merely reported to their leader or leadership council their desire to attend the game. Otherwise, one needed only go to an official AS Roma store with a ticket office to buy away game tickets. Even as identification papers were required, so that each ticket holder's name could be printed on each ticket, one person could carry all of the papers for his group and make a group purchase. Unless the game was of an importance that made availability an issue, one could easily acquire tickets to any AS Roma away game. However, after the Amato Decree, as a way to sever the ties between Ultras and the clubs, the latter were forbidden to sell tickets to away games; and tickets could no longer be sold in groups.

Thus, acquiring tickets now requires Ultras to struggle and sacrifice, which they see as 'doing their duty to the *Curva*.' Ticket One, a service similar to America's Ticketmaster, distributes the tickets for USC Palermo. To buy tickets for the game, AS Roma fans could go to any locale serving as a Ticket One ticket office. However, it was normal to arrive at one of these locales, usually a bar or tobacconist, only to be told that, in fact, they had no blank tickets for USC Palermo and, therefore, could not sell tickets. Given that there would normally be only one or two designated ticket offices in Rome for each sporting club, it made purchasing tickets difficult.

Some teams, like the two teams from Milan, used Milanese banks as ticket offices. One or two branches in Rome would sell tickets to various sporting or cultural events. These banks, though, were notorious for refusing to sell tickets to Ultras. On one occasion, my wife and I purchased tickets to a game against Inter Milano. While waiting at a nearby bus stop an unfamiliar AS Roma fan asked us the location of the bank. Moments later he returned saying that he was told the bank did not sell tickets.

In other instances, a team would use a local retailer as ticket office. Livorno's team, for instance, used a perfume store on the northern edge of Rome. Others were linked to List Ticket, who had only one branch of Banca di Roma near the Termini train station that sold tickets. All told, it took time and effort to buy tickets, especially from the banks, because, their prejudice against rowdy fans aside, their hours of operation usually prohibited anyone with a job from easy access. Difficulties buying away game tickets became regular conversation on Lorenzo Contucci's *AS Roma Ultras* website in 2007. Anyone, myself included, who found a bank branch or otherwise that would actually sell him or her a ticket invariably posted that information online.

Because of the hardship suffered merely to buy tickets, the Ultras have incorporated this into their conception of what one must do to be or become an Ultra. There is no distance here between the in-game behaviors and the mundane everyday life of the Ultras. If one does not sacrifice oneself during the week then it matters little what one does on game days. In the past, day-to-day sacrifice might have meant community service or being present at group meetings. Now it includes hunting for tickets, which they use as an example of the distance between themselves and normal fans.

The Ultras assumed that the State was making it difficult to purchase tickets to away games because it did not want them to travel. Instead of banning travel, which would be unconstitutional, the State would ensure that very few Ultras would make it to the games. Given the difficulties I faced in acquiring tickets, regularly having to travel from one side of Rome to the other in search of a vender who was willing or able to sell tickets, I feel confident in expressing the Ultras' idea of sacrifice as a part of the away game process. For most of the Ultras I met, free tickets were a given until February 2007, but these free tickets were replaced by a maddening system of confusion that might take someone two days to acquire one ticket.

Ticket costs were usually minimal, between twelve and eighteen euros. This allowed access to the guest section, the only section an Ultra would enter. The premise of the away game is to be with one's group or friends, amassed in the small guest section against the superior numbers of the home fans. To be mixed with the home fans, as will be explained later, was seen as a sign of vulgarity and pointlessness.

Transportation

After acquiring tickets, one must arrange transportation. Even though the Amato Decree has made this more difficult as well, the options available to most Ultras do not involve the State or the clubs but other Ultras. To make the trip from Rome to Palermo for a Sunday game starting at 3 PM takes commitment. To arrive by automobile one needs nine hours; by train, almost thirteen. To fly takes only two hours but one expects to pay around 200 euros. Because spending money is not considered a sacrifice, and because many Ultras refuse to spend great sums of money to follow their team, most travel by train or automobile. This is true even for Ultras who have jobs and disposable income.

Although it is more difficult today than in the recent past to take trains without paying, it is still part of the Ultras' form of life to travel for free. On numerous away trips, I saw Ultras walking from one train car to the next, and back again, in a constant attempt to avoid the ticket checker.

Another strategy was to lock oneself in the bathroom. I asked Giorgio, an Ultra of thirteen years about the practice. 'Our goal is to pay as little as possible to follow AS Roma. Money should never be a substitute for one's worthiness to be in the stadium,' he explained, before adding that in the 2006–2007 season he took a seventeen-hour trek to Milan by way of small regional trains because these very rarely have ticket checkers. He could have taken a high-speed train, as I did, and arrived in Milan within four hours. Upon learning that I simply went to the ticket counter and bought a ticket to Milan, he laughed and said, 'You will never be an Ultra until you sneak aboard a train. We never pay.'

Therefore, the idea of using airlines to travel to away games is generally ruled out unless the game is outside of Italy. Before the 2006–2007 season the Italian state railway would organize special trains to transport large groups of fans to their destinations and back for free. However, the Amato Decree outlawed this practice in order to curtail the movement of the Ultras. It is still possible for Ultra groups to organize private buses, however, because they do so for profit, and because so few Ultras travel now, most buses are canceled in mid-week due to lack of interest. Hence most travel to and from away games these days takes place in automobiles.

For the 2006–2007 Palermo game, however, most Ultras chose to arrive by train. With the game beginning at 3 PM on Sunday, they took the overnight train from Rome, leaving Saturday at 9 PM in order to arrive in time. Being on a train with Ultras is a unique experience. One witnesses fandom, camaraderie, affection, aggression, horseplay, and an array of insults. The trip began as was usual during my time with the Ultras: with flags and scarves waved from windows and twenty minutes or so of songs. Being unobserved by the authorities someone invariably made their way to the intercom and broadcast the performance to all of the train's passengers. After this trip's performance, the Ultras found seats and sleepers near their friends and group-mates. On the train to Palermo were approximately 100 Ultras. Of these, I only saw eight females, four of whom were traveling with *Fedayn*. The group of Ultras as a whole was typical of those that traveled long distances. There were many leaders from the most important groups in *Curva Sud*, along with the most committed of their members. Ages ranged from approximately nineteen to forty-six, the age of Alessandro, a longtime member of *Fedayn*.

Mangiamo![7]

Within each group, or group of friends, there seems always to be someone who always travels with food. Each time I enquired about the food's origin, I was told with a knowing smile that, 'mamma made it.' Normally, when the group arrived at a stadium, the food carrier would open a backpack and begin distributing individually wrapped sandwiches to his friends. However, in Parma for a *Coppa Italia* game, I watched a small group of Ultras share a portion of perfectly sliced Prosciutto di Parma while discussing its merits relative to Friuli's *Prosciutto San Daniele*.

Other times food is central to the post-game experience. Returning by train to Rome from Empoli, a small town near Florence, my hunger was sated by a young Ultra whom I had never met. He passed sandwiches to his friends and caught me observing intently. He asked my wife and me if we were hungry. She politely answered, 'No thank you', while I said, 'Yes thank you.' Seconds later we were sharing a sandwich. Similarly, in one of the buses arranged by the city of Milan to transport AS Roma fans from the San Siro stadium to the Milan Central train station after a game against Inter, a group of friends devoured a sack full of sandwiches as a machine-gun toting *Carabiniere* observed. They laughed as someone asked his permission to eat in jest.

Water and beer are also consumed communally. On a bus to Milan organized by *Boys Roma* for the second-leg of the 2006–2007 *Coppa Italia* final, there was constant circulation of water, chips, and cookies provided by whoever brought or purchased them. On this trip, no alcohol was allowed. While it is prohibited by the State to consume alcohol in automobiles I was told that it is normal for Ultras' buses to be awash in alcohol. *Boys Roma*, however, does not allow anyone to drink during travel to away

---

7   Let's eat!

games, as they demand strict order and discipline. The water consumed this day was pleasurable but on other occasions water seems an issue of life and death.

A large group of nearly two thousand Ultras went to Livorno in January 2007 — our last away game before the death of Raciti and the crackdown that followed — on a special train. From the station, special buses transported the Ultras to the stadium. Once the buses entered the enclosed area beyond the guest section it was impossible to leave, making hunger and thirst a virtual guarantee for anyone without food and drinks. This is standard practice for away games, although Livorno took security especially seriously, given the political nature of the rivalry between AS Roma and AS Livorno. Even when the Ultras are not forced to go directly to the stadium, as in Udine, Reggio Calabria, and Turin, they normally arrive between 10 AM and noon on Sunday mornings when only a few snack bars and cafés are open for business.

The guest section of Livorno's *Stadio Armando Picchi* has only one concession stand that guests can reach only through a small hole in the back wall. Thankfully, Ultras cut this hole in the chain-link fence surrounding the concession, allowing one to hold out a handful of euros and retrieve the ordered items, trying not to get snagged on the ragged fence. On my two trips there, the concession either ran out of food and drinks or simply closed well before half time. This meant that one had to wait at least an hour until the end of the game with very little to eat or drink. On top of this, it is also standard procedure for away fans to be held in their section until all home fans, especially opposing Ultras, have left the stadium area. This usually translates into an additional hour.

Once we were loaded on the buses after the game and post-game wait we faced another twenty-five minutes of driving to the station. In order to keep us separated from any *Livornesi* (inhabitants of Livorno), they drove us to a deserted strip of land behind the station. When the doors opened, we sprinted to the train cars in order to find seats. Everyone laughed at the situation and cursed the police and *Livornesi* until the train pulled away from the station. It was only when we settled in for the four-hour journey that we realized we were thirsty and had nothing to drink.

For most of the Ultras, lack of food and drink was just an inconvenience to be overcome, an example of their willingness to suffer in order to be present at the game. For two Ultras on the train, though, the situation seemed more serious. After singing and screaming themselves hoarse for the game's ninety minutes, and now facing the prospect of a water-less journey back to Rome, these two almost reached the point of panic. At our first stop in Rosignano an attempt was made to exit the train, buy water from a vending machine, and re-enter the train. However, the fickleness of the machine left the Ultras scrambling back on the train without water just as the doors closed and minus thirty cents. Cecina offered no vending machine on our platform. This prompted the Ultras to cease from insulting the locals and begin asking politely for water. No results. Not at San Vincenzo, either. Finally, at Campiglia Marittima — an hour into our trip — a young girl, perhaps flattered by the commotion she and her glistening bottle of spring water caused, handed up the partially drunk bottle through the open window. The two Ultras most desperate for water took excited sips and then handed the bottle to the person next to them, who passed the bottle not back to them but on to someone else.

The Arrival

Returning to the Palermo trip referred to above, after we ate and everyone calmed down and settled in for the night's journey we arrived at the Naples central station to make our scheduled stop. Out came the flags and scarves. Then came the anthem of the CUCS and several rounds of 'Odio Napoli' (I hate Naples). As we pulled into the station, the platform was populated by a handful of waiting passengers and perhaps one-hundred policemen. Beyond them, we could see and hear a small crowd of SSC Napoli Ultras, singing 'Romanisti pezzi di merda' (AS Roma fans pieces of shit) and 'Roma Roma Vaffanculo' (Rome go fuck yourself). Some of the AS Roma Ultras attempted to exit the train, but were stopped by the police. The scene lasted approximately fifteen minutes, but after the initial exchange of insults there was only sporadic singing or yelling. The sizable police presence kept action to a minimum, despite the hostilities.

AS Roma has no such rivalry with Palermo. We faced no opposition from the Palermo Ultras even outside the *Renzo Barbera* stadium, which lies west of central Palermo. The entrance to the guest section of the stadium was even opened this day to normal Palermo fans who sat above the section itself (normally a position advantageous for showering various objects upon the guests). Perhaps the police felt secure in this arrangement because they understood that only under extreme circumstances would Ultras engage in violence with non-Ultra fans.

Or perhaps it was because they were interrogating on video every person who entered the section wearing *giallorosso* (yellow and red, the colors of Rome). They asked our names, what time and how we reached the city, and what time and how we were leaving. Then, another officer looked through knapsacks and backpacks, I assumed to search for bombs and flares, while another confiscated all flagpoles. Anyone carrying a flag or homemade banner had them inspected and some were confiscated as well.

Hold Your Colors High!

Upon entering our cage-like section, two more policemen waited to inform each and all that the displaying of team and city colors was prohibited, due to their being a provocation to other fans. Therefore, no flags, no banners, no scarves could be held aloft. Many of the Ultras immediately removed their shirts just to carry the point further. Despite the protests of the leaders of *Fedayn*, *Boys*, and *Ultras Romani*, a pile of flags and banners was created below us at field level and the officers stood guard over it throughout the game.

To be interviewed on camera, so as to be identifiable on Closed Circuit cameras in the stadium, was unusual but sufferable. However, to be forbidden to stand behind and under AS Roma's (and Rome's) colors and the names and symbols of their groups was particularly stinging for the Ultras. Meanwhile, the detractors of the Ultras use the issue as proof that they are not true fans but only go to away games to be seen behind their banners. Far from being a mere vanity or truly the only reason they travel to away games, the banner is the symbol of the group.

English hooliganism developed the 'taking of one's end' as the ultimate humiliation of one's opponents. This entailed raiding the *curva* of the opposing team and, after fighting or because of being uncontested, being able to stay there for a period of time. In Italy, the Ultras were never free enough to move within stadiums to invade another team's *curva*. Since the creation of *Serie A* in the 1920s, rivalries have been so heated as to warrant harshly segregated stadiums.[8] Thus they stole opponents' banners as a similar humiliation. These would then be displayed and sometimes burned in the opposing *curva* during a game. The most common way for a group's banner to be stolen was during fighting before a game. However, since the death of Genoa Ultra Vincenzo Spagnolo at the hands of his AC Milan counterparts in 1995, the police have made a concerted effort to keep opposing Ultras separated before and after games.[9] Thus, while such encounters and thefts rarely occur, when they do it is a devastating blow to an Ultra group.

The Ultras place so much value on having their banner seen because it is a form of validation of the energy expended going to and from away games. As Antonio of *Razza Romana* told me, he explained to the police in Palermo that, 'we came a long way to be here to feel the pride of hoisting our colors above our heads in a stadium full of people who will hate us for doing so.' Later that evening I asked him to elaborate. 'Have you seen the *Boys* scarf?' he asked, referring to their latest model which reads *'odiati e fieri'* (hated and proud), 'well, that sums up who we Romans are. Everyone hates us because we are so proud to be Roman. Going to Palermo shows them that we will go anywhere and hold our colors high, with pride and dignity.'

I asked about hanging the banners. 'The banners are only slightly different because they belong to the groups; and the groups are the ones

---

8   Foot, 2006, pp. 302–324.

9   Mariottini, 2006, pp. 111–127.

who suffer to support *la Roma* (AS Roma). Yes, I may go, or you may go, but we go as representatives of groups — friends, comrades, brothers, or sisters. When I hang our banner in Palermo I do so for them, especially if they cannot come to the game.' I then asked him about sacrifice, but he misunderstood me. 'Exactly!' he said, 'it is their sacrifice to miss the game. They might help me get here, as we help one another always, and I am only here because of them.' In that vein, I asked about the prospects of getting his small banner stolen. '*Porco dio*,' he replied in classic Roman style, with the '*por*' exaggeratedly annunciated, 'how could I face them? Sure, I would have to get a new banner made, but then the history, the kilometers, the blood and sweat that stained this one would be lost. If this banner were lost our group would probably fold. In this climate [post-Raciti] it would be too difficult to begin again. There is no way to remake the memories contained in this banner.' As we spoke he was keeping the folded banner in a backpack, which he held all the way back to Rome.

In Lisbon for a Champions League game between Sporting Portugal and AS Roma, I witnessed a fight between a former leader of *Opposta Fazione* and a well-known 'club fan' because the latter had placed his banner over that of the Ultra's group *Brigata Caciara* (one of the small, away-game only groups). The 'club fans' are the other form of organized fandom in Italy. Instead of being Ultras, they are social clubs, for example *Roma Club Testaccio*, and consist of older and more bourgeois fans. They are always present at away games and in Rome, occupying the *Tevere* grand-stand, but do not share the Ultras *mentalitá* or style of fandom. Given the nature of the combatants, the fight was short, nasty, and ended with the ejection of the Ultra. Importantly, his banner remained.

The groups compete to arrive at stadiums earlier than the others so as to have choice of the best space to hang their banners. The glee of arriving early to find an empty section is matched only by the horror of arriving late and finding space for neither the banner nor the group. This is one of the main reasons groups create alliances, to save space for one another at away games. For the 2006–2007 and 2007–2008 seasons, the largest groups worked together to save space, repeatedly elbowing out many smaller groups who hang banners away from Rome. In their mind, the hundreds standing behind the larger groups' banners outweigh the three to five standing behind a small group's banner. There would be no solution in a group hanging its banner and standing elsewhere as no one would want to stand behind a banner that was not their own.

Because most guest sections are small, holding less than 1000 persons, the groups seek to accommodate one another by hanging smaller versions of their normal banners. To compensate, the group might carry more flags. *Ultras Romani*, early in the 2006–2007 season, was not following this protocol. They consistently carried their large banner, created for their space in Rome's stadium, and measuring approximately twenty feet across and four feet high. Leaving no space for the banners of other groups, this was interpreted as a provocation. *Boys*, *Fedayn*, and various smaller but still substantial groups first conspired to arrive at away stadiums before *Ultras Romani* in order to procure the most banner space. Eventually, *Fedayn* united (on only this issue) with *Ultras Romani*. Both agreed to save space for one another, with *Ultras Romani* carrying their smaller banner as part of the agreement.

The act of hanging the banner is a serious matter. Each group carries various forms of tape, twine, and rope in order to be best prepared. Only the most select members of each group carry the banner, who are also responsible for having it hung properly. Unless there is no other choice, a banner will never be visibly crooked or creased. Often, as in Parma, Messina, and Reggio Calabria, hanging a banner in the optimal space requires climbing and sitting on a ten foot partition topped by jagged metal pieces designed to keep the Ultras from breaching their designated space. In these cases, a human pyramid may form, which the banner hanger climbs in order to reach the top of the partition.

For as long as it takes — in Reggio Calabria it took forty minutes for *Razza Romana* to hang their banner in this manner — an Ultra will endure pain and fear to get the banner hung. If the situation is pathetic or comical enough, another group might offer to help. The most adept hanger of group banners in all of *Curva Sud Roma* is Luigi, the leader of

Arditi. In Parma, he climbed the partition freehanded and proceeded to hang almost every present group's banner. He also used his time atop the barrier to harangue opposing players, stewards, officials, photographers, and TV personalities. Upon returning to earth he was given a rousing ovation by the large contingent of AS Roma fans.

The cooperation between the groups while away from home gives us a sense of the spirit of camaraderie and brotherhood that develops amongst those who regularly travel to support AS Roma. *Arditi* has been aligned with *Boys Roma* since its inception in 1992. In Rome, its leaders and members converse with a very small number of Ultras, almost exclusively of the Right and well known in the *Curva*. Yet away from Rome, Luigi, the group's leader, lends his time to anyone who asks. Similarly, *Fedayn* members paid me little mind in *Curva Sud*; yet, away from Rome they would regularly interact with my wife and me. On two occasions, in Parma and in Milan, I was even commanded to wave one of their large flags. On the latter occasion, Filippo, a twenty-eight-year-old veteran of *Fedayn* who was known to everyone in *Curva Sud* — or so it seemed because everyone was familiar with his flags — called to me over his shoulder, 'American Boy *vieni* [come here].' I climbed down two rows to where he was waving his flag and he handed it over to me.

I met Filippo during my first away game, which happened to be a long trip by train to Udine. He was amongst the *Fedayn* Ultras I naively approached to introduce myself. He said little, as another Ultra advised me to read the *AS Roma Ultras* website if I wanted to learn about Ultras. However, after seeing me in Milan on a cold Sunday night, cheering on a historic win by AS Roma — and in various other cities — he began to warm to my presence. By the time of the *Coppa Italia* game in Parma — which occurred on a Wednesday night — he knew I did not take my presence among them lightly. That night I waved his flag and received the praise of a few *Fedayn* members. A month later in Turin, he began calling me 'American Boy,' in homage to the 1954 Alberto Sordi film *Un Americano a Roma*.

It took months, though, for me to be accepted by Filippo. And, because accepted by him, I not only came to be accepted as a fixture amongst the select Ultras who travel to every away game, but I also came to understand that one did not enter their brotherhood without a sacrifice.

Incidentally, as a way to explain their understanding of the away game, the week before Filippo Raciti was killed in February 2007, I received a text message from Filippo. He was again in Milan, this time on a snowy Thursday night to support AS Roma against AC Milan in the *Coppa Italia*. He asked where I was, having noticed my absence. My wife was ill, I explained, but told him I was watching on TV. 'Can you see my flags?' he asked. 'Yes,' I said. He then replied with apparent glee, 'there are only 200 of us.' Filippo thought that only the most dedicated Ultras would regularly travel to AS Roma games. To have that dedication made someone a true Ultra. And, being present each week, Filippo and a few others knew the faces of their compatriots. They knew who was only at the games that were easily attended (in Florence on a Sunday at 3 PM, for example). Thus, for the most committed of Ultras, it is not a mass phenomenon but one that involves the very few who are willing to sacrifice their time and energy to be present.

The Ultras know that the major press, as well as Ultra publications like *Fans Magazine* and *Ultrà Tifo*, will carry photos of the *curvas*, which they use for publicity as well as a way of measuring their worthiness and relative strength within this domain. The press and personal photos also form a memento of the occasion. Upon entering an Ultra office, or even the bedroom of committed Ultras, one finds fewer photos of players and game action than photos of their group away from, and in, Rome. To go away from Rome and hang, and stand behind, the banner of one's group, is seen as a way of immortalizing the group. Someone somewhere will always have a photo.

Thus, to be seen and photographed in Palermo without colors was not only insulting for the Ultras but also demeaning and, in a way, tragic. To have the colors prohibited defeated what many had traveled so far to do. And, like many of the other laws passed and enforced after Raciti, the prohibition was interpreted as having less to do with maintaining public order than with eradicating the Ultras altogether.

The Game

Along with the police in the guest section guarding over the pile of Roman colors, that day in Palermo was also hot. Unlike Rome's Olympic Stadium, Palermo's stadium has no awning covering all spectators. We suffered under the afternoon sun. After AS Roma scored to lead 2–0, the normal fans seated above and behind us began showering us with water and other drinks. Given the heat most did not complain. And even though by the sixtieth minute of the game many began thinking of the return trip that would follow, the Ultras were glad to be there.

They sang the entire first half. Like every game, whether home or away, the Ultras began with the anthem of CUCS. Then they sang various songs from their 'songbook,' a collection of songs now around 40, with two or three songs added each year. If the away game is against a rival of AS Roma or *Curva Sud,* the Ultras will spend most of the game singing against their opponent. In Palermo, with no rivalry in either case, they sang only to support AS Roma. Only occasionally did they sing '*Palermo, Palermo, Vaffanculo,*' (Palermo go fuck yourself) as they would in any host city (with that city's name replacing 'Palermo'). It is the goal of the Ultras to sing regardless of what is happening on the field; '*oltre il risultato,*' beyond the results, they say. Whether AS Roma is winning or losing is of no consequence. This goal is becoming more difficult to sustain, however, because of the spread of unaligned fans in the *Curva.*

The second half began as the first, but with less urgency for the Ultras. With AS Roma winning comfortably they began to feel the heat a little more. The small group of Ultras began singing songs against SS Lazio and in support of certain AS Roma players. *Fedayn* eventually began moshing (a form of gang 'play fighting') amongst themselves in order to reanimate the section. They formed a loose circle and began singing a *Curva* favorite that I called '*Tutti allo stadio*' (Everyone to the stadium). As the song progressed, they began pushing and shoving each other through the center of the circle in order to be pushed back from the other side.

Eventually Palermo scored, cutting AS Roma's lead to one goal. This brought both sets of Ultras to full attention, and the game concluded in fiery fashion. They honored themselves and each other with many rounds of '*Curva Sud Ale*'' (Come on *Curva Sud*) late in the second half. And following the game, the team honored them as well, with many players coming '*sotto la curva*' (under/below the *curva*) to throw their shirts and shorts into the crowd, the maximum show of respect from the players to the fans. The Ultras' sacrifice, even without their colors, had brought the team glory.

The Return to Rome

The return trips to Rome are much the same as the trips to the game, albeit more subdued. Usually the Ultras are tired, thirsty, and hungry after a game. They want to find a comfortable seat, then eat, and sleep. If the trip or game has been particularly nasty, however, this may be impossible. An example was the trip to Florence to witness the AC Fiorentina-AS Roma game in 2008, when a line of AC Fiorentina Ultras attacked the *AS Roma Ultras*' cars with stones and bottles as they exited the enclosed and guarded guest section of the parking lot. Some Ultras had to drive for two hours in forty-degree temperatures without a windshield. I asked one of the Ultras who had to drive this way about the damage to his car. The driver said little, just shrugged his shoulders as if to say, it comes with the territory. I myself had been offered a ride back to Rome by a friend who did not want me journeying back into central Florence to catch a train because I would be unprotected.

As I will explain in Chapter Five, the act of going to an away game is warlike and militarist. The groups move 'in formation,' always looking out for attack. The singing is far more aggressive and negative than at home. And, it is only after returning to Rome that the Ultras relax and let down their guard. However, there is no relinquishing of their 'liminal status' because the boundaries between Ultra and non-Ultra are never crossed.

In other words, the *mentalità* and sense of life in terms of opposition and heroic struggle do not reign only on game-days. Still, there is a different feeling to games played in Rome. They are no less serious but tend to be more festive.

Figure 6. Game day in *Curva Sud*, 2007.

The Ultras at Home

For AS Roma's Ultras, their greatest moments of solidarity and celebration of being an Ultra and a Roman occur in Rome. The safety of being at home, where there are no travel restrictions, and being amongst a large group of AS Roma fans, make home games less warlike than the away games. At home, one might stand with friends who are absent away from Rome, and one's group will be more fully present. Nevertheless, the ritualization of violence is still present, and warring actions still takes place, but these are subtler, and meaningful only within the world of the Ultras. Two aspects are highly visible: the choreography — a coordinated display of color, image, message, and fireworks that is the ultimate expression of the Ultras' passion for the team, the game, and being Ultra; and the *striscione* — the long, hand painted banners with messages of various themes.

Game Days

Game days at home tend to begin only on game day. There is no need for the Ultras to buy tickets because they are, to a man, season ticket holders. According to AS Roma, *Curva Sud* has been sold out each season since the Olympic Stadium was restructured in 1990 (for that year's FIFA World Cup). Although home games are no less structured or ritualized than away games, they tend to unfold in a more solitary manner for many Ultras. Whereas the away game happens strictly within a group setting, the Ultra is more likely to arrive at the Rome stadium alone. This is truer for day games, though; Ultras often meet at the group's office or at a bar before going to the stadium at night.

Day or Night?

Night games tend to be reserved for more important and 'TV worthy' opponents. Games against SS Lazio, FC Juventus, AC Milan, and Inter FC, the club's biggest rivals, are usually played on Saturday and Sunday nights. Aside from fans meeting beforehand to eat, drink, and socialize, these games also carry with them the opportunity for violence. Ultra violence occurs in groups, as will be explained later. The groups will amass an hour before game time in one of three places: the River Bar along the Tiber across from the stadium; under the Mussolini obelisk in front of the stadium; or as close as possible to the fenced in guest section 'holding area' near *Curva Nord*. There they simply await any groups of opposing Ultras that might come into their midst. If any do so, a group of *AS Roma Ultras* will run to them, prompting either shameful flight from the opposition or a quick skirmish of kicks, punches, and whacks with flag poles. If the police have properly contained the visitors and no one arrives, the Ultras come into *Curva Sud*. Today it is rare for inter-city violence to occur, but in the past, especially before the Spagnolo death in 1995, it was a normal part of coming to the stadium.

Traffic

Oddly enough, an issue the Ultras face at home that they do not on the road is traffic. Because they usually have a police escort to away stadiums, they are unencumbered by the worry of arriving on time. This is always true when arriving by train and often so by bus or car. I arrived in Milan by bus with *Boys Roma* and our bus, along with many private cars, was made to stop outside of town before being escorted to the stadium *en masse*. I was never able to learn how the police knew we were AS Roma fans, as no colors were visible from outside the bus. In Rome, however, the Ultras know to allot enough time for idling on the way to the stadium. The time I spent like this in cars with Ultras was passed listening to pre-game radio shows. However, the most common way to see Ultras before games is in pairs, weaving through traffic on a motorcycle or scooter, with the Ultra seated behind the driver holding folded flags and banners. Once parked, the Ultras waste little time making their way to the stadium.

Meeting the Group

Unless there were reasons to meet outside the stadium, such as the opportunity for violence or a structural issue like transporting props for the choreography (see below), most groups will meet under the *Curva* beyond the turnstiles. There, if the group sells merchandise, as do *Boys Roma*, *Ultras Romani*, and *LVPI*, they have a small display of items for sale. Coffee, water, or beer is consumed, along with sandwiches. Otherwise group members socialize and intermix, although only after the group's banner and flags have been put in place in the group's section.

Standing

Even though each seat corresponds to a specified season ticket, no one in the *Curva* uses his or her assigned seat. Instead the Ultras consider the *Curva* to be a 'general admission' area. In this way, the groups are able to claim and maintain sections for themselves, regardless of the seats they were assigned. It is up to the groups to maintain the boundaries of their respective sections. For the larger groups like *Fedayn, Ultras Romani, Boys Roma, Ultras Primavalle-San Lorenzo,* and *Padroni di Casa* this is not a problem, as everyone in the *Curva* knows their territory.

For the numerous smaller groups, however — not to mention the myriad groups of friends who have been standing together for numerous seasons — the issue is pressing and addressed anew with each home game. Usually someone from the group will arrive early, approximately two hours before kick-off, and mark out the group's section with newspapers or scarves (laid upon each seat). I witnessed a small seven-person group protect its territory on numerous occasions. Gabriele, the group's leader, an Ultra of twelve years who was formerly a part of *AS Roma Ultras*, once cleared the section of other fans just as a game was beginning (his group had been outside at the River Bar and no one was free to 'save the seats') just by explaining that 'this is where we stand.'

Despite now having no chance of finding room for ten to stand together for the game, the others vacated the area in question. I asked Gabriele about the incident. His response was a knowing smile (as if to say, 'they know who I am') and a simple explanation. 'I have stood with my friends in [that] spot [five seats along three rows] for ten years,' he said, 'We earned the right to be [there] by taking care of some bad situations.' From Giorgio, another member, I learned that they had fought another small group called *BVB Ultras* for part of their space. They did it during a game so that everyone nearby would know the victor and rightful holders of the space. The two groups are now friendly and share a porous border and numerous hugs when AS Roma scores a goal.

Fare Tifo (The act of being a fan)

There are now two basic elements of fandom in the Ultra style: singing and waving flags. In *Curva Sud* before the 2007 death of Raciti, each of the large groups contained a person who handled a megaphone and directed songs to be sung by large numbers of Ultras at once. The groups traded turns directing the *Curva* as a whole. Since Raciti, however, megaphones have been outlawed — the 2007 Amato Decree (discussed in detail in later chapters) made 'organized fandom' illegal and punishable by three-to-five years' banishment from all Italian stadiums — and now each of the larger groups attempts to begin *Curva*-wide songs just by singing amongst themselves. When the Ultras are disciplined the system works well enough. Usually, the *Curva* has more than one song being initiated at the same time.

Coinciding with each song may be a coordinated pattern of claps. If not, many Ultras wave flags or hold *stendardi* (banners or standards on two vertical poles in the style of the Roman *vexillum*). Flags are a part of the history of the many smaller groups in the lower section of *Curva Sud*; the larger groups in the upper-*Curva* use them less often. In the lower zone, flags of various shapes and sizes fly throughout the ninety minutes of a game, whereas elsewhere in the *Curva*, individual Ultras hold aloft their flags as the mood strikes them. Before Raciti, flares and powerful fireworks were also central to the Ultra style of fandom. Now, however, they have largely been relegated to history.

There are two extreme forms of Ultra fandom remaining: the chore-ography and the banner. The choreography, which is the more extreme, rare, and inspiring of the two, will be discussed in Chapter Six. Instead, the *striscione*-style banner is the veritable mouthpiece of the Ultras phenomenon.

Striscioni

While the massive choreographed displays have given the Ultras fame beyond the realm of fandom, many remain unaware of their subtler practice of unveiling banners with various messages of scorn or devotion. According to Stefano Pivato, the practice was adopted from the behavior of political protesters in the 1960s and 1970s, who would march behind or demonstrate in front of the long message-filled banners.[10] The Ultras use the banners to 'speak' on any issue on the mind of the writer. Typically, though, they are used to insult, to protest, to motivate, or to memorialize.

Historically, the most popular use of the banners has been to insult opponents and opposing Ultras; for instance, against the Milanese Inter fans in 2004–2005: '*È una questione di avi, noi legionari, voi nostri schiavi*' (It is a question of ancestry, we are legionaries, you are our slaves). This is also a good example of the way Ultras use Rome's classical history as a means to aggrandize the present. Other insulting uses of banners can be as simple as the *Inter Ultras* greeting Napoli fans in 2007–8 with '*Fogna d'Italia*' (Italy's gutter).

The Ultras use banners to protest against *Calcio Moderno* and various political issues, such as attacking journalists as the agents of big business, the State, and morality. In the semifinal of the 2006–2007 *Coppa Italia* against AC Milan, one banner asked: '*Scrivete al giornale, parlate alle radio, ma quando ci venite allo stadio?*' (You [all] write in newspapers and speak on the radio, but when do you come to the stadium?). This banner was in response to accusations against the Ultras of destroying soccer by turning it into a war-zone unsuitable for families and children.

In 2005, the *Decreto Pisanu* introduced a set of laws designed to end 'soccer violence' by improving stadium security, having electronically named tickets, assigning stewards to the *curvas*, and in making the prosecution of those involved in soccer violence easier and more severe. Although generally unenforced, the decree was used to keep AC Fiorentina Ultras from standing together with the same colored shirt (white) on the grounds that this represented an 'unauthorized choreography.' In response, those Ultras displayed a banner reading '*Nessun decreto cancellerà le nostre tradizioni*' (No law will cancel our traditions).

---

10   Pivato, 2000, p. 173.

AS Roma's Ultras also use banners to help motivate the squad during an important game, or after having lost one. In the latter case, after a recent loss to SS Lazio, the *Curva* displayed a banner telling Francesco Totti, Daniele De Rossi, and Alberto Aqulani to '*Imparate da noi*' (learn from us) after having been less than impressed with the effort of the three Roman players during the loss. The Ultras wanted the players to put as much passion and hostility into the game as they themselves did.

Finally, another popular use of these banners is in celebrating Rome and memorializing or monumentalizing Romans. One of the most succinct of these was created by *Razza Romana*, a small group in *Curva Sud*, for AS Roma v. Inter 2006–2007, which read, '*La nostra superiorità si chiama Romanità*' (Our superiority is called Romanness). This banner will be discussed in Chapter Six as an expression of the Ultras' feelings of devotion to, and responsibility for, Rome.

Almost every week during my time in the *Curva* a group would raise a banner to announce the death or birth of someone close to the group or the *Curva*. What the Ultras wished to accomplish with these banners was to keep the recipient of the honor alive in the *Curva*. They also hoped to make the readers aware of the issues surrounding the death of the subject, whether it be cancer, immigrant crime, driving while intoxicated, or, in the case of Alessandro Bini, the dangers of playing soccer on improperly cared-for fields.

Alessandro Bini was a fourteen-year-old member of the Cinecittà team in a league sponsored by AS Roma. He was playing a league game on February 2, 2008 when he fell violently upon a pipe used for irrigating the field. The impact to his chest caused a heart attack. He lost consciousness and could not be resuscitated. Given the proximity of Cinecittà to Quadraro, it was not long before both *Fedayn* and *Ultras Romani* delivered scarves and flowers to the scene. In the days following the death, the local news was full of explanations and demands for justice. It emerged that Bini's favorite player was a former AS Roma player named Vincent Candela. He was contacted in France and agreed to attend the child's funeral.

The funeral took place at San Giovanni Bosco in Quadraro and Ultras hung banners on all sides of the piazza. Among these were ones saying, '*Ale piccolo angelo*' (Ale little angel) and '*Ora abbiamo 12 giocatori in campo*' (Now we have 12 players on the field). Luciano Spalletti, the head coach of AS Roma spoke at the service, saying that Alessandro would always be remembered as a player of AS Roma. Vincent Candela wept openly. At the end of the memorial, William Spadino, leader of *Ultras Romani*, announced that the entirety of *Curva Sud*'s activities at the next home game would be dedicated to Alessandro. No one could remember such an honor being bestowed on anyone before.

When AS Roma hosted Reggina Calcio four days later, everyone who entered the stadium was greeted with a banner hung in the hallowed space reserved normally for *Brigata Roberto Rulli*, a *Fedayn* banner which commemorated the founder of the first Ultra group in *Curva Sud Roma*, and one of the most sacred items in the world of AS Roma's Ultras. The banner read, '*Nel tuo riccordo piccolo Alessandro. Il coro della Sud è tutto per te*' (In your memory little Alessandro. The chorus of *Curva Sud* is all for you). The groups did not hang their banners; instead each held one aloft to honor Alessandro. *Fedayn*'s said, '*Piccolo nuovo angelo lasci un grande ricordo. Ciao Ale*' (New little angel you leave a big memory. Goodbye Ale.). *Ultras Romani*'s said, '*Piccolo Ale nel cielo con gli angeli . . . fai vedere il campioncino che sei noi tutti tifiamo per te. Ciao*' (Little Ale in the sky with the angels . . . you showed us the little champion you are . . . all of us 'root' in your honor. Goodbye).

There were as many tears as smiles in the *curva* that evening. Two Ultras recounted to me how their mothers, who had watched the game and ceremonies on AS Roma Channel, hugged them sobbing upon their return home from the stadium. At half time, Spadino was allowed to exit the *Curva* to deliver flowers on behalf of *Curva Sud* to Alessandro's mother, who sat with the club's directors in the Monte Mario grandstand. In return Daniele De Rossi, an AS Roma player born in Rome to a former player and current coach on the team, delivered flowers under the *Curva*.

For the Ultras, honoring Romans goes beyond just a singular memo-rializing action. The act itself is full of meaning and reverence because the Ultras take being Ultra and being Roman so seriously. The honor given Alessandro Bini was not meant to end that day at the stadium. Thus, the Ultras were instrumental in helping to establish the Alessandro Bini Association for Safety in Sport. Already by late-summer 2008 the organization was successful in having new laws for safety in sport for the Lazio region drawn up. The Ultras used their platform to ensure that no one forgot to act in honoring Alessandro by making Rome a safer city for other young soccer players.

Conclusion

As we begin to move toward a deeper analysis of the Ultras' *mentalità* and the more extreme aspects of their behavior, it is important to appreciate the mundane aspects of being an Ultra: going to stadiums to take part in the games of AS Roma. The *trasferta*, or away game, was presented as the essence of the Ultra experience. Away from Rome, AS Roma's Ultras are far more aggressive and united as Romans or fans of AS Roma. While there is always time for play, as in transit to and from stadiums, and oc-casions for humor, the away game tends to be a serious affair. For one, until 2007, the Ultras experienced away games as veritable war zones, with the potential for violence existing at every moment. What is more, the away game has traditionally been the domain of only the hardest, most committed Ultras. The away game, then, fosters an elite within the Ultra phenomenon. These elite Ultras understand themselves as the quintes-sential Ultras, ready to sacrifice time, energy, health, safety, and more to support AS Roma in hostile territory. It is not by coincidence that most of the Ultras with whom I developed close relations come from this group. In fact, it was only because of my willingness to join them away from Rome that I was able to get to know them at all.

Back in Rome, the games are perhaps more grand and festive. The occasional choreography charges the air of the pre-game period, as does being with a large group of friends and cohorts. While the away game is given electricity because of the hostility involved, in Rome it is the opportunity to be in *Curva Sud* that does so. As was demonstrated in the previous chapter, however, being in the *Curva* is not without its conflicts and dangers, the more so because ideological differences are always present. Away from Rome, such differences largely disappear, as a more cohesive group forms. In or away from Rome, the Ultras support AS Roma in the same manner: with songs, flags, and occasionally flares, bombs, and choreography. *Striscioni* banners, the traditional voice of the Ultras, are also displayed in and away from Rome. However, these, like much of the Ultra in-stadium experience, are being policed into extinction by a government that is increasingly at odds with the Ultras' worldview.

CHAPTER THREE

Ultra Practices and Their Consequences

In the last chapter I gave a sense of the emotional, temporal, and financial investments the Ultras make to being Ultras. Whether going to an away game or creating a choreography or banner for one at home, the Ultras are Ultras *'per tutta la vita'* (for their whole life) as they say. The language used in the chapter was designed to ease the reader into the discursive world of the Ultras, and into the 'language regime' through which their *mentalità* is made real.[1] This was more obvious at the end of the chapter, which examined the creation of banners and the purpose they serve within the Ultra phenomenon.

The banners and game-day experiences inform the beginning of this chapter, which seeks to explain the most extreme forms of Ultra behavior and its consequences. I begin by introducing the Nietzsche of the Ultras, who will take center stage in Chapter Four, and explaining how the Ultras utilize what he called 'monumental history.' This form of history promotes the creation and celebration of heroes, as well as strictly defined codes of co-identification, wherein the race or nation are often diminished for the sake of more particular groupings. Finally, it allows the Ultras to bask in

---

1   Kroskrity, 2000, p. 23.

the importance of their every action, so that the act of following AS Roma away from Rome becomes a series of opportunities to define one's self and create one's own value.

The chapter then describes in detail the events surrounding the death of SS Lazio Ultra Gabriele Sandri in November 2007 and how these relate to the period following the death of Filippo Raciti, eight months earlier. This section takes the form of a newsreel so that the confusion, anxiety, anger, and compassion of those days predominate. It is written from the perspective of the Ultras, which I find valuable for presenting their understanding of what transpired.

The section demonstrates what Michel de Certeau theorized regarding the imposition of textual and professional knowledge on the 'knowability' and experience of everyday life. The Ultras resisted, in his terms, the 'view from above' which painted them as terrorists, but in doing so became thoroughly ensnared in the language of the authorities aligned against them.[2] Finally, the chapter uses the Sandri murder and subsequent Ultra violence as a way to introduce the Ultras' war against *Calcio Moderno* (the business of football).

Monumentalism and Ultra Practices

In October 2007 *Boys Roma* elected a new leader. A leadership council had governed the group since the death of Paolo Zappavigna in June 2005. Instead of promoting from within that group, *Boys* decided to reward the loyalty and radicalism of a former hierarch under Paolo. His name is Maurizio, but the *Boys'* Ultras call him *Duce* because of his physical resemblance to Mussolini and, now, because he is their leader. I stopped by the group's office soon after Maurizio's ascension, and I stood outside with a group of Ultras looking at the *Boys'* graffiti that covered the area walls. My attention focused on the message painted on the front of the office: *'Chi l'ha fatto, aspetta'* (He who did it, expect [retaliation]), I asked some of the Ultras what they thought of it.

---

2   de Certeau, 1984, p. 13.

Maurizio, the Duce, said sternly (in English), 'if someone messes with us, we gonna mess with them,' before smiling and asking if I liked his imitation of Robert De Niro. Of course I did, I said, and then asked, 'This is central to the Ultras *mentalità*, yes?' He responded, 'Life is for the purpose of fighting. We search for enemies from history and the present, all the same.' I had witnessed in other Ultras the commitment to having long memories. Fading graffiti tags in Rome had been explained to me with enough venom to make me think the confrontation that prompted them had taken place yesterday instead of nine years ago. Locales along a train route were explained similarly, always in terms of rivalry, confrontation, and someone or some group acting heroically to avenge its honor.

Figure 7. Graffiti, Monteverde, Rome, 2007.

Maurizio and the others made it clear that for the Ultras, the past is never dead. One must act unhistorically or suprahistorically in order to keep it alive, but in The Eternal City this makes sense. The Ultras act unhistorically by seeking a present that changes only by way of the meanings and will of a highly subjectively understood past. Conversely, they act suprahistorically by being keenly motivated to maintain distance from others and proximity to their *mentalità*.[3] In the second of Nietzsche's *Untimely Meditations*, 'On the Uses and Disadvantages of History for Life,' he distinguishes between three kinds of history: critical, antiquarian, and monumental. He implores his readers to 'employ history only in the service of life' instead of 'enslaving life' to a particularly modern (and in his estimation, decadent) understanding of history.[4]

Critical history is of use to those who seek to cast off the burdens of the present. It is a history that judges and condemns the past for its role in creating the present. It is also a nihilistic history, in that it condemns all that lies beyond the 'good' as being unworthy of life.[5] Antiquarian history is of use to those who aspire to familiarity. It is a history that preserves and reveres the past. But in doing so, it is romantic and condemns the present for the sake of every past triviality. In both cases, life is mummified, because the preservation of life is valued above the expansion of life.[6]

Monumental history, by contrast, is useful for those who aspire to 'greatness.' It takes its cues from heroes, grandeur, warfare, victory, and the value of battle (found in sacrifice, honor, duty, and commitment). It is a history that uses the past as inspiration to act in the present. Monumental history is less interested in the study of the past, or in the construction of models of causation. Instead, its interest lies in affect. It diminishes the 'motives and instigations' of an historical act in order to fully monumentalize its affect 'as something exemplary and worthy of imitation.'[7] With such a focus on affect, history is made poetic and mythical, just as myth and poetry themselves become important sources of history. As Nietzsche says, 'the past itself suffers harm' for the sake of those heroes, saints, and

---

3   Nietzsche, 1997, pp. 59–123.

4   Ibid, p. 116.

5   Ibid, pp. 72–76.

6   Ibid, p. 74.

7   Ibid, p. 70.

vistas that fire the blood of the present.[8] Monumental history, then, is a history alive in the present moment.

Nietzsche uses this conceptualization of history as a critical way to understand the relationship between history and culture. The 'natural' relation between the two is always to serve life at the moment; it is never to undermine the present.[9] The weakness of modern culture, he explains, is in part due to its lack of monumentality. In critiquing modernity through its uses of history, in its critical and antiquarian guises, Nietzsche seeks to make us aware of the dangers of consuming knowledge for its own sake and without purpose or affective base — in the mode of 'culture-less' 'career-minded consumers.'[10]

More powerful is the way Nietzsche explains this in *Twilight of the Idols*: that the modern West suffers from 'atrophy of the spiritual instincts' because of its faith in, and celebration of, the universal and concurrent dismissal of the particular and unique.[11] This attack on the universal (and concomitant celebration of 'spiritual instincts') is the key to understanding the Ultras in terms of Nietzsche, for as the Ultras act against modernity they do so primarily because they critique it (and what it promises) as a promotion of the universalization of modern-or-global-capitalism.

I discerned this same monumentalism in the banners displayed in the *Curva* and in the strong desire to display one's colors away from Rome. The Ultras have become cognizant of their ability to influence both public discourse and other *curvas* because their displays are captured in film and published both online and in print. The groups themselves hire photographers located in other areas of the stadium to take photos of their banners so that they are recorded for posterity. Thus, there is always a sense amongst the groups that what they are doing is historical and creative, a marker of the Ultra *mentalità*. The banners that were intended to honor Vanessa Russo are perfect examples of how the Ultras use monumentalism.

---

8   Ibid, p. 71.

9   Ibid, p. 77.

10   Ibid, p. 139.

11   Nietzsche, 2005, p. 188.

On April 28, 2007, Vanessa Russo was attacked and killed by two female Romanian prostitutes while leaving the Metro at *Termini* (Rome's central rail station). After arguing in the subway because the Romanians thought she was looking at them, one, Doina Matei, sixteen years old, jabbed the closed end of an umbrella in Vanessa's left eye. She died of a massive brain injury. The city was outraged. It was the first of what would be a long summer filled with accusations and attacks against Romanians and Roma for criminal behavior.

The game following her murder was April 29: AS Roma — SS Lazio, the biggest game of any season for the Ultras and the city. Early in the day, a small group calling itself *BD Ultras Roma* reached the staging area beyond *Curva Sud*'s entrance. They carried a banner that said simply '*Ciao Vanessa*.' As Sandro, the group's leader later told me, it was meant to show Vanessa's family, and all the sisters, daughters, and mothers in the city that what happened to Vanessa would not be tolerated or forgotten.

'For me and my friends,' he said, 'the murder of an innocent Roman girl at the hands of illegal immigrants was like a call to arms.' However, the police would not allow the group to enter the stadium with the banner because it was unrelated to AS Roma or the game per the terms of the 2007 Amato Decree. The mood in *Curva Sud* that day was murderous. Hardly anyone followed the game. Ultras were on cell phones explaining to one another and others beyond the stadium what had happened to *BD Ultras Roma*. 'If the State wants to destroy the Ultras,' an unfamiliar Ultra roared, 'that is one thing. We are at war with them already. But to defend murderous *zingari* [derogatory term for Roma gypsies — plural of *zingaro*] by disallowing a salute to Vanessa's family was treasonous.' As word spread through both *curvas*, the AS Roma and SS Lazio Ultras united in protest against the banning of the banner. Both *curvas* began taking down all banners and colors. Neither *curva* displayed any *striscioni* banners, even though some *Curva Sud Roma* groups had been able to enter the stadium with their banners honoring Russo.

The protest of the State's treatment of *BD Ultras Roma* demonstrates an interesting aspect of how the Ultras use fandom. In order to do honor to something, in this case Russo, her family, or Roman women in general, the *Curva* creates banners announcing their sentiments and intentions, and then performs their unique form of fandom. Conversely, when the Ultras are protesting something, usually their own treatment by the State, they will deny themselves the act of fandom. Because the Ultras act as fans for themselves, and for the eleven players on the field, there is no sense that they are denying the general public the thrill of the spectacle they create. Using history and creating history as an affective force, then, are inseparably linked, as the Ultras do not assume that the other fans seated in the Olympic Stadium comprehend their actions or worldview. The selection of history to use and to make, in other words, is done so to honor *Curva* Sud, Rome, and AS Roma, for the sake of *Curva Sud* and not the non-Ultra audience that may be watching.

The War for Sandri or The Sack of Rome

In the morning of November 11, 2007, Gabrielle Sandri, a twenty-seven-year-old Roman fan of SS Lazio, and three friends were driving to Milan to support their team against Inter Milan. Sandri was well known in Rome, and famous amongst Ultras, as one of the city's most respected DJ's. His parents own a men's clothing store in the Trionfale neighborhood that had supplied countless Ultras with the 'casual' clothing that defined Ultra fashion since the 1990s. Through DJ-ing and his parents' store, Sandri was also well connected with several SS Lazio players. His entire family was involved in the Ultras and was fans of SS Lazio in some form.

Sandri had worked until 6 AM and was then riding to Milan for the 3 PM game. In an Autogrill parking lot near Arezzo he and his companions encountered a carload of FC Juventus fans and engaged in taunting and insulting them. The yelling alerted two local police officers assigned to keep the peace at the Autogrill, as these stops on the highways have become among the favorite meeting places for Ultras traveling to away games. As both cars were pulling away shots were fired. Moments later, the car in which Sandri was riding came to a stop. He was dead, having been shot in the neck.

Initial news reports said only that a young Roman had been killed in what appeared to be an accidental police shooting. As midday approached, reports were lengthened to say that the dead youth was an Ultra of SS Lazio. These reports said nothing about games being cancelled, but most Ultras believed that Inter-Lazio would be postponed if nothing else. Then it was announced on the radio that Inter-Lazio would not be played but that the other games of the *Serie A* calendar would start after a fifteen-minute delay (as a show of respect). Indeed, newly elected FIGC President Giancarlo Abete said on live television that Inter-Lazio *could not* be played but that 'the other games will be played in order to avoid problems.' One had to assume he referred to 'problems' with the Ultras.

In Milan and Bergamo

At the opening of Milan's San Siro stadium at 1 PM (at that time the game was still going ahead), very few fans entered. The few that did sang songs against the police and Juventus. The most popular song in Italian *curvas*, perhaps the only one common to all, is against the *Carabiniere*: '*La disoccupazione, ci ha dato un gran mestiere, mestiere, di merda, carabiniere*' (Unemployment has given us a great profession, profession of shit, *carabiniere* [the militarized State police]). It is this attitude toward the police that truly unites, and creates, what could be called 'the Italian Ultras.' Where otherwise the joys of agon and celebrations of local particularity override common values, ultimately hindering the Ultras' ability to unite as a true social movement, the police act as a rare stimulus to unity.

Instead of entering the stadium directly, a group of Inter and Lazio Ultras sought to enter through the tunnel used by buses carrying the players. They went to secure a promise from the players that they would not play. When told the players had yet to arrive they left to amass under *Curva Nord*. It was there that they learned of the cancellation of the game.

Outside the stadium other Lazio and Inter Ultras joined together to smash the TV camera of a reporter who insisted upon filming their activities and to parade behind two banners. These read, '*Amato Dimettiti*' (Amato Resign) and '*Per Raciti Fermate il Campionato, La Morte Di Un*

Tifoso Non Ha Significato' (For Raciti you stopped the championship, the death of a fan means nothing).[12] They shouted *'Assassini'* (Assassins) and *'Un Saluto a Gabriele'* (A salute to Gabriele) as they marched behind the banners to the police headquarters on Via Novara. Once there, the group of approximately 400 launched bottles and stones against the office. Along with them was also a small group of Ultras of AS Varese, a small but historic team from the Milan suburbs who, like the Ultras of Inter and Lazio, are known to have Far Right convictions.

Figure 8. SS Lazio Ultras graffiti: 'Our rage wants your blood, Gabbo (Gabriele Sandri) lives,' Rome, 2008.

Meanwhile, in Bergamo the Atalanta BC Ultras had a skirmish with the police before the game between Atalanta BC and AC Milan (around 1 PM). The Atalanta Ultras, among the most active and aggressive in

---

12   Giuliano Amato is a former member of the Italian Socialist Party (PSI) and then Minister of the Interior. He authored the April 2007 *Decreto Amato* which outlawed many Ultra traditions.

Italy, first attacked a police jeep with rocks; those inside received minor head wounds. They then began a more serious engagement with the police amassing near the stadium, raining stones upon them. AC Milan Ultras attacked train guards at the Treviglio station (between Milano and Bergamo) and then evidently fought with Atalanta BC Ultras outside the station in Bergamo.

In the 2 PM hour Atalanta BC Ultras outside their *Curva Sud* attacked the police with rocks and sticks. The police responded with teargas. Nearby the Milan Ultras engaged the police but most were already in the stadium. When they realized the Atalanta Ultras were fighting the police elsewhere they tried to exit the stadium but were charged by the police and constrained to stay inside.

As game time approached the situation calmed, but the Ultras had already decided that under no circumstances was the game to proceed. As the game started they used a manhole cover to blast a hole in the partition separating the field from the *Curva* as an attempt to get the game stopped. The most popular video of the day is of them smashing a hole in the glass barrier, while Christiano Doni and other Atalanta BC players pleaded with them to stay calm. During the interruption, the AC Milan Ultras exited the stadium and were escorted back to the Bergamo central station. At the announcement of the game's abandonment, the Atalanta BC Ultras gave a victory yell. After exiting the stadium, there were no serious incidents. The Atalanta BC and AC Milan Ultras, as much as it pained Claudio of *Ultras Romani* to say of their bitter rivals, 'had done their duty.'

In Other Cities

There was Ultra activity in other Italian stadiums, as many acted with fury that the games had been allowed to go ahead as scheduled. In Florence, a small number of AC Fiorentina Ultras sang songs against the police but were drowned out by the whistles and singing of the 'other Ultras' (according to Mediaset's TG1 newscast). Lorenzo Contucci wrote on the website of *AS Roma Ultras* that this news was actually saying that there are only 200 or so people in Florence worthy to call themselves Ultras.

Songs against the police were sung in Reggio Calabria and Siena. In Reggio, there were no colors. In Turin, the Torino Ultras left the *curva* in protest, followed in kind by the Catania Ultras. Initially the Torino Ultras decided against displaying colors in the *curva*. It was only after the game started that they decided to leave the stadium. They were joined outside by the *Catanesi* (people of Catania), where they too sang against the police.

In Parma, where Juventus was playing, there appeared a banner reading '*La morte è uguale per tutti*' (All deaths are equal). As the game began, the Juventus Ultras had all their banners turned upside-down (a common sign of protest among Ultras). Then, in accord with the Parma Ultras, both groups followed the game in silence (except to sing against the police).

The Ultras' reaction was seen also in smaller cities. In *Serie C*, Taranto Ultras pelted the field and forces of law and order stationed under their *curva* with stones and other objects, thus bringing their game to a halt. The police responded with tear gas. In Potenza, six Brindisi fans were arrested for violence against a public official. In the Lazio *Lega Eccellenza* (amateur league) game between Boville and Latina, three *Carabiniere* officers were injured by a bomb thrown from the Latina *curva*. Otherwise the league's games were played without incident.

After Raciti was killed in February 2007, I heard no Ultras say they were glad that a police officer had been killed. No one mentioned his death at all, except to acknowledge its role in the government's subsequent crackdown on the Ultras. After Sandri was killed, however, the smoldering tension created by the months of what they saw as repression exploded into a spontaneous nationwide uprising. Although not in all cities were the Ultras' actions violent, but there was still a collective will toward expressing grief and frustration. As a violent, militant, and militarist brotherhood, the Ultras' dedication to a radical anti-bourgeois worldview put them at odds with the police. Rather than uniting as oppressed victims of injustice, the Ultras exploded in rage because that was the logical way to express their anger and to honor the sacrifice of Gabriele Sandri. Likewise, there was no similar night of violence following Raciti's death. Instead, it was only after Sandri that cries of '1,000 Raciti's' could be heard amongst AS Roma's Ultras.

Figure 9. Ultras graffiti calling for the deaths of 10, 100, 1000 Raciti (police officer Filippo Raciti), Rome, 2007.

The Italian Football Association President Giancarlo Abete seemed completely dismayed at the violence in Bergamo, insisting repeatedly that what was happening had neither a connection with soccer nor the relationship between the police and some Ultras. He then said that it was not parallel with Catania, which, in his mind, involved a premeditated attack on the police. This death was just accidental, he repeated.

Rome

By late afternoon, news began circulating of huge protest marches in Milan and Rome. In Rome, AS Roma and Cagliari Calcio were scheduled to play at 8:30 PM. Ultras from SS Lazio and AS Roma were discussing ways to ensure that the game would be stopped. Word reached the media around 5 PM that the two *curvas*, *Curva Sud Roma* and *Curva Nord Lazio*, were uniting in order to force the game's postponement.

Around 6 PM the game was officially postponed. In the minds of the Ultras, though, it was not abandoned out of respect for Sandri and his family, but out of fear of public disorder. Meanwhile, at 6:15 PM, Luigi Conti, the lawyer for Sandri's family, announced on RAI's TG1 newscast, along with Gabriele's brother Christiano, that the shooting could not have been accidental based on eyewitness accounts. He called it a murder and said that, based on early evidence, the shooting must have occurred 'like target practice.' Sandri, he vividly explained, was shot while seated in the backseat of a car that was leaving the Autogrill. At this time, there were already SS Lazio fans arriving in Arezzo, shouting '*Assassini*' outside the police station.

A Guerilla War in Rome

As the sun fell on Rome, Skynews 24 was reporting that away games would be banned, possibly forever, as the Ultras were 'holding the season hostage.' Accompanied by live scenes near the Olympic Stadium of Ultras throwing unidentifiable objects at police-lines and passing cars, Giancarlo Abete now said that the violence was proof of 'structural hatred' of the police amongst the Ultras. The death of Sandri had sparked, he said, 'a guerilla war in Rome.'

By 8 PM all Ultra websites were shut down. The Ultras use their own sites for news. The largest of these is *Tifonet*, which collates news from various *curvas*. It reads like an hourly update on the Ultra experience. The most important website for Ultras happens to be associated with *Curva Sud Roma*. It is that of the now disbanded *AS Roma Ultras*. Its Webmaster, Lorenzo Contucci, is still involved in the *Curva*, however, as he is one of the most important lawyers and advocates for the Ultras and other political dissidents in Italy. The sites closed, asking for '*giustizia per Gabriele*' (justice for Gabriele). I was later told by Federico of *Antichi Valori* that they closed because the Ultras believe that the government monitors the sites for information just as do the Ultras.

The main body of Lazio Ultras marched to Piazza Euclide, but by 6 PM had already attacked one police station near the Olympic Stadium.

According to *Il Messaggero*, the general battle was between Ultras with flares and bombs and police with teargas. As they marched, the face-covered Ultras torched scooters and trash bins, as well as a police bus and several cars.

Elsewhere, twenty Ultras attacked police on Via Bosis, near the stadium, with bottles, bolts, and pieces of iron. One person from this attack was arrested. Then, the Ultras assaulted the headquarters of the Italian Olympic Committee (CONI), which is located next to the stadium in one of the buildings comprising the *Foro Italico*. Over one hundred Ultras broke into the lobby of the building. The unarmed security guards locked themselves in the offices while the Ultras destroyed the lobby. According to Skynews 24, after one group had entered the building, another group waited outside, seeking to draw in the police. They refused the chase and the Ultras instead entered the building.

They ignited a bomb that damaged the marble, destroyed the China Olympics countdown clock, all the windows, and a computer at the reception desk. After CONI, a group of Ultras entered the stadium (but did no damage). At this point the Ponte Duca d'Aosta (which spans the Tiber at the Mussolini obelisk that marks the entrance to the stadium) was barricaded with crowd control barriers and garbage bins. Many Ultras could be seen armed with iron bars and with their faces covered. They set about burning the trash bins at the mouth of the bridge before crossing it and moving out of the area. Small groups formed and split from the main group of Ultras. Some of these smashed car windows and burned cars, scooters, and trash bins. The largest group assaulted police stations.

The biggest attack on a police station occurred on Via Remi, near the *Flaminio* Stadium. Around two hundred Ultras amassed in front of the station. They set fire to a bus and a row of trash bins. They then broke the windows of the station and attempted to set it afire with flares and bombs. The tactic was repeated elsewhere. The police station at Ponte Milvio and another on Via Flaminia were attacked with flaming trash bins, stones, bottles, bolts, and other pieces of iron.

Around midnight, the bulk of the action stopped when the police pulled everyone out of the area for fear of reprisals. According to Alessandro Marchetti (secretary of the Policeman's Union) the pull-out left the city in the hands of the '*teppisti*' (hooligans).[13] While walking far enough from the stadium area to find a bus to the center of town I met a young Ultra who admitted to throwing stones at a police-line and a few passing cars near the stadium. He was an AS Roma fan but had joined a group of SS Lazio Ultras as they crossed the Duca d'Aosta Bridge. At that point, he was advised by one of the Ultras leading the group that he was better off not getting involved with them. He was only sixteen years old and did not share the 'hardened' appearance of most of the Ultras who were out that night. He stayed around the stadium to look for friends and, as he put it, 'to see how [he] could help.' As we walked he spoke of his disgust at the news coverage that had replaced soccer for the day. 'The Ultras are always [presented as] animals,' he said.

The Media Responds

When I arrived home, well after midnight, the twenty-four-hour RAI news channel was wrapping up the day's events. They still called the shooting of Sandri accidental, but by now the shooting was a distant memory for the press. The real story was what happened in Bergamo and Rome. Various MP's had their say. Maurizio Gasparri and Ignazio La Russa of *Alleanza Nazionale* attacked Amato for not stopping all the games — if not out of respect then out of concern for public safety. *Forza Italia*'s Fabrizio Cicchitto seconded their thoughts, saying that Amato had the power and responsibility to keep the violence of Bergamo and Rome from happening. Giovanna Melandri stated her support for Amato's decision to cancel only Inter-Lazio and to start the others after 'a moment of reflection.'

---

13   The Italian language tellingly does not translate Ultra as 'hooligan,' as hooliganism is associated with rowdiness and vandalism — neither of which are general behaviors of the Ultras.

Rome's mayor Walter Veltroni received news of what was happening while in Cracow. He said it was a terrible day for all of Rome, but that the situation again showed that violence of any sort has no place in a civilized society. Veltroni then asked a group of two hundred students visiting a synagogue in Cracow to perform a moment of silence for Sandri. Piero Marrazzo, president of the Lazio Region, said that work must be done amongst children in order to create a culture of sport that refutes all forms of aggression.

The next day, the press was universal in its condemnation of the Ultras. The major dailies sold in Rome (*Il Messaggero, Il Tempo, La Repubblica, Corriere dello Sport, Corriere della Sera, La Gazzetta dello Sport,* and *Il Romanista*) each carried a photo of either Rome or Bergamo. Two of them used '*NO*' as a headline; two others used '*BASTA*' (ENOUGH). As the night before, the reactions to Sandri's death were more prominently covered than his death. In the morning, the name of the officer and details of the shooting were still undisclosed. By extension the jury was still out on Sandri's culpability for what happened. The facts that were available seemed tame given the images of the previous evening: three arrests (of which one was a female), twenty policemen with minor injuries, and four policemen under medical supervision in a Rome hospital.

Most of the news consisted of negative moralistic profiles of the Ultras. A typical article in *La Gazzetta dello Sport* identified the Ultras as 'misguided thugs with a warped reality . . . who show up to games hoping for trouble.' The author added that the Ultras are 'dangerous rabble with power over the peace-loving masses that just want to enjoy soccer.'[14] The Italian media used '*teppisti*' and even 'hooligan' instead of 'Ultras' when talking about Rome, understanding well the moral implications of the switch in descriptive terms.

At a café in my Monteverde neighborhood, the morning regulars all spoke of the previous day and night. The vast majority parroted the press in the assumption that the events of the morning and the evening were unrelated. This assumption could only be made with no understanding

---

14   *La Gazzetta dello Sport,* Nov 12, 2007, p. 1.

of the Ultras' *mentalità*. The owner, who was aware of my involvement with the Ultras took me aside and explained to me in his best Italian (he usually spoke Roman dialect) that the Ultras were criminals who were killing the game. He suggested I come with him on Saturday mornings to watch his young son play if I wanted to see what was important in sports: sportsmanship, fun, innocence. The Ultras, he explained, with their 'stupid rivalries and war against the police,' had nothing to do with soccer.

The midday TG1 newscast on RAI1 led with an update on the shooting and the subsequent violence. The State news agency ANSA identified the police officer who shot Sandri as thirty-five-year-old Luigi Spaccatorella of Arezzo. It was assumed that he would be facing charges of involuntary manslaughter. Through his lawyer, he issued a statement calling the shooting a terrible accident. According to the statement, a warning shot from two hundred meters was made, followed by an accidental firing as the gun came down. He said he was not aiming as he was running from two hundred meters.

But on the 5 PM broadcast, the Police Chief of Arezzo, Vincenzo Giacobbe, stated that numerous witnesses saw Luigi firing with both hands, apparently in the belief that Sandri's car had just robbed the petrol station at the rest area. The bullet (perhaps shot at the car's tires) hit Sandri in the neck as he sat in the back driver-side seat. Back in Rome, the police injury list reached forty, with the most serious being an officer assaulted with an iron bar during one of the station raids.

The Ultras Explain

Talk amongst the Ultras was much like that amongst non-Ultras. Everyone wanted to know what had happened and why. There was a great disparity, however, in how the previous day was explained. Whereas the general public, politicians, and those involved in the business of soccer (including the media) spoke about Sandri's death as a tragic accident unrelated to soccer and of the Ultras holding the game and its fans hostage for the sake of their anti-social war against the police, the Ultras spoke about honor, sacrifice, commitment, brotherhood, and, indeed, warfare.

As I briefly explained above, the Ultras' *mentalità* utilizes a model of history that deploys and creates heroes. Monday evening, a large group of Ultras met at the Cutty Sark Bar near Piazza Bologna. Many of them were at the stadium the previous evening. They were reluctant to talk about anything, and more importantly, anyone they had seen. This was a group of older Ultras — those who had seen the *Curva* become not only more ideologically influenced and violent, but also the prey of the police and various 'governmental agendas.'

The Ultras feel that they are used not only to justify the creation of a Police-State, but also the creation of myriad divisions and offices within the governmental bureaucracy that are charged with controlling soccer-related violence. The most vocal of those gathered allowed themselves the pleasure of being in the company of other Ultras. Unable to speak freely during their workday, they asked each other, among other things, 'What do they want us to do?' It was in situations like this that the hegemony of the State and media in control of the image of the Ultras was most telling.

Despite the Ultras' attempts to create public awareness (through banners, choreography, websites, offices, and even radio shows), they were still an isolated minority. And despite their self-representation as an elite phenomenon, in the aftermath of the Raciti death and the killing of Sandri, what the media and State say of them is far more powerful than what they say of themselves. Instead of merely speaking past one another, however, the more the media described the Ultras as a violent mob which threatened the security of the State, the more the Ultras acted as a violent mob, albeit one incapable of threatening the State. For the Ultras present at the Cutty Sark, this was also apparent. 'They speak, we act,' said Fabio of *Boys*, 'and this shows their cowardice and our courage.'

The state of affairs also demonstrated that against the State, in the person of the police, the Ultras have an opponent that will at least confront them with arms, so to speak. It is never a fair fight when one battles with guns and teargas and the other with stones and bolts, but it is a battle nonetheless. Against the power of the media, dissident groups such as the

Ultras find the rules of engagement far less equal, if no less consequential.[15] Oddly enough, the Ultras are perfectly equipped to fight on both fronts. They will be violent, which suits the first, and they understand imagery, ideas, and how they interact in the production of information (even if many of them are verbally unaware of the connection) which suits the second. Although the Ultras made it clear that they understood what happened the day before, and what was happening to them as a phenomenon, they were still incapable of making anyone beyond other Ultras listen to their position. This is because of the distance between their values and those of their opponents.

In the entirety of Italy, they said, there were only two groups who had acted honorably and nobly: the *Atalantini* (the Ultras of Atalanta BC, the team of Bergamo) and us (the AS Roma and SS Lazio Ultras). The Ultras in Bergamo had risked much to show their disapproval at the games being allowed to continue. They had acted not out of uncontrolled aggression but out of respect for Sandri, honoring his sacrifice with one of their own. It is rare to hear *AS Roma Ultras* speak positively of the *Bergamaschi*, as people from Bergamo are known, for the rivalry between the groups is deep, politically driven, and violent. Despite both sets of Ultras being of the Far Right, those of Atalanta BC are also aligned with the *Northern League*. As the League has gained notoriety, so too has its vehement denunciations of Rome as a cauldron of corruption and southern backwardness. When the two *curvas* meet, no punches are pulled. But these *AS Roma Ultras* were sympathetic to their Atalanta counterparts because they acted beyond themselves and stood up to the greed and might of *Calcio Moderno*.

Not just the State, nor the police, but *Calcio Moderno*. As Fabio of *Boys* explained, 'The games continued not to benefit the communities in which the games are played nor the youth or families, which the media claims are the true victims of our behavior. They continued for SKY, Mediaset, Telecom Italia, and the other corporate sponsors of soccer on television.' And now, the Ultras, who understand themselves as the only true fans

---

15   Massumi, 1992, pp. 104–105.

of the game, as well as the only ones fighting (literally) to keep the game connected to its roots, expected to face a lengthy, perhaps permanent, ban from the stadiums.

Speaking in this way made them think, too, of their situation. They were certainly facing a lengthy stadium ban. Their response, though, was sobering. *'Macchì se ne frega un cazzo?'* (Who gives a fuck?) Who cares about soccer or AS Roma when an Ultra was killed for doing nothing more than supporting his team? What does any of it matter when the game is in the hands of those who care only about maximizing corporate sponsorship and then making that sponsorship as profitable as possible? Thus, the Ultras echoed the cries heard in the media and from the offices of FIGC, although looking at the situation from an opposing point of view: we are witnessing the death of Italian soccer.

Consequences
Raciti and the Policing of the Ultras: The *Decreto Amato* and *Osservatorio*

To better understand the thoughts of the Ultras, we must return to the aftermath of Raciti's death in February 2007. Following the actions of the Catania Ultras, all of Italy's Ultras were demonized. It was impossible to watch television, listen to the radio, or enter a piazza or café without hearing someone speaking of the Ultras. There was no mention of the life devoted to honor, commitment, and sacrifice that I had come to know, but instead talk of criminals, hoodlums, and delinquents. I took it upon myself to wear a *Boys Roma* hat around Rome after the killing and was asked to remove it one morning by a barman at Tazza d'Oro (one of Rome's most venerated cafés). Ironically, on January 31, 2007, just two days prior to Raciti's death, and on an evening when AS Roma played AC Milan in the second-leg of the *Coppa Italia* semi-final, *Curva Sud* unfurled the banner asking, 'You (all) write in newspapers, and talk on the radio, but when do you (all) come to the stadium?' Even before the media barrage surrounding Raciti, the Ultras understood themselves to be at war with the media.

More important than the press, post-Raciti the government was talking about the Ultras, making it clear that life as the Ultras had known it before was officially over. Not only, they were told, would organized travel to away games be outlawed, but also all of the performative elements of the Ultra form of life: bombs, flares, banners, and (certain) songs. Those speaking most vociferously against the Ultras were Giuliano Amato (Minister of the Interior), Giovanna Melandri (Minister of Youth and Sports), and Antonio Matarrese (President of *Lega Calcio*). While Matarrese spoke of cracking down on delinquency and making soccer safe for families, Melandri spoke of the ills of Italian sport (especially when compared to England's policing of hooliganism) and of her desire to implement a *modello inglese* (English Model) based on strict and aggressive policing, all-seated stadiums, and zero-tolerance of violence. For his part, Amato spoke of ridding soccer once and for all of the Ultras.

On Thursday February 8, Amato announced that he and the National Observatory of Sporting Events had devised a set of amendments to *Legge 401* (Law 401—the set of laws dating from 1989 that set the terms and conditions of policing and penalizing violent acts relating to sporting events). The Observatory is a governing body made up of various governmental departments, including the Ministry of the Interior, the police and the *Carabiniere*, as well as Trenitalia and Autogril (restaurants and gas-stations located along Italy's highways) that has advised policy and policing decisions for sporting events since 1999. Until 2007 it had only an advisory capacity regarding the reduction of 'soccer-related violence' but now was given the authority to change the face of Italian soccer. Autogril was included on the Observatory board because, as violence was defeated in the stadiums, and organized travel to-and-from away games became more diligently policed, the Ultras adapted to the changing situation began traveling in smaller numbers and using these highway stops as the setting for their conflicts.

The proposal motivated by Raciti's death, quickly dubbed the *Decreto Amato* (Amato Decree), consisted of seven points:

1. Any act of violence against a public official will be punishable with a prison term of between four and ten years. Any act resulting in grave bodily harm will be punishable of a prison term of between eight and ten years.

2. The displaying of any banners containing incitements to violence, racial, cultural, or bodily insults or insensitivity, will be punishable by expulsion from all Italian stadiums for between one and five years. Further, all banners must be pre-approved by the club hosting the event in question. Approvals are based upon the criteria set out by the Amato Decree. Displaying of unapproved banner will result in expulsion from all Italian stadiums for three years.

3. The 'statute of limitations' for arrest after the event of soccer-related violence is extended from thirty-six to forty-eight hours.

4. Any stadium unable to reach the security plan set forth in the Amato Decree will be prohibited from hosting spectators. Included in this section is the prohibition of the selling of blocks of tickets (more than four) to traveling supporters. Any club found to be doing so will face financial penalties and possibly criminal charges.

5. All tickets must include the holder's name, location of purchase, and, if applicable, a *codice fiscale* (fiscal code — similar to American Social Security Numbers). Also included is the instruction that seat assignments must be respected and adhered to.

6. The creation of the designation DASPO (*Divieto di Accedere alle Manifestazioni Sportive*—Prohibited from Entering Sporting Events) assigned to persons prohibited from attending sporting events, including criminal charges that can result in prison terms (see 1).

7. The mandatary placement of one steward for every two hundred
    spectators in a stadium, a move that subtracted seats from spec-
    tators in a stadium's various sections.

Many Ultras, if not all of them, understood the Amato Decree as not having the intention of diminishing soccer-related violence, but of destroying
the organizational bases of the Ultras. As Fabrizio of *Boys Roma* explained
it, it was a declaration of war against the Ultras, done so with the conceptualization of the Ultras as hooligans — *maleducati* (ill-bred or bad
mannered) hoodlums with no interest in soccer or cultural traditions, but
only in causing trouble. When asked about the cultural traditions upheld
by the Ultras he explained:

> The new measures seek to make everything illegal. No more political flags,
> songs, or messages in stadiums; no more flares, smoke bombs, or bombs; no
> more standing with your group — organized or of friends; no more songs against
> the other team. We are now to come to the stadium to buy overpriced beer and
> watch in silence as overpaid illiterates kick a ball around. Instead of the beauty
> that is "*il calcio*" (soccer) we now get organized intermixing of "real fans" in the
> expensive seats, calls for changes to Italy's culture, and a stadium experience
> exceptional only for its sterility and anonymity.

When I pressed him on what was in fact being outlawed, he answered
'politics, theatrics, community, and fierce rivalry: in a word, dissent.' We
talked some more about 'the beauty of soccer' and Fabrizio explained the
Ultras as the encapsulation of what was greatest in Italian history. The
country's greatness was not cultural production (in his mind a material phenomenon) but 'the unrestrained passion for, and celebration of,
something greater than ourselves [indicating me and him].' This was not
the first time one of my Ultra informants spoke in extreme terms about
the importance of the Ultras, but it was the first that I heard this theme
connected to a general model of Italian history.

I pressed him further, asking how the Ultras embodied this greatness.
'There are two things,' he said, 'we live like children of an old mentality. For
us the first thing is rivalry. I am Roman and for me Rome is the preemi-
nent city in the world. I don't give a damn about other Italian cities. And

two, we dare to risk our lives every week for Rome. For this we are Ultras.'
He continued a while, talking about Ancient Rome, Renaissance rivalries
with Florence, the Northern League phenomenon, and even the *Decima
Flottiglia MAS*, a Special Forces division of the Italian Royal Navy. 'In all
these,' he said, 'are the examples of how a Roman and how an Ultra is to
live: daring, honorably, fearlessly, defensively, passionately and exaltedly.'

What the Ultras exalt, he continued, is not violence or drunkenness, as
do hooligans, but 'the willingness to suffer to defend the honor of Rome
against the infidels. When they say that we can be adversaries and not
enemies they are saying that our culture is dead. Do you understand?
Italy's is a history of rivalry, division, and suspicion, indeed hatred. Why
should we change what has made us so particular and beautiful, and for
whose benefit?'

Fabrizio's conceptualization of himself as an Ultra and a Roman
matches the Ultras' monumental use of history in that it operates selec-
tively. For Fabrizio, the Ultras are connected to, as he said, the greatest
things about Italian history. Rivalry and *campanilismo* aside, however, he
made it clear that what is greatest about Italian history is Rome. Nor is
Fabio alone to be enveloped in a world that simultaneously exalts Rome
and the Ultras; all of the Ultras with whom I developed a relationship
are. What became clear in the moments of crisis, after Raciti and Sandri,
was that they saw the Italian State as an imposition that attempts to break
the connection between Rome, or more specifically *Romanità*, and being
an Ultra.

This of course would not be the case for an Ultra in Genova, for instance, but this points to the fractured and highly local nature of being
an Ultra. For the Romans, the strength and courage they speak so much
about as central to being an Ultra is inspired by Rome. The State's attempt
to destroy the Ultras is in essence the attempt of a modern, bourgeois
nation-state to destroy something primal, a spirit of *Romanità*, which
predates the State. In other words, the State is a foreign imposition
seeking to impose its will upon the 'true Romans,' as they call themselves in song.

Federico, formerly of *Antichi Valori*, does not believe the State's desire to eliminate the Ultras is motivated by the latter's violent proclivities. Mirroring the comments of Fabio concerning *Calcio Moderno's* culpability in the death of Sandri, he argues, rather, that the Ultras are bad for business. 'We are the last voices of freedom connected with soccer in Italy,' he said via telephone in 2010. 'We have been in the stadium since 1972 teaching the youth and anyone who could hear us about the evils of consumption and the joy of a pure connection between city, people, and team. We protest everything the new business of soccer attempts to do, be it foreign ownership, hyper-advertising, teams as commodities, and most importantly, fans as consumers. Besides,' he concluded, 'I used to fight every-other weekend, from 1999 to 2004, and often during the off season [he told an incredible story of some unsuspecting foreign tourists wearing AC Milan gear in Rome whom he and the rest of *Antichi Valori* set upon near Piazza Navona], but no one I know has been in a fight since. Ultra violence is over.' 'Because of the State?' I asked. 'Yes,' he said, 'but more importantly because the Ultras who would fight are all outside the Ultras now. The State is fighting ghosts if it is truly fighting the violent Ultras.'

Indeed, the Observatory's own documents show that violence related to soccer, at least in *Serie A*, is largely a thing of the past. During the 2004–2005 season, there were thirty-five games at which fighting occurred between fans. In 2005–2006 the number was reduced to sixteen, rising to eighteen in 2006–2007. The total number of injuries occurring during these encounters was fifty-one in 2004–2005, forty-four in 2005–2006, and thirty-two in 2006–2007. Injuries occurring to police officers fell from one hundred and seventeen in 2004–2005, to fifteen in 2005–2006. They climbed to forty-eight in 2006–2007, the season in which the large-scale violence in Catania claimed the life of Filippo Raciti. Arrests have remained steady. In 2004–2005 and 2006–2007 there were thirty-seven arrested. In 2005–2006 the number dropped considerably to seventeen. Despite consistency in arrests, the number of charges filed climbed from one hundred and forty-three in 2004–2005 to one hundred and seventy-six in 2006–2007.[16]

With the State's own statistics demonstrating a diminution of violence between Ultras and the police, it makes the stark measures and strong words aimed at marginalizing the Ultras after the deaths of Raciti and Sandri even more conspicuous. The deaths and the Ultras' responses to them were used by the State as excuses to repress the Ultras. The State even considered the violence of the Roman Ultras on November 11, 2007 to be an act of terrorism aimed at overthrowing the government. As preposterous as this sounded to the Ultras, such language served the purpose of legitimizing the crackdown on all forms of Ultra action, even those as benign as carrying flags and colors into a stadium. Similarly, any acts of coordinated Ultra action, such as manifestations against club malfeasance or potential foreign investment, are roundly attacked in the press. It is easy to conclude, therefore, that the State is using violence as an excuse to rid the business of soccer of the Ultras.

From personal experience, it is clear that policing methods are working to reduce violence at matches. In the approximately sixty games that I attended during fifteen months of research (from October 2006 to January 2008) I did not witness any incident that could be called fighting by the Ultras or police. I saw posturing, heard insults, and occasionally felt menaced because I was at the mercy of home fans with a position of strategic advantage (to throw items into the guest section). Despite standing amongst the hardest of the most reviled Ultras in Italy (according to another Observatory document from 2002, AS Roma's Ultras were involved in 15% of all fighting in Italy, regardless of league) there was simply nothing to report in terms of actual violence. However, the attitudes toward violence I observed were another matter and will be examined below.

---

16   http://www.interno.it/mininterno/site/it/sezioni/sala_stampa/documenti/2008/index.html, accessed 2010

Whistlegate

As the days passed after the February 2007 death of Raciti and the polemics and promises piled up, the Ultras were in limbo. They knew from past experience that tough talk was followed by little action and even less change. Still, they worried that this time it was not an Ultra who was killed, but one of the State's own, which might incite retaliatory action. This prompted a variety of actions. One longtime Ultra I met during the week when the games were cancelled (to plan for a soccer without Ultras as well as honor Raciti) was at once convinced that nothing would change and that the Ultras were now a dead phenomenon. He was not speaking thus because of the bankruptcy of the Ultras' *mentalità*, as some older Ultras had said, but because 'the government will not allow us to be Ultras.'

On February 11, 2007, the games recommenced. AS Roma hosted Parma FC, and because the Olympic Stadium had long ago implemented the electronic ticketing system with corresponding turnstiles, AS Roma was allowed to 'host its public.' Outside the stadium there were long lines waiting to enter *Curva Sud*. The police were frisking every entrant, as well as unfurling all flags and banners. In *Curva Sud* there were a few more stewards visible than normal, but otherwise, nothing had changed. The fear that an army of stewards enforcing seating assignments would destroy the groups de facto was, in the end, unfounded. If anything, the pre-game mood was festive. All the groups hung their banners and unfurled their flags. Friends hugged and laughed. Food was shared, and many beers.

It was just as the *Curva* is meant to be. Then something incredible happened. After the players entered the field to the stadium's singing of 'Roma Roma' (the club's anthem) by Antonello Venditti, they gathered around the center-circle. It was announced that a moment of silence for Filippo Raciti would be observed. Within seconds, the *Curva* was awash in a cacophony of whistles — an act of supreme disrespect, and one that forced the rest of the stadium to clap for the minute, in the hope of salvaging the dignity of the occasion. (It is customary in Italy to clap during moments of silence, but the press claimed the authorities had hoped instead for stone silence in order to accentuate the solemnity and seriousness of the occasion.) After the game, Francesco of *Fedayn* agreed that the whistles were disrespectful. They were meant, as he said, to match the disrespect shown the Ultras by the State and media during the week. From my position in the *Curva*, I could tell the whistles began in the upper-left section occupied by *Fedayn*. However, according to radio reports of the whistles, they were begun by *Boys*. For their part, *Boys* silently turned their backs on the proceedings in another premeditated protest at their being forced to join in the commemoration of Raciti's death and the degradation of the Ultras.

The media described the Ultras as 'disgraceful,' 'stupid,' 'idiotic,' 'a minority of barbarity in a sea of gentility,' 'ungrateful,' and, finally, 'defeated.'[17] Callers to post-game radio shows said the Ultras should be banned for life from attending games. At a meeting between some members of *Boys* and *Ultras Primavalle-San Lorenzo* in midweek, the discussion was dominated by the press reactions to what I was calling 'whistlegate.' Matteo of *Primavale* was dismissive, saying, 'It was of no consequence to the Ultras what was printed in newspapers, as the journalists know nothing and invent what they write.' It was expected, then, that they would *strumentalizzare* (instrumentalize, or exploit for profit) any situation against the Ultras.

'The press,' Matteo said, 'has an agenda, to promote the interests of *Calcio Moderno*, and to moralize against the Ultras. This happens all the time — well, anytime there is violence. We see the world from opposing vantage points: when they say virtue [*virtu`*] we say cowardice [*vilta`*], when they say moderation [*moderazione*] we say mediocrity [*mediocrità*].' Jean-Paolo of *Boys* agreed, giving me some examples of how the press 'has sided with a form of life which seeks to diminish the hardness [*durezza*] and clarity [*chiarezza*] of the Ultras. Among other things,' he said, 'the press had been pleased that Prodi and his government of neo-liberals and communists had passed [sic] a law that forces the state to recognize gay marriages, while the nation was aghast at such a defeat of the holiness

17 Quoted in the newspapers *La Repubblica*, *La Gazzetta dello Sport*, *Corriere della Sera*, and *Il Tempo*.

of the family.[18] It had also been silent when three Italian women were gang-raped, stoned [intentionally to death], and buried alive in Cape Verde by the very people to whom it would willingly give the nation in an effort to show how multicultural and liberal it can be. The same press had celebrated when Prodi was in India attempting to create more ways to import cheap fabrics from people that would hammer another nail in the coffin of [Italy's] own legendary textile industry. So it is only natural that the Ultras are the true enemy of the press,' Jean-Paolo said.

Protesting *Calcio Moderno*

With the resumption of the season came the return to normal routines as well, except that the Amato Decree forced the closing of all but four stadiums expected to host games in *Serie A*. Even Milan's famed San Siro was to be closed to the public for failing to install electronic turnstiles. However, around-the-clock work crews insured the stadium could at least host season ticket holders. The closings forced AS Roma to play four consecutive away games in empty stadiums. The first of these, at Empoli, was attended by members of *Fedayn* and *Ultras Romani*, who hung their banners from a fence outside the stadium and listened to the game on a car radio. Their being outside the stadium was meant as a reminder to the players that, 'we will never leave you,' as goes a popular song of *Curva Sud Roma*, and to Amato, the government, the police, the press, and the monied agents of *Calcio Moderno* that, despite the bans and laws, the Ultras were going nowhere. Lorenzo of *Ultras Romani*, present in Empoli, prophetically (considering the killing of Sandri nine months later) made the point: 'They will have to kill us to be free of us. We risk everything for the things in our hearts and because of this we are dangerous to the system [of *Calcio Moderno*] that wants passive consumers.'

Each home game in that eight-game span began with fifteen minutes of silent protest by *Curva Sud*. The first was against Reggina Calcio, the team

---

18   In Chapter Seven I describe the Ultras' responses to DICO, the bill seeking rights for cohabitating couples. The bill never reached the floor of the Upper House (Senate) of the Italian Parliament.

from Reggio Calabria. As the game began, the *Curva* was instructed to remain seated and silent for a protest by way of a banner reading '*15 min di silenzio ... sono urla di rabbia.*' (15 minutes of silence ... [as] shouts of rage). As no other sections of the stadium sing, cheer, or clap like the Ultras, it was noticeably quiet. Somewhere close to ten minutes into the proposed fifteen-minute protest, however, groups of fans in the section next to *Curva Sud*, began to sing. Their songs were quickly met with derisive whistles and a barrage of insults from the *Curva*. The Ultras were instantly as furious as I ever saw them in my time with them. Their derision began as whistles and yelled insults (destined to fall on deaf ears). It progressed into organized chants of '*Distinti, Distinti, Vaffanculo*' (Distinti, go fuck yourself), and then, '*Cantate solo quando volete*' (You only sing when you want) — the latter being an insult designed to show the bourgeois nature of those fans who do not support AS Roma as a duty. The Ultras ended the fifteen-minute protest with chants of '*Curva Sud Alè*,' (Let's go *Curva Sud*).

The short scene captured many elements of the Ultra phenomenon. First, the Ultras understood that they were protesting the media and its ability to portray them in unflattering ways. They had been portrayed as expendable for weeks. What better way to show what they bring to the games than by remaining seated and silent? Second, they must be well-organized to get a section of seventeen thousand people to go along with a protest that was unannounced to the vast majority of those in the *Curva*. Third, the distance between the Ultras and the 'normal fans' was made apparent. The song sung against the *Distinti* section was designed to show them the vacuity of their singing only 'when they want' instead of the Ultra-style of singing for the entire ninety minutes (and more) of the game. To sing at one's leisure removes the sacrifice and commitment from the act. Fourth, the act of silence as protest is difficult for the Ultras. Contrary to how they had been portrayed in the press, their actions as fans are most dear to their movement, so much so that many long-time Ultras condemn anyone who puts political affiliations or ideologies above performance in the *Curva*.

Conclusion

The Ultras, as we are beginning to see, live and act within a distinctive form of life driven by a language of honor, sacrifice, glory, and daring — what they call '*antichi valori*' or a '*vecchia mentalità*'. They use a form of history that promotes the celebration of heroes and heroism while at the same promoting the particular at the expense of the universal. Thus, Romans and Ultras are glorified and magnified while others are ignored or vilified. As we will begin to see, the Ultras' *mentalità* takes its clearest form as an understanding of the world in starkly oppositional or agonic terms.

Their monumentalism keeps history alive and present in their every action as Ultras. Whether it is the memory of fallen Ultras, friends, and colleagues, the glory of Ancient Rome, or the long history of Italian intercity rivalry, the past plays a powerful role in the way they understand themselves. On the evening of Gabriele Sandri's death, when the Ultras of AS Roma and SS Lazio united to confront the police and rampage through the streets of Rome, they did so believing not only that Sandri's death deserved a violent response but also that they were making their own history in doing so. In other words, they would not have acted as Ultras if they stayed passively at home, nor would they have set a proper model to be emulated by later Ultras.

The night of what the media called the 'sack of Rome' as well as the months following the February 2007 death of Filippo Raciti begin to make clear the relationship between the Ultras, the State, and media. The Ultras are adept at using the media for their own ends. The media coverage of performance of fandom, be it choreography, flares, smoke torches, or banners, is counted upon in order to gain notoriety for groups and *curvas*. For the same reasons, it is also hoped that the media will acknowledge the Ultras' social initiatives and protests. However, there is a great distance between these and the expectation that the media will attempt to understand the complexity of the Ultras, their worldview, or their critique of modern bourgeois life. Likewise, the State had long accepted the Ultras and the small-scale violence they perpetrated amongst themselves. They made great shows of force in attempted to quell these but made no moves to prohibit Ultras' access to stadiums. However, after the death of a police officer and a night of what was also called domestic terrorism, both in 2007, the State finally moved to rid soccer of the Ultras. Although the media and State play peripheral roles for the Ultras, whose self-conception, while political, is so insular that the impossibility of being understood by non-Ultras is often assumed, they are critical in determining the discourse of being an Ultra and the freedoms thereby advanced.

In the coming chapters, the media's power to moralize situations will be analyzed more fully, as will the State's ability to determine which forms of violence are legitimate and which are markers of subversion. All the while, the Ultras, their agonistic culture full of the language of premodern warriors, and their connections with neo-Fascism, Rome, and political philosophy will be examined. What emerges is a kind of cultural movement, very political and critical of modernity, also violent, and dedicated to preserving the traditions they feel sustain them and the people of Rome.

CHAPTER FOUR

Ultras, the State, and Violence

I n the previous chapter I described some of the most extreme moments during my time amongst the Ultras. The deaths of Raciti and Sandri became the bookends of this project because they brought to light so many elements of the Ultras: their *mentalità*; violence; and their relationship with the Italian State, soccer, and *Calcio Moderno*. In this chapter, I continue the discussion of their relationship with the State, this time focusing on the distance between the Ultras and the State and media. While the Ultras maintain an ethic that focuses on the virtuous and heroic aspects of violence that are said by Sorel and Nietzsche to lead one beyond the bourgeois form of life, the State and media combine to create and disseminate against the Ultras, a counter-ethic that promotes the legitimacy of State violence and condemns instances of interpersonal violence. Because the chapter requires an examination of the discourses and moralities of violence I also explore the attraction of Nietzsche to AS Roma's Ultras.

AS Roma's Ultras and the State

In the Introduction, I explained that the State and media exist as meta-natural opponents of the Ultras for two reasons — they are not amongst the natural or soccer-related rivals of the Ultras, and they are able to comment upon and define the context of all of the Ultra rivalries. In order to best understand the contention between the Ultras and the State, it is crucially important to understand the ways in which the physical power of the State is bound up with the morality of bourgeois liberalism. Through both of these, the hegemony of the State is legitimized and maintained.

Sorel distinguished between the violence of a revolutionary proletariat and violence in the name of the State.[1] Interestingly, Sorel includes the capacity of intellectuals and bureaucrats to act violently in the state's service. Given their feeble natures, they do so primarily through the wielding of morality and an ethic that condemns violence. What we find in Sorel, then, is an acknowledgment that morality is a tool used by the bourgeoisie against any eruptions that would seek to disturb the peace of the modern marketplace.[2]

Agamben goes further in explaining the links between the state's monopoly of legitimate violence and the incorporation of the modern political subject into a system of protection and happiness. The modern State, he explains, is able to bring all of the 'objects' that dwell within the State's confines to 'subjecthood' by demanding that these (human) objects conform to the State's inclusionary/exclusionary model of humanity.[3] As a corrective to Foucault's 'bio-power,' which proposed that the state lords over the care of the individual, Agamben says that in the modern State, the bare life, or natural life, along with morality and truth, coincides to the point of 'irreducible indistinction.'[4]

Once the State makes a political issue of something formerly excluded from the political — as was the 'bare life' in the classical period, for

---

1 Sorel, 1999, p. xvi.

2 Sorel, 1999, pp. 231–238.

3 Agamben, 1995, pp. 8–12.

4 Agamben, 1995, p. 9.

example — it then has the right to decide in its interests and to bring these interests in-line with those of the State.[5] The State then becomes the sole interpreter of a political meta-language that includes not only narratives of self, but also 'the ability to define 'good and bad,' 'victim and aggressor.'[6]

Within this system, which is totalitarian by definition — in that it offers promises of personal redemption and happiness, thus providing completely for the individual's wellbeing, at the price of mere unthink-ing devotion to the bourgeois form of life — the State and the individual are mutually affirming.[7] What is good for the one is good for the other. However, Deleuze and Guattari propose that at the edges of modern States — if we momentarily conceive of their territoriality as a metaphor for zones of inclusion and exclusion — there are also marginal spaces or thinkers who offer cracks in the order and critiques of its functioning and systemic completeness. They call these 'smooth' or derelict spaces because they are contiguous to every one of the State's spatial coordinates yet offer sites of such unorthodoxy that they cannot be brought within the State's system of reality. One of the most important of these spaces, according to Brian Massumi, is the thought of Friedrich Nietzsche, which he calls 'an immanent outside,' because it signals a plane of exteriority to, or a moving beyond the realm of, bourgeois capitalist modernity.[8]

In thinking of the relationship between the State and the Ultras, *Curva Sud Roma* exists as a derelict space. The contiguous nature of such a space to the reality of the modern State is important because of the circularity of power and discourse that exist between the State and its dissidents.[9] This circularity is predicated upon the State and its media having the ability to control the dissemination of knowledge about its subjects, who then re-spond with a counter-vision informed by their dissident status.[10] For their

---

5   Schmitt, 1976, p. 7.

6   Sunic, 2007, p. 125.

7   Agamben, 1995, p. 10.

8   Massumi, 1987, p. 105.

9   Wolf, 1999, pp. 252–257.

10   Wolf, 1999, pp. 44–45.

part, AS Roma's Ultras respond to the State and its bourgeois prohibition against violence with a discourse informed by revolutionary philosophy that promotes the positive value of violence and aggression — precisely because of their opposition to bourgeois peace and security.

Not only is there a circular nature to the discourses of the State and the Ultras, but also of power and the use of force. According to Maurizio Stefanini, when the State began cracking down on Ultra groups following Raciti's death in February 2007, there began an exodus of the hardest and most politically motivated fascist Ultras from the Italian *curvas* in order to act politically beyond them.[11] The same phenomenon was witnessed in *Curva Sud Roma*.

Because of the ability of the State to make life difficult for Ultras whose political affiliations threaten the State's security, some opted to fade away from the stadiums and fall in with the organized Far Right. Not all Ultras needed to respond in this way, however. Many of the smaller or politically unaligned groups shunned political commitments beyond the *Curva* or AS Roma, fearing danger to the future of the phenomenon. Those in *Boys Roma* and *Padroni di Casa* argue instead that the Ultras are threatening to the State regardless of political affiliation. Manuele, a thirty-one-year-old member of *Padroni di Casa* who works as a paralegal in a small industrial law firm, told me in 2010 'the Ultras represent a 'free space' in Italy that calls into question the rationale of consumption and civic irresponsibility that is becoming the norm.' As the State closed in on that free, or derelict, space, bringing the *curvas* within the domain of its legitimacy, rightist Ultras felt compelled to act more aggressively in the outside world. This was the argument supplied by Fabio, one of the leaders of *Boys Roma*. 'Many of the previous generation of *Boys Ultras*,' he said, 'didn't bother coming back to the stadium after the policing increased in 2007. It was easier to go in the streets, or to join *Forza Nuova* or *Fiamma* [Tricolore]' — radical parties of the Far Right. 'It is easier to be a political extremist in Italy than an Ultra,' he told me.

---

11   Stefanini, 2009, p. 74.

What we see then, is that policing measures might unintentionally create spaces of possible Ultra action that are also more extreme and threatening to the State. It is too soon to tell. What is knowable, and what the rest of this chapter will demonstrate, is that the Ultras offer a form of life that is a direct challenge to the legitimacy of the modern State.

Violence, the State, and the Media

Max Weber's understanding of the modern State has influenced not only each of the above theorists, but Sorel, Agamben, Schmitt and even Deleuze and Guattari too. 'A State,' says Weber, 'is a human community that (successfully) claims the *monopoly of the legitimate use of physical force* within a given territory.'[12] The right to use force, he continues, is restricted to those authorized by the State to do so.[13] Thus, Sorel says, true power is held by those authorized to use violence, and political subjects of the 'dangerous classes' (i.e. proletariat and sub-proletariat, but in reality anyone who stands against the bourgeoisie) exist largely as those capable of being victims of violence.[14] If we take this as a given, that the State exists as the sole right to legitimate violence, what are the consequences for groups like the Ultras who practice a form of violence, often against the police, that, when coupled with a critique of the bourgeois form of life, puts them at odds with the legitimacy of the State?

The Italian State has had an ambiguous relationship with the Far Right since the fall of Fascism in 1945. Although Fascism and its symbols have been outlawed since that time, the intellectual currents that flowed through the Fascist regime and ideology remained. By 1969, when the international student movement formally identified with the summer of 1968 reached Italy, the Far Right was re-organized as bands of urban guerillas and terrorists.[15] Although the Christian Democrats, led by Giulio

---

12   Weber, 1958, p. 78.

13   Weber, 1958, p. 78.

14   Sorel, 1999, pp. 185–187.

15   Ferraresi, 1996, pp. 16–50.

Andreotti, were firmly entrenched in control of Italian politics, this control was based on a shifting coalition of centrist parties of the Left that
came to include the Italian Socialist Party. In the early 1970s, however, the
socialists' involvement was shaken by increased tension between union-
ized industrial workers and the State, causing Andreotti to move tempo-
rarily to the Right for coalition partners before turning back to the Left
in 1973.[16] In this environment, guerilla groups of the Far Left and Right
(including anarchist groups that fit with neither) began exchanging ter-
rorist acts in Italian cities, highlighted by the 1978 abduction and murder
of Christian Democrat leader Aldo Moro by the Leftist Red Brigades and
the 1980 Rightist bombing of Bologna's central train station that killed
eighty-five people.[17] The Rightist guerillas, however, were often aided, or
at least unhindered, by the State, which sought to use the destabilized
environment caused by domestic terrorism to shore up support for the
Andreotti government.[18]

It was in this milieu that the first groups of Ultras originated. Despite
having groups in major cities being founded along extreme political
lines (*Fedayn* and *Boys Roma* in Rome, *Fossa dei Leoni* and *Boys SAN* in
Milan), the State did not conceive of these groups as a threat. Instead, the
Ultras were allowed to thrive as soccer fans, seemingly at a remove from
the political instability of the day.[19] However, that idyllic period came to
an end when the Italian *curvas* began shifting from Leftist or apolitical
leanings toward the Far Right in the mid-1990s.[20] Ferraresi explains that,
while the Far Right was able to thrive in the crisis years of the Christian
Democrats, it was seen as threatening to the stability of the neoliberal
regime of Silvio Berlusconi. Additionally, the Right from the 'years of lead'
(1969–1980) had attempted to connect the Right with a 'movement ideology' in contrast with the Rightist radicals who developed in the 1990s,

---

16   Ginsborg, 2003, pp. 333–337.

17   Ferraresi, 1995, pp. 159–160.

18   Ferraresi, 1995, pp. 116–143.

19   Stefanini, 2009, pp. 11–16.

20   Podaliri and Balestri, 1998, p. 89.

who instead sought a more extreme ideological form that championed 'being beyond' the State rather than a victorious turn to liberal power.[21] It can be surmised that State officials felt the Ultras belonged to this new form of the Right — with its less clearly defined boundaries, allegiances, and pronounced sense of autonomy from the bourgeois form of life, especially as Ultra violence became endemic to soccer matches during the same period. And as the police presence at soccer games increased steadily from 1994 to 2004, so too did the tension between the Ultras and the police.[22]

During this same period, organizers of *Serie A*, Italy's top professional soccer league, began to seek greater profits from the game. England's Premier League, the quintessence of modern, consumer-based soccer, began in 1993 and reaped immediate financial gains by way of domestic and international television rights contracts. *Serie A* would become the world's richest league by 1999, paying the highest player wages, as well as becoming a popular advertising vehicle for Italy's most important industries.[23] The Ultras, with their organized mob violence and manifestoes and protests against *Calcio Moderno*, appeared to be 'bad for business;'[24] that they attracted more police attention in the 1990s could also be because they threatened the stability of soccer, Italy's most stable industry.[25]

What is certain is that the interactions between the State and the Ultras have been defined by hostility. Returning to Weber's understanding that modern states must control the use of violence in their territories, Agamben argues that modern neoliberal States utilize states of emergency or a 'state of exception' to strengthen the security of the State at the expense of individual liberties. During a state of exception, the 'well-being of the State' is used to justify an increase in suspicion and surveillance of

21   Ferraresi, 1995, pp. 190–194.

22   Roversi and Balestri, 2002, p. 43.

23   Foot, 2006, pp. 489–495.

24   Garsia, 2004, p. 36.

25   Foot, 2006, p. 7.

private individuals.[26] For the Ultras, just such a state of exception exists. Each professional soccer game that takes place in Italy is a militarized zone, as the police make use of the 'show of force' technique to enforce the peace. Surveillance is also a normalized part of the Ultras' experience of soccer, especially after the 2005 Pisanu Decree, which demanded that Closed Circuit Television systems be installed in all Italian stadiums hosting professional matches.

The consequences of this militarization of soccer games can be deadly, as both Raciti and Sandri attest. However, it is important to remember what it tells us of the State and its responsibility toward the Ultras — some of whom are professionals, students, and even fellow police officers. With soccer games being militarized, they are essentially states of exception. Therefore, the Ultras, by definition, lie beyond the moral obligation of the State.[27] The State alone is able to define what is included and therefore excluded from its purview. In doing so it also defines the expectations of those who are excluded. As Agamben argues, the policing of any 'agent of chaos' becomes part of the legitimation not only of State violence but also of the State itself.[28] In this way the physical repression of the Ultras comes to mirror the terms of their condemnation by the media (delineated below).

Agamben was motivated to interrogate the liberal State in these terms by the juridical scholarship of Carl Schmitt, which explained how the liberal State defined its enemies and violence. The State must be free, as sovereign, to determine who and what is the political and mortal enemy of its people.[29] What the Ultras question are these very definitions. By seeking hostility and extremely restricted modes of altruism, they challenge the bases of liberal consumer-based passivity and freedom.[30] In so

---

26   Agamben, 2005, pp. 32–40.

27   Agamben, 1998, p. 18.

28   Agamben, 1998, pp. 17–29.

29   Schmitt, 1976, pp. 35–36.

30   Sorel, 1999, p. 216.

doing, though, they also take exception to the State's legitimate power to maintain such a state of passivity amongst its populace.

Through the media, the State is able to maintain its hegemonic grip upon public (liberal) discourse on violence, inclusion/exclusion, and the enemies of the State. As Gramsci explained, it is not simply a matter of enforcing discipline upon the public, because the State's discourse of 'the public good' is already based on a high level of consent within civil society. In other words, hegemonic ideas are already received as natural truths. But, when the hegemonic fabric is torn — when consent is withdrawn (as in the 'derelict spaces' described above) — State policing is justified in order to maintain hegemony over the main body of the public sphere.[31] The relationship between the State (and its repression of the Ultras) and the media (and its condemnations of the Ultras) is seemingly contradictory. If the press is in business to sell newspapers or gain viewers and listeners, then Ultra violence is conceivably 'good' for the press. However, the press is also in business to maintain the hegemony of the bourgeoisie over the 'subaltern classes' that threaten its dominance of the 'cultural and political' fields.[32]

In describing the circularity or mutually dependent nature of the discourse and violence of 'being Ultras' with the media discourse about the Ultras, I do not intend to give the impression that the former's self-understanding is merely reactive. Instead, their knowledge, and use, of the Counter-Enlightenment philosophies of Nietzsche, Sorel, and Evola all demonstrate a high level of awareness of the image they project as well as the historical nature of what they are doing. The rest of this chapter will focus upon the discourses and ethics of violence and inclusion/exclusion that the Ultras and State utilize against each other.

---

31 Spanos, 1993, p. 158–160.

32 Crehan, 2002, p. 104.

Discourses of Violence and Morality: Sorel and Ethics of Violence

Just as Nietzsche provides a rationale for rejecting the morality of the modern world, Georges Sorel provides justification for maintaining a counter 'ethic of violence' to that of the modern West. Contrasting the modern aversion to violence with the 'cruelty ... [and] brutality of past times,' Sorel explained that, by example, the Roman celebration of strength and dominance was accompanied by 'uprightness, sincerity, a lively sentiment of justice, [and] pious respect before the holiness of morals.' Instead, the modern democratic world is characterized by an extreme aversion to violence — so much so that any violators of passivity may be considered insane — but also by 'lies, duplicity, treachery, the spirit of deception, the contempt for property, [and] disdain for instinctive probity and legitimate customs.'[33]

Sorel's analysis stems from his considering violence only from the position of its 'ideological consequences.'[34] Thus, the violence of the State and its capitalist rulers, for instance, is justified, but no more so than the derelicts who fight its hegemony. Elsewhere, he borrowed from Paul Bureau to relativize the modern aversion to violence. He explained that in Norway it was possible to find populations that subscribed to strict moral systems, but who were also averse to passivity. 'A stab given by a man who is virtuous in his morals, but violent, is a social evil less serious and more easily curable than the excessive profligacy of young men reputed to be more civilized.'[35]

Sorel's examination of modern precautions and prohibitions against violence began, though, where the Ultras — like the Fascists — based their critiques of modernity. Modern thinkers, he said, favor industrial societies, over military societies, because peace, while being essential to consumerism, has 'been considered the greatest of blessings and the essential

---

33   Sorel, 1999, pp. 187–188.

34   Ibid, p. 178.

35   Ibid, p. 176.

condition of all material progress.'[36] Fascism — especially while under the influence of the Futurists and Syndicalists — condemned pacifism and neutralism as properties leading to the creation of 'economic men' at the expense of 'heroic men.' Thus, it praised the purifying effects of war and dynamism. The Ultras, likewise, understand that occasional violence can be useful in reducing the value of Italian soccer to those attempting to engulf it within *Calcio Moderno*. For the soccer of the Ultras is full of rivalries, antagonism, aggression, and violence — the characteristics associated with the heroic life.[37]

Although the Ultras have shown an ability and willingness to think through the 'ideological consequences' of violence, it must be remembered that violence is more useful to the Ultras as a salve of sorts against modern life. For this reason, Sorel and Nietzsche provide important lessons on the possibility of violence to coexist within a moral-ethical system (like the Ultra *mentalità*) that is enmeshed in myth and narrative — significant when we consider that the Ultras largely reject the world of wealth, materialism, and consumerism.

The Moral Prohibition Against Violence

There are two intertwining elements that will alternate as the focus of this important section: one, the morality of the Italian political class and media which seeks a prohibition of violence; and two, the Ultras and their understanding of violence. Both of these combine to make knowable what I, following Sorel, am calling an Ultra 'ethic of violence.' In other words, both sides of the opposition have developed ways of talking about violence. And, both of these distinct ways mirror the visions held by each side of the optimal state of soccer (and life in general): egalitarian and sporting for the one and hierarchical and warring for the other. Where one speaks of delinquency, the other speaks of *vivere pericolosamente* (living dangerously), contemptuous of life that has been stripped of confrontation.

---

36   Ibid, p. 175.

37   Koon, 1985, pp. 3–5.

The Media and Violence

The Italian press has an ambiguous approach to the Ultras. On the one hand, they are presented as the color and excitement of soccer. Most broadcasts of games begin with a montage that includes Ultras with flags and flares, even as the latter are now banned from stadiums. Additionally, journalists occasionally praise the social initiatives, and even the commitment to fandom, of the Ultras. However, these occasions are offset and rendered strange by press hostility toward the Ultras, which centers on its violent aspects. Past aggressions against one another and current aggression toward the police are frequent media topics.

That the media presents the Ultras negatively is not a concern for many Ultras. Indeed, many take responsibility for the image; entranced by the media attention they received in the 1990s. Most Ultras, at least those in the large cities or those of teams in *Serie A*, were conscious of the media and even strategized how best to make it into newspapers and news telecasts. The notoriety of many groups like *Boys Roma* or *Irriducibili Lazio* was established by media coverage, leading these groups, among others, to be revered and feared throughout the Italian *curvas*. The clippings from various newspapers of their history of violent encounters fill two notebooks at the *Boys Roma* office.

By focusing only on aggression and violence, the media fails to understand or clearly present the Ultra *mentalità* or to specify the targets of their enmity, which come across only as rationales for violence. In many respects, the Ultras are what the press makes of them: aggressive, violent, and driven by agonism and rivalry. Nor would they deny this. Where there is a glaring contradistinction between the Ultras of the media and the Ultras' self-understanding is in the press's moral oppositions to rivalry, violence, and aggression, and associated utopian vision of soccer — a vision without the Ultras. In the end, the media demonize the Ultras as a way to moralize against aggression, violence, and conflict, omitting these from the legitimate concerns of Italy's passive liberal subjects.

From the perspective of the Ultras, what the media wants is a world in which all are seated and clapping politely as twenty-two actors present an evening of entertainment; in which the peoples and cities of Italy and the world exist in perfect harmony; in which communities no longer appear homogeneous and teams are made up only of low-priced Africans and Asians; and in which games take place at times and places only designed for a television audience — in short, the world of *Calcio Moderno*.

The Ultras' understanding of the media's motivations is formed by the daily coverage of Ultra activity in the Italian press. For the purpose of brevity, only two periods of media coverage will be analyzed here: the immediate post-Raciti period of February 2007, and the period before AS Roma's *Serie A* meeting with SSC Napoli in October 2007 (just one week before the killing of Gabriele Sandri).

How to Cure a 'Sick Culture Of Sport'

After the death of Filippo Raciti in February 2007, the press was united in condemnation of the violence that led to the officer's killing. Many *opinionisti* (columnists) worried that Italy was suffering not only a hooligan problem but also a generally negative culture of sport. Government ministers like Giovanna Melandri, Minister for Youth and Sports under both Prodi and Berlusconi, supported their view. Melandri, a member of one of the Left parties that emerged after the collapse of Communism — Democrats of the Left, subsequently renamed the Democratic Party — was one of the most vociferous opponents of the Ultras' view of soccer (as a system of rivals and enemies) in the days after Raciti's death. What she proposed in place of Italy's overly extreme sense of *rivalità* (rivalry) was an 'English model' of sport, in which sportsmanship, tolerance, multiculturalism, and deterritorialization replace rivalry, discrimination, Italianness, and localism.

In Rome, the local sports newspaper, *Il Romanista*, championed this attitude most loudly. In a week's worth of editorials, the paper's director Ricardo Luna, a former editor with the center-Left Espresso group (which includes *La Repubblica*, the leading center-Left newspaper in Rome), made it clear that 'rivalry was killing Italian sport.' The tradition and cherished practice of vociferous *tifare contro* (rooting against) on the part of many Italians was 'archaic in a world striving for oneness.'[38] Luna took up the theme of a 'sick culture of sport' the day after Raciti's death. His answer to this problem (for no one in the media was asking if this was perhaps a positive element of Italian life) was 'education;' not of the current generation of fans, which included the Ultras, but the next. 'The next generation,' he said, 'should be made to see that "*si può essere avversario, non nemico*"' (one can be an adversary without being an enemy). A few days later, Luna, buoyed by the positive response to his understanding of the problem, gave his vision of what could be done to facilitate this utopia.

First, rid soccer of the Ultras, for while Italy itself was sick, the Ultras were sickest of all. Second, fill the *curvas* with children. And third, close all guest sections and allow fans to intermix.[39] While the first two were unlikely to be accomplished, the third was worth trying, according to Luna. For one week, *Il Romanista* promoted the idea of integrating fans. As the February 11, 2007 game against FC Parma approached, Luna realized that AS Roma was powerless to change the Italian Football Federation's ticketing policies, so instead of insisting that the guest section be closed, he invited Parma fans to buy tickets in the Monte Mario grandstand as a demonstration of support for this new vision of sport and soccer in Italy.[40] Although only a handful of Parma Ultras attended the game, standing in the designated guest section, it was reported that some Parma fans did sit in Monte Mario.[41] In the end these matters were overshadowed by *Curva Sud* having whistled during the moment of silence to remember Raciti.

AS Roma-SSC Napoli: *A Braccia Aperte* (With Open Arms)

The AS Roma and SSC Napoli Ultras share a vehement hatred for one another. Although the games on the field tend not to manifest the aggression

---

38   *Il Romanista*. Anno IV, n. 39. 9 February 2007, pp. 1, 4.

39   *Il Romanista*. Anno IV, n. 35. 5 February 2007, p. 1.

40   *Il Romanista*. Anno IV, n. 37. 7 February 2007, pp. 1, 4.

41   *Il Romanista*. Anno IV, n. 42. 12 February 2007, p. 2.

and combativeness characteristic of the derby games between AS Roma and SS Lazio, for the Ultras the rivalry with the *Napolitani* is more intense. Both sets of Ultras boast of provocation of, and victory over, the other, and for AS Roma's Ultras Naples has value as the dark pole in a Manichean scheme. Indeed, it represents or symbolizes the lowest value one can have and still be Italian. I asked Maurizio of *Romulae Genti* to clarify, especially as his father's family hails from a small town between Naples and Rome. 'There are *zingari* [Roma or gypsies], *stranieri* [strangers or foreigners] like Africans and Muslims,' he told me, 'and then *Napolitani*. It is enough to be from Naples to be disliked.'

For example, the insults AS Roma's Ultras sing to other Italians tend to be structural or situational. The Juventus fans, whose team has long been owned by the Agnelli family (of FIAT), are insulted for being 'slaves to the Agnelli.' *Livornesi* (people of Livorno) are insulted for being Communists. *Veneziani* (people of Venice) are insulted for living in a lagoon. *Milanesi* (people of Milan) are insulted for being Lombards and former Roman slaves. *Napolitani* are insulted, however, just for being from Naples.

Compared to other rivalries, AS Roma's Ultras are less articulate when explaining their opposition to the *Napolitani*. Whereas the songs they sing against the other fans point to the above-mentioned specific reasons for rivalry, and whereas they speak with a sense of irony or playfulness against other cities, teams, and *curvas*, when asked about the *Napolitani*, many say matter-of-factly that they hate Naples and *Napolitani* and leave it at that.

So it was that the Roman Ultras were looking forward to hosting their biggest rivals and to opportunities to make the SSC Napoli Ultras pay for past disputes. The media treated the October 20, 2007 game as the biggest test yet of the post-Raciti security measures. The common assumption among the Ultras and the press was that the authorities would simply prohibit the SSC Napoli fans from traveling to Rome for the game. Although it is unconstitutional to ban travel itself, the government is able to ban ticket sales beyond the city or region hosting the game. They can also prohibit selling tickets for the designated guest section.

Il Romanista began covering the October 20, 2007 game against SSC Napoli on October 6, 2007. On that day, Felice Ferlizzi, the President of the National Observatory of Sporting Events, was interviewed, saying in essence that AS Roma's Ultras had behaved impeccably in the young season's games, but that one misstep and AS Roma would face a stadium ban. This was because of their past reputation for incidents, in spite of previous promises by the Observatory that each team would begin the season with a clean record and that it would act only to punish current wrongdoings.[42] A warning was issued that even singing racist songs would be considered grounds to close the Olympic Stadium or ban travel. Two days later, AS Roma's Ultras traveled to Parma and caused no problems. Therefore, the next game against SSC Napoli was under no threat of being played entirely behind closed doors. The same day, though, Inter Milan's Ultras unfurled banners calling *Napolitani tubercolosi* (tuberculosis sufferers) and *colerosi* (cholera sufferers), which implied that Naples was a Third World city.

Normally *Il Romanista* devoted itself to AS Roma on the morning following an AS Roma game. On the morning of October 9, 2007 however, well before October 20th, the headline screamed '*Siamo Tutti Italiani*' (We are all Italians) and the banners from Inter Milan-SSC Napoli were displayed on the cover.[43] The tone of the issue was that the 'anti-violence laws' enacted after Raciti were failing. There had been no fights in Milan, it is true, but this was because there had been no SSC Napoli fans. (Actually, there was a small group seated in the grandstands with SSC Napoli scarves and flags. They were obviously not Ultras but their presence in Milan was noted — as defiance of the travel ban — in the eventual decision to ban the *Napolitani* from traveling to Rome.) Yet, the media had understood the banners as a form of provocation.

---

42   *Il Romanista.* Anno IV, n. 275. 6 October 2007, pp. 8–9.

43   *Il Romanista.* Anno IV, n. 278. 9 October 2007, p. 1.

Figure 10. Ultras graffiti, notably, '*Curva Sud*, Strong and Roman,' and 'Neapolitan Jew,' *Stadio Artemio Franchi*, Florence, 2007.

For the next two days, the local media turned on the *AS Roma Ultras*, who had gone from destroying train cars two years earlier (during a trip to Naples for a *Coppa Italia* game) to doing little more than eating and sleeping in them. Nonetheless, the Roman media, led by two center-Left papers, *La Repubblica* and *Il Romanista*, went into attack mode. By October 11, 2007, Ultras were writing to *Il Romanista* saying they, as Romans and Ultras, were not to be co-identified with the *Napolitani*, and that they hated Naples. Finally, one Ultra wrote that if the *Napolitani* arrived in Rome the Ultras were prepared for World War III.[44] Of course, normal fans wrote to say that hatred was abhorrent and that the Ultras were animals. For every opinion supporting the Ultras there were two opposing. The back page of the issue said simply, '*Sono Romanista ed odio nessuno*' (I am an AS Roma fan and I hate no one). The question of the day on the newspaper's website asked if one hated Naples, to which more than 90% responded 'No.'

Also on October 11, 2007, *La Repubblica* published an exposé on politics in Italian *curvas*. According to the article, there are two hundred and sixty-eight political Ultra groups in Italy and all of these share a common enemy: the forces of law and order. It said that political extremism and its concordant violence are the biggest concerns of the Observatory and other forces of Italian law and order; and that extreme political parties like *Forza Nuova* seek fertile ground in the *curvas* today amongst young males between fourteen and sixteen.

La Gazzetta dello Sport, the nation's most popular sports daily, joined in. On October 12, 2007, it announced that the 'good times are over for the Ultras.' It explained that the forces of law and order had begun a new strategy that ultimately bans away travel if the Ultras misbehave (by fights with Ultras or police, unfurling unauthorized banners, or singing offensive songs); or the game is considered too risky for fans. The paper also announced that this new State strategy, called 'Operation Clean *Curvas*', would keep the ten worst offending *curvas* in the country under constant surveillance. The Ultras of AS Roma and SSC Napoli were first and second on the initial list of ten.

The next day, October 13, *La Gazzetta* explained the inclusion of the ten Ultras under surveillance. SSC Napoli was on the list because of the fifteen or so of their fans who were at the Inter game, as well as an ongoing investigation into *Curva A*, the home of Napoli's Ultras, extorting tickets

---

44   *Il Romanista*. Anno IV, n. 280. 11 October 2007, p. 16.

from the club. AS Roma was on the list because 'it is a *curva* of the Far Right' (the same rationale that landed *Serie C1* team Lucca on the list). It singled out *Boys Roma* as being the most violent group in Italy and cited as evidence that they turned their backs on the Raciti moment of silence back in February.

Meanwhile on October 12, 2007, the Observatory decided that the game would take place without SSC Napoli supporters. Five days later, after conferring with Roman police authorities, it was decided to have only AS Roma season ticket holders in the stadium. As expected by the Ultras, this was met with disappointment by the media, who desperately wanted a mixed stadium with no guest section in order to show the world that Italy was a civilized nation.[45] With this in mind, *Il Romanista* created an issue devoted entirely to distancing what it called 'true fans' (the bourgeoisie) from the 'delinquents' (the Ultras). On the cover was an open letter written by AS Roma's beloved coach Luciano Spalletti.

Under the headline 'we must unite to defeat the violent fans,' he wrote that the game should be a party and not an opportunity for partisanship. He asked all fans to help Italy move beyond the need to have police forces outside stadiums in order to keep the peace between the opposing fans. He concluded by saying that the only way forward for soccer was without any 'divisions and barriers, either ideological or material.'[46] Inside, one found two full pages devoted to fans pledging their allegiance to stop the Ultras from destroying the game with their violence. They were, as the headline said, '*tutti uniti contro i violenti*' (all united against the violent). For two days Rome and Italy spoke in glorious terms of Spalletti's letter. He was 'courageous,' 'correct,' and 'a real man' for having stood up to the Ultras and their 'delinquency' (according to RAI's TG2 on October 15, 2007).

Then on October 16, 2007, *Il Romanista* allowed a counter-voice to the moralism against violence and published an interview with Giuliano Castellino, co-founder of *Padroni di Casa*. Castellino wasted no time in

---

45 *Il Romanista*. Anno IV, n. 281. 12 October 2007, p. 8.

46 *Il Romanista*. Anno IV, n. 282. 13 October 2007, p. 1.

pointing out that the '*a braccia aperte*' (open arms) theme that the media had taken with AS Roma-SSC Napoli was not only utopian but also '*moralistico*' (moralistic). He said that Padroni di Casa was disciplined and organized and thus rarely involved in violence. But, he added, the 2001 game in Naples was 'like Iraq' and included the mistreatment of AS Roma's Ultras by the police. Because of this AS Roma-SSC Napoli could never be contested as if the fans were 'brothers.' When asked about Spalletti's letter, Castellino chastised the manager for being manipulated by the media against the *Curva*, saying 'Spalletti should concentrate on training the team.'

As for those who condemn the Ultras for being political, he explained that 'life is political. Life does not end when one enters the *curva* but is more amplified. After all, *Padroni di Casa* loves Rome above all else and thus works to help Romans who are without homes or meals. Some come to the stadium and are enraptured for ninety minutes and then go home and do nothing. For us [*Padroni di Casa*], that energy remains throughout the week and it is used, along with the efforts of *Fiamma Tricolore* [at the time, one of two popular movement-based neo-Fascist parties in Italy, along with *Forza Nuova*], to make Rome a better place for Romans and Italians to live.'[47]

Turning to the press, Castellino accused reporters of turning a blind eye toward the positive things that Padroni di Casa and other groups had done in various Roman neighborhoods, only to descend upon the Ultras, even when the only thing to report were whistles, as if they were criminals and '*mafiosi*.' He asked specifically why, although no one came to file a report after fifteen armed Leftists ransacked the group's office, when four SS Lazio Ultras of the Far Right were caught with weapons the entire national press '*sono ai ferri corti*' (have their knives out).

As for the police, he said only that the Ultras are against any form of arrogance and overbearingness, whether by police or a fan that, for instance, insults someone in the presence of his wife and children. The Ultras, he said, are about being extreme, or 'beyond' as he called it — beyond the

---

47   *Il Romanista*. Anno IV, n. 285. 16 October 2007, p. 5.

law, beyond the State, and beyond the stadium. As for the whistles against Raciti, the *Curva* was not protesting Raciti but the moment of silence and the arrogance of a State that insults dead Ultras every weekend.[48]

The bourgeois fans exploded in indignation over the interview. The cover of *Il Romanista* on October 17, 2007 announced that, 'the *curva* that had insulted the Napolitani [Inter's *Curva Nord*] is closed for one game,' and that 'the Ultra [Castellino] is no fan of AS Roma.'[49] Both headlines were followed up inside with articles saying 'clean up this shame' in reference to Inter Milan's Ultras and 'a chorus of "shut ups"' to *Padroni di Casa.*' An ex-police chief of Rome said that having people like Castellino in Rome was justification for closing the doors to the stadium for good — that way they could 'keep the animals out.'[50]

Although one would have to turn all the way back to the emergence of Judeo-Christian morality in order to find the moment when it became hegemonic in the West, it is clear from the discourse on violence, rivalry, aggression, and hatred that enveloped the build-up to AS Roma-SSC Napoli in 2007 that there is a fundamental distance between how these are understood by the Ultras and the media. For as Nietzsche argues, there was a form of life and morality that pre-existed the morality of the modern West. Below I will demonstrate how the morality and ethics of the Ultras more closely resembles Nietzsche's pre-modern morality than the modern. What we must understand first is that the model of soccer and bourgeois life espoused by the media and private individuals who interacted with it through polls and letters is on the level of a 'common sense' that cannot be separated from the practical, everyday behavior of modern bourgeois subjects.[51] After all, Castellino had not demanded that all of Italy understand soccer as do the Ultras, only that the Ultras themselves be allowed to understand it this way. He had not defended the Ultras' right to violence, but instead their right to hatred and discrimination. In

---

48   *Il Romanista.* Anno IV, n. 285. 16 October 2007, p. 5

49   *Il Romanista.* Anno IV, n. 286. 17 October 2007, p. 1.

50   *Il Romanista.* Anno IV, n. 286. 17 October 2007, pp. 3 and 4.

51   Crehan, 2002, pp. 173–174.

the end, this is exactly what *Il Romanista* and the media could not abide. As Riccardo Luna wrote, 'there is no room in soccer for these kinds of "prejudices."'[52]

Ultras, Violence, and Nietzsche
The Purposes of Violence

Although I am arguing, based on the evidence I gathered, that the ethic of violence employed by the Ultras is more prevalent than actual violence, it must be remembered that the history of the Ultras in all parts of Italy, but especially Rome, shows it to be a fundamentally violent phenomenon. Returning to Sorel, who asks us to think of the purposes of violence, we see that the purpose of State violence against the Ultras is to maintain the State's monopoly of legitimate violence in the Italian territory. At the same time, and more mundanely, the State is violent against the Ultras in order to protect the moneyed interests of the business of soccer. In later chapters I will examine the diminution of soccer-related violence in recent years. For now, it is clear from public statements and actions that the State is intent to eliminate all forms of violence from soccer matches, and especially violence between Ultras and the police.

As with the statistical data on violence between soccer fans reported in the previous chapter, according to the National Center of Information on Sporting Events violence between soccer fans and the police has lately been severely diminished. From 2003–2004 to 2007–2008 violence between fans and the police is down 79%. After reaching a high of two hundred and fifty-seven incidences in 2004–2005, by 2007–2008 the incidences of violence between police and fans was fifty-three. In that period, injuries to police have also plummeted, from one hundred and eighty-one in 2004–2005 to twenty-two in 2007–2008. However, while injuries to fans have also dropped, from seventy-six to thirty-one, 2007–2008 showed more injuries to fans in violent encounters with the police than to police officers. Concurrently, arrests for acts of violence against police

---

52   *Il Romanista*. Anno IV, n. 287. 18 October 2007, p. 1.

or other forces of law and order are up from fifty-eight in 2004–2005 to seventy-three in 2007–2008. This has also happened as attendance has plummeted 23% in the same period.[53] In examining these statistics, the Observatory proclaimed that the State is winning its battle against soccer-related violence.

Returning to the purposes of violence, this time of the Ultras, we see the crux of the issue. The Ultras use violence just as Sorel proposed for the French sub-proletariat: as a way to maintain the distance between themselves and the bourgeois form of life.[54] They use violence as a way to distance themselves from the State and its morality of peace, tolerance, and inclusion. But, because the Ultras have no political revolutionary intent, but instead focus upon what Emilio Gentile has called an 'anthropological revolution,' — which seeks to create a new type or form of man — they remain too closely bound up with the State and the industry of soccer to be able to practice their ethical violence with impunity. As the examples above demonstrate, the media is as concerned with the Ultras conceptualization of soccer and their form of life as it is with their actual violent encounters.

The Ultras' Nietzsche
The Anti-Liberal Nietzsche

Through their politics and deeply ideological *mentalità*, the Ultras find themselves aligned with Nietzsche's critiques of modernity and 'the modern man.' Nietzsche's place in this narrative is complex, for while he offers me instruction for understanding clashes of morality and forms of life, he offers the Ultras a way to formulate and create distance between themselves and modernity. It is where these intersect that the affective power of these words lies. That being said, Nietzsche plays an active role in how the more ideologically committed Rightist groups understand the Ultra phenomenon. The leadership of *Boys Roma*, *Romulae Genti*, and

---

53   CNIMS, Campionato di Calcio 2007–2008 — Punto di Situazione, pp. 1–11.

54   Sorel, 1999, p. 85.

Padroni di Casa all utilize a Nietzschean reading of the distance between the Ultras and the bourgeoisie. In the large groups (*Boys* and *Padroni di Casa*) these ideas are disseminated through hours of spirited conversation that occur at the groups' offices. For *Romulae Genti*, the small size of the group (less than twenty people) and exclusive membership ensure that each member is already familiar with Nietzsche before joining. Some of these are former members of *Antichi Valori*, which used to find inspiration from *The Gay Science*. Beyond these groups, AS Roma's Ultras acted in accord with Nietzsche's philosophy, regardless of how deeply he was known by the mass of Ultras. Most fundamentally, AS Roma's Ultras' critique of modernity parallels that of Nietzsche. For the Ultras mentioned above, this is purposeful.

For Nietzsche, modernity was problematic because of three foundational features: the relentless process of democratization; the tendency to exalt compassion and pity; and a cult of facile painlessness. These three combined to act as corrupting agents turning European civilization into a rest home for sheep-like herd animals.[55] To arrest the corrosive influence of modernity, Nietzsche attacked the moral and ethical system that he argued provided the intellectual, spiritual, and philosophical impetus toward mediocre standardization. He did so not to leave Europeans without value but in order to further the re-establishment of heroic pre-modern values. These he consistently identified as strength, honor, discipline, spiritualism, hierarchy, distance, and veneration (among others).[56]

Because his critique was designed to destroy so as to create, Nietzsche proposed that the weakness promoted by modern life could be overcome in the present. Modern weakness he characterized by 'indolent peace, cowardly compromise,' preoccupation with triviality, extreme tolerance, and a desire to forgive all through 'understanding.'[57] To combat these instincts of modernity, Nietzsche demands that one 'thirst for lightening and action . . . to stay as far away as possible from the happiness of

---

55 Cate, 2002, p. 472.

56 Nietzsche, 2001, p. 241.

57 Nietzsche, 2005, p. 173.

weaklings.'[58] Modernity, he explained, and its normalization of middle class mediocrity, has diminished the species and made 'us' smaller. Our goal is now a soft life of comfort, with hands for mediocre work but unfit for making fists.[59]

While there is much to be gained from Nietzsche's (postmodern) deconstruction via genealogy of modern hermeneutic concepts, his rationale for pursuing such a project is often lost when one ignores the political aspects of his motivations. Put somewhat differently, by ignoring Nietzsche's 'great politics,' — wherein he distinguishes between the higher, aristocratic and noble, and the lower, democratic and cosmopolitan, forms of life, and urges his readers to liberate themselves from the latter at any cost — one is able to use Nietzsche to support the most liberal of projects which he himself would never have countenanced.

But those who ignore 'great politics' would be unable to appreciate the deepest implications of Nietzsche's thought: namely, how even those on the most radical edge of modernity are still children of *ressentiment* as long as they think with bourgeois modernity's image of thought. In embracing the characteristics of the Nietzschean noble, the Ultras, better perhaps than the Far Right with which they are most often associated, transvaluate the foundations of bourgeois modernity. This is important for the obvious macro-political ramifications of such a transvaluation, but perhaps more so for the micro-political transformations that it affords.

For in transvaluation there can be no simple Manichean shift between active noble forces and reactive slave forces in order to transcend what is modern in each of us. In other words, there must be 'no simple substitution' of values, but a radical conversion of valuing itself.[60] Transvaluation thus becomes less about a genealogy of oppositions between the Classical world and Judeo-Christian modernity than about re-constituting the very ground of human thought.

As Gilles Deleuze says:

---

58   Ibid, p. 4.

59   Cate, 2002, p. 440.

60   Deleuze, 2006, p. 175.

The instinct of revenge is the force that constitutes the essence of what we call psychology, history, metaphysics, and morality. The spirit of revenge is the genealogical element of *our* [i.e., modern] thought, the transcendental principle of *our* way of thinking. [. . .] We do not really know what a man denuded of *ressentiment* would be like. A man who would not accuse or depreciate existence — would he still be a man, would he think like a man? Would he not already be something other than man? To have *ressentiment* or to not have *ressentiment* — there is no greater difference, beyond psychology, beyond history, beyond metaphysics.[61]

Deleuze is clearly talking about the *Übermensch*, but whereas other thinkers — perhaps drunk on Nietzsche's poetic proclamations of his arrival — discount the sacrifices necessary for moving men in his direction, Deleuze is unsparing in connecting *ressentiment* with the very tools of modern consciousness:

Evaluations, in essence, are not values but ways of being, modes of existence of those who judge and evaluate, serving as principles for the values on the basis of which they judge. This is why we always have the beliefs, feelings, and thoughts that we deserve given our way of being or our form of life. There are things that can only be said, felt, or conceived, values that can only be adhered to, on condition of "base" evaluation, "base" living, and "base" thinking. This is the crucial point: high and low, noble and base, are not values but represent the differential element from which the value of values themselves derives.[62]

The intense physicality of the Ultras, and the ways that they not only use it to defend their life of rivalry and hostility, but also incorporate it into that life, take transvaluation to this second level, leaving behind what the bourgeois fans or passive political subjects of the State need to survive. In their place, the Ultras justify small — pack-like — social aggregations with philosophies and actions that, as we have seen, place them beyond the purview of the State.

---

61   Ibid, p. 35.

62   Ibid, pp. 1–2.

Nietzsche, Ultras, and Conflicts with Fascism

In language closer to Deleuze and Guattari's spatial dynamism of *A Thousand Plateaus*, Nietzsche creates thoughts no longer suffering the administrative machinery or moral economy of the State, but that are instead displaced into frontiers and labyrinthine streets where new movements and distributions become possible.[63] This is apparent in the violent and aggressive form of life celebrated by the Ultras, just as it was in the interventionist position and revolutionary politics of D'Annunzio, Marinetti, and Mussolini before World War I.[64] However, there is a current of elitism that runs through Nietzsche's philosophy that is at odds with Fascism.[65] This is because his thought is presented primarily to individual readers and with a deep suspicion of mass-based political organization.[66] He demands readers who are able to cast-off the need for broad co-identification, especially in the terms of modern liberal politics. Thus, Nietzsche's ideas come at the cost of some level of social disengagement. Although it cannot be put to the influence of Nietzsche alone that makes AS Roma's Ultras less inclined to unite with other Ultras, there is no denying that the groups tend to be fiercely independent, while those in the *Curva* who refuse to join a group are even more so.

But even amongst the groups, the tension between the macro-and-micro-political levels is not always alleviated. At the December 2, 2007 Ultras protest against the killing of Gabriele Sandri and attempts by the State to remove the Ultras from soccer stadiums, held at Rome's *Circo Massimo* (discussed at length in Chapters Seven and Eight), the group *Romulae Genti* formed. This group of former *AS Roma Ultras, Monteverde,* and *Antichi Valori* members calls itself a '*Fascio Nietzschiano*' (Nietzschean band, but also in the sense of a Fascist organization) in an attempt, as

---

63   Flaxman, p. 197.

64   Schnapp, 2000, pp. 40–41.

65   Nietzsche, 2001, p. 160.

66   See Part Three of *Thus Spoke Zarathustra* for an example of how Nietzsche cultivates an audience of those who have, evidently, overcome their modern peers. Nietzsche, 2006.

Federico, one of its founders told me, 'to bridge the gap between Nietzsche's noble *superuomo* (superman) and the Fascism of *Romanità*, order, hierarchy, discipline, and *squadrismo*. In this way,' Federico concluded, 'we have an Ultra [group] that is committed to Rome and to understanding the city as a site in the war against the modern world.'

A longtime acquaintance of Federico is Lorenzo, a twenty-eight-year-old political science graduate of *La Sapienza* University who now works for a multinational consulting firm but spends many free evenings at the office of *Foro 753*, a Fascist social-cultural education center on Rome's north side. In January 2008 Federico and I met Lorenzo at a nightclub just off of Piazza Navona. Although Federico was there to celebrate his fiancée's birthday, he and I were able to speak with Lorenzo about the new group (*Romulae Genti*) and Federico's conception of the Ultras as a form of the Nietzschean superman. However, where Federico understood the superman to have Fascist possibilities, Lorenzo related the superman to a form of Anarchism. 'This is the man,' he told us, 'that has overcome the morality of others and can create his own ideas and thus his own freedom.'

'*Odio Napoli*' (I Hate Naples)

Returning to the media build-up to AS Roma- SSC Napoli in October 2007, the Ultras of *Boys Roma* understood the situation, particularly the offensive between the press and the Ultras, as a war between a 'moral regime' against the Ultras' right to '*tifare contro*' (root against) and to '*odiare Napoli*' (hate Naples). In the offices and locales of these Ultras I heard one word above all: '*moralismo*' (moralism — a form of discursive control akin to 'political correctness' in the USA). According to Jean-Paolo of *Boys*, 'what is at stake in this battle is our rivalries, not our ability or willingness to throw punches, flares, or rocks at one another. What the media, and *Calcio Moderno* have always wanted,' he continued, 'is a soccer without enemies.' To make sure I really understood, Melo, also of *Boys*, went further. 'Just as the hyper-capitalists want an Italy without defense against foreign invasion or cultural destruction,' he said, 'the soccer industry wants to be rid of those who will defend the "old ways" and "old times" when being Roman and *Romanista* (fan of AS Roma) actually meant something.' Melo is a typical *Boys* Ultra. He is twenty-one years-old, lives at home with his parents and older sister, and attends *La Sapienza*, majoring in history. He began going to games with *Boys* when he was seventeen and was convinced to major in history by Paolo Zappavigna who told him 'the only way to make the future you want is to know the past.'

When pressed to explain his comments about Rome and capitalism, he gladly did so. 'Only last week,' he began, 'there was a police raid on a Roma camp in which dozens of underage prostitutes were arrested and no one wanted to talk about anything but the Ultras; or that Muslim women are allowed to cover their heads because "we" have to respect their difference. Yet if we [Italians] respect ourselves we are racists.' The same, he said, was true for the Ultras. 'We are now violent criminals if we hate Naples.'

On October 20, 2007, as AS Roma hosted SSC Napoli, the lower half of *Curva Sud Roma*, including *Padroni di Casa*, silently protested against the decision to refuse the SSC Napoli fans the right to travel to Rome. The other groups of *Curva Sud* decided not to protest during the game, focusing instead on the one thing that was being denied them: their hatred for Naples. In place of the silence of the lower *curva*, and the polite clapping for both teams by the bourgeois fans, vast sections of the *Curva* sang '*Odio Napoli*' (I hate Naples) for most of the ninety minutes. They seemed exceptionally proud to sing and wave scarves with the same message. The most interesting aspect of the day was that the Ultras were singing not to the *Napolitani* (SSC Napoli fans), because there were none, but to the rest of the stadium. The press and the people of Rome had two weeks to call the Ultras animals and delinquents. The Ultras had ninety minutes to be Ultras. After their game that same afternoon, AC Milan coach Carlo Ancelotti was asked by SKY about AS Roma's Ultras singing '*Odio Napoli*.' 'It is a form of racism,' he said.

Conclusion

The Italian State is fighting a war with the Ultras over the right to the legitimate use of violence within its territory. It is in the interests of the

State to limit the Ultras' aggression and opportunities for violence. Thus, the Ultras are increasingly prohibited from attending games away from their home stadium. This chapter utilized a narrative of events and statements surrounding the AS Roma-SSC Napoli game of October 20, 2007 as a way to demonstrate how the media disseminates a bourgeois 'political meta-language that includes not only narratives of self but also the ability to define good and bad, victim and aggressor.' It used the philosophy of Agamben and Schmitt to explain how the modern State reduces the lives of its citizens to 'subjecthood' by demanding that they affirm its model of inclusion and exclusion. In this way, the interests of the (bourgeois) individual are aligned with those of the state. Conversely, the Ultras of AS Roma were presented as the inhabitants of a 'derelict space' in which bourgeois morality and ethic against violence are acted against. While the purpose of State violence is to protect not only the State's monopoly of legitimacy, but also the interests of the business of soccer, Ultra violence is associated with a space beyond the hegemonic force of the bourgeois form of life.

CHAPTER FIVE

The Agonistic Form of Life of the Ultras: Opposition and Life as War

The preceding chapters presented various aspects of the Ultras, from their stadium-based behaviors and oppositional interaction with both the State and media, to a description of how *Calcio Moderno* not only promotes radical changes to the temporal and spatial aspects of fandom by ascribing it value primarily within the terms of capital accumulation, but also invigorates the Ultras' will to counter the forces of global capitalism with a narrative of local belonging and a counter-modern ethic of violence.

This chapter continues the discussion of the Ultras' *mentalità*, in order to explain their agonistic, or 'oppositional' form of life. In Rome, it became clear to me that, above all else, a warring form of life guides the Ultras' behaviors. Antagonism and contest, as I explained in the first chapter, play crucial roles in determining the mode of Ultra interactions with soccer. As such, the Ultras mirror the Italian tendency toward national ambivalence that is marked by the extreme localism called *campanilismo*.

Likewise, the Ultras engage globalization and other current political issues. These examples further the idea that division and discrimination are central to the Ultra experience. But these divisions are themselves better explained as products of the Ultra agonistic form of life, rather than as material stimulants of that form. To explain this crucial aspect of the Ultra phenomenon I will begin the chapter with an explanation of what I mean by agonism, then continue with a discussion of the moral basis of altruism, and the Ultra war against 'modern man.' Finally, I will explain war and militarism from the perspective of the Ultras.

Agonism

As I noted in the introduction, I have taken 'form of life' from Friedrich Nietzsche as a way to describe the distinctive characteristics of the Ultra phenomenon. Nietzsche was not concerned with categorical precision when using the concept, so it is difficult to know the boundaries of a conglomeration designated a 'form of life.' This is because Nietzsche understood forms of life as characteristics and, more specifically, characteristics of morality and ethics. As such different forms of life could exist within the same organism or phenomenon. Still, he did use 'forms of life' to explain not only inter-cultural difference, such as between the Classical and modern worlds, but also intra-cultural difference, such as between noble and common elements of the Modern West. 'Forms of life' were based primarily in morality and were always at odds with other forms of life or morality.[1] It is this aspect of the concept that I find most applicable to the Ultras.

An Agonistic Form of Life

In his essay 'Homer's Contest,' Friedrich Nietzsche begins one of the most vital themes of his work, the distance between the Classical and modern understandings of the world, or 'forms of life.' He uses Hesiod's explanation of *eris* (jealousy, envy, and grudge) and Homer's battle scenes to demonstrate that the Greeks had a 'trait of cruelty' which allowed the Greek world to 'rejoice' over the excessively descriptive (to our modern

---

1   Nietzsche, 2002, pp. 151–177.

mind) scenes of battle in *The Iliad*.[2] That we find them disturbing where the Greeks found them elevating and exhilarating gave Nietzsche cause to reflect on what we can discern from a 'form of life's' view of battle and victory. He decided, ultimately, that 'forms of life' are separated largely by their conceptions of battle and victory; and that early ethics were derived from those conceptions.[3]

The Greeks, he explains, lived a life of 'combat and victory' in which warring competition and pleasure in victory were acknowledged and even colored their ethical concepts like *eris*.[4] When there were no wars in which to take pleasure, physical contests between cities were arranged. It was the centrality of contest and strife to Greek life that prompted Nietzsche's calling it an 'agonic form of life.'[5]

Living 'agonically,' the Greeks valued ferocity and strife. To battle was a means of salvation, not just for one's people or city but also against the very chaos of the natural world. Perpetual peace, a very modern utopia, would not have been desirable to the Greeks because their lives were given meaning by the struggles and victories associated with war and contest. Indeed, the 'life affirming' qualities of the agonistic Greek 'form of life,' so admired by Nietzsche, were created, in his estimation, by agonic op- positions.[6] The very engagement of an enemy on an athletic or battlefield, he said, was an act of strength and courage. The warring nature will seek resistance at every turn and through surpassing opponents, become even stronger. Thus, one needed enemies and not mere adversaries.[7]

The value of enemies is another theme central to Nietzsche's work. As it was proudly put to me by *Antichi Valori* founder Federico, consciously paraphrasing Nietzsche's *Ecce Homo*, '*poter essere nemico, già questo pre- suppone una natura forte*' (to be able to be an enemy already presupposes a

---

2   Ibid, pp. 174–5.

3   Van Boxel, 2005, p. 72.

4   Nietzsche, 2007, pp. 176–177.

5   Ibid, pp. 174–181.

6   Van Boxle, 2005, p. 78.

7   Nietzsche, 2005, p. 82.

strong nature). Thus, it is only those with a 'strong nature' that are capable of engaging in agon. Although they did not put it in these terms, there was a sense after the death of Genoa Ultra Vincenzo Spagnolo that the Ultras needed to commit themselves to a form of violence that did not necessitate killing.[8] Seeking a form of mutual engagement between equal powers is central to the Greek agon, as agonistic behavior must take place in a setting that allows commensurable 'strong types' to 'project power outwardly, assertively, and affirmatively.'[9] Agon, in other words, is 'life affirming' in that it does not depend upon destruction of the enemy but rather in engagement.[10] Nietzsche understands the agonist to compete or fight in order to elevate their self-status, and the status of their city. The fight may well be controlled and even symbolic but the rewards are nonetheless thought to be a form of salvation.[11] The life and wellbeing of the city, and culture, were dependent upon victory.

When the Ultras engage a particularly nasty rival, even if there is no literal intent to murder there is still violence involved. In many cases, violence is not directed at a person but at a city. Although it is impossible to properly entertain the idea here, the conflation of civic identities amongst the Ultras most likely makes the attack of a city block, for instance, congruous with attacks on a person. In other words, if it is impossible to attack an Ultra of AC Milan, destroying the light fixtures in a subway station will suffice. This form of violence was not a normal part of Ultra behaviors away from Rome, but it did occur. As I explained earlier, in 2006 AC Milan Ultras attacked a group of AS Roma fans, of which I was a part, being led on foot by a police escort from the *San Siro* stadium to the nearest subway station. After being restrained, and unable to engage the enemy Ultras, the *AS Roma Ultras* instead turned their aggression toward the light fixtures in the subway station. Once inside the subway car they further attacked the advertising and emergency bells.

---

8   Roversi and Balestri, 2002, pp. 47–48.

9   Johnson, 2010, p. 70.

10   Cox, 1999, pp. 232–233.

11   Nietzsche, 2007, p. 179.

It is this 'will to transgression' in the Ultras that the State finds unacceptable. As Valerio, a ten-year veteran of the *Curva* and now of *Ultras Romani* explained, 'it used to be that if we traveled and someone got arrested it was a good trip. Now if we go and no one gets arrested it's good. We used to go to harm and destroy; now we go only to be fans but we get in more trouble for that.' The Italian State has no choice but to see something sinister in even the most playful of Ultra violence, as if all Ultra violence were as violent as the Sandri uprising in Rome. This is because the violence of the Ultras serves no bourgeois purpose. While it gives too much credit to Ultra violence to speak of it as Sorel does proletarian violence, which in the inter-war context was truly revolutionary, his understanding of violence against the bourgeois State is applicable here.

Figure 11. Ultras stencil, Pasticceria Pulcini, Monteverde, Rome, 2007.

Violence, he explained, seems to operate from a different, mythological, vantage point than the strict rationality (or myth of rationality) that unites the individual to the State. It seems, then, to undercut or circumvent the motivating narratives of the State, leaving a void of responsibility between the perpetrators and victims of violence. One gets the sense that Sorel speaks of victims of violence with tongue in cheek, as it is the bourgeoisie that is the only possible victim of proletarian violence; the same bourgeoisie whose own violence is normally a tool directed at strengthening, instead of undermining, the State.[12]

However, while I am emphasizing the revolutionary potential of violence from the perspective of the State — which justly filters violence and its potential through a bourgeois lens that delimits both as merely political — what the Ultras ultimately demonstrate is that violence has the unique potential to effectuate an 'anthropological' revolution within the psyche and instincts of individual men, leading to a form of life that is incompatible with the needs of the bourgeois State and its economy. This type of revolution, then, should be considered when I speak of an 'ethics of violence,' or 'ethical transformation.'

If the Ultras act violently without concern for the consequential breakdown of law and order, or State legitimacy, then they must be dealt with as enemies of the State. As discussed in the previous chapter, the State is the sole purveyor of legitimate violence in the liberal order. Any violent individuals or groups are seen as a form of order breakdown. As Foucault demonstrated, the purpose of State violence is often coercive and is always dispersed throughout the institutions of the State.[13] The most obvious institution of social coercion is the police, whose task he identifies with far more than mere 'policing.' Simply put, the police 'see to the benefits that can be derived only from living in society.' The police are charged with caring for the good of the body, soul, and economy of the State.[14] What the police are policing amongst the Ultras is exactly this idea of order and the bourgeois 'good' that comes from the liberal State. What the State seeks, in other words, is to bring the Ultras within its own model of freedom.

---

12 Sorel, 1999, pp. 16–20.

13 Foucault, 2000, pp. 298–325.

14 Foucault, 2000, p. 321.

When scholars and journalists identify war as the dominant metaphor in the Ultras' vocabulary (of fandom), perhaps they say more than they intend. Indeed, I have taken that metaphor much further and connected it with the overall *mentalità* and ethical structure of the Ultras. As war promotes the idea of an organic community united by commitment, suffering, and sacrifice, as I argue below, it is a threat to the system of rights which legitimizes and normalizes the relationship between State and individual, especially given the 'peacetime' context in which Ultra violence occurs. From within, a group of Ultras standing their ground and refusing to show fear to a rival group looks poetic and romantic, like an elite legion defending the honor of Rome to the (symbolic) death. From without, however, it looks like two gangs of thugs attempting to break the social contract that maintains the order of the State.

Perhaps this is why I find the Ultras ambiguously concerned with the State. While they neither explicitly discuss the State, nor desire its overthrow *as Ultras*, they still act largely outside its legitimizing embrace. Weber spoke of State domination by virtue of a general belief in the validity of legality and the obligations it presupposes in the liberal individual.[15] He also understood that the warrior castes of pre-modern Europe, with their honor codes, restricted halls of brotherhood, and heroic forms of violence, would have been, and were, out of step with the State's technologies of dominance and institutionalization. Warrior coercion, as it was, became anathema to State coercion and its monopolization of violence and warfare, as did its codes of ethics.[16]

It would be hyperbole to say that AS Roma's Ultras are committed to a war against State legality. However, they are at war with the obligations that legality imposes on the person. This is precisely because their ethics fall closer to the pre-modern warrior than the bourgeois individual. Thus, physical transgression may have major consequences for the Ultras even as it plays a smaller role than their ethical transgressions. But while two nights of violence in 2007 were the rationale to begin the State's

---

15   Weber, 1958, p. 79.

16   Weber, 1958, pp. 257–260.

suppression of the Ultras, it is the latter, ethical transgressions, I believe, that set the State against them to begin with, and the reason I have focused more upon the Ultras' ethic of violence than actual violence.

The Morality of Altruism
Progress Towards the Universal?

The Ultras' ethic of violence not only puts them at odds with the State's system of law and order but with the guiding ethical components of Western liberalism. The Ultras place little value on safety, security, or peacefulness — in short, the values of the marketplace. Yet they are not mere hoodlums bent on destruction for its own sake, but are guided by reverence for a form of life that simply does not fear violent confrontation. Because of this, and because of the rarity of violence in the lives of bourgeois subjects, the Ultras are condemned as criminals.

However interesting the criminalization of non-legitimate violence is, I find the ways in which violence makes knowable the relationship between truth and morality more so. This relationship was central to Nietzsche's works and, oddly enough, has become a major aspect of the Ultras' conflict with the liberal State. This is because of the moralistic nature of the media's portrayal of the Ultras' agonistic form of life. As I demonstrated in the previous chapters, the Ultras seek to maintain a high level of rivalry and hostility in Italian soccer, primarily because these point to a form of interaction and experience that transcends the marketplace.[17] The system they call Calcio Moderno, however, seeks to mitigate enmity precisely because it destabilizes the marketplace, as well as the peace and wellbeing of the bourgeois soccer fans.

For example, when AS Roma's Ultras explained their desire to 'hate Napoli' and to sing 'I hate Napoli' during the 2007 game between the two teams, they were condemned in the press as 'racists' and as representatives of a non-evolved and not-quite-modern aspect of Italy's collective unconscious that the liberal cosmopolitan press found abhorrent (see

---

17   Nietzsche, 1995, pp. 17–21.

Chapter Three). Seemingly as a consequence of the weeks of discourse around the AS Roma-SSC Napoli game of 2007, one of Italian soccer's major sponsors, Volkswagon, produced a pamphlet that was handed to those entering Italian stadiums during the tenth round of games on October 31, 2007 (two weeks after AS Roma-SSC Napoli). Called the 'Handbook of the Good Fan,' it consisted of ten points, among them to 'go to the stadium "armed" only with enthusiasm,' to 'never express joy in an aggressive fashion,' to 'never assume a racist attitude,' to 'appreciate the nice play of the adversary,' (in other words, to clap for the opposition) and to 'not imitate those who act in an "incorrect" and "miseducated" way.'

Aside from cynicism about the intentions of a corporate sponsor seeking only profits from their involvement with soccer, the *Boys* Ultras with whom I spoke during the game understood the moral implications of the pamphlet. 'The system' said Manuele, a lithe twenty-three-year-old member from the ancient Testaccio neighborhood, 'is telling children not to be Ultras, plain and simple. Each of the things presented as good are the opposite of what we do. The children are being told to live as good, modest, normal people.' Fabio, standing next to us but facing the crowd and not the action on the field, as do most leaders so they may direct songs to their group, made the point more eloquently. 'The children are to be good — that is enough to say multiculturalists, consumers, and desirous of comfort, fun, and peaceful coexistence even with mediocrity. But they will discover, at least some will, that the promises being made [by the marketplace] pale in comparison to the traditional Roman life.' He then, referred to a list of Roman characteristics made by Evola that he and other members of the group had been discussing in the week prior to the game (examined in Chapter Six).

With the pamphlet of the model bourgeois subject converging, in one place, with the raging fandom of *Curva Sud Roma*'s Ultras, I again began to wonder about the relationship between truth and morality, or more correctly, morality and altruism. I wondered how it made sense to the liberal world to propose ecumenicalism as a way to live a fulfilling life. As the bourgeois fans clapped politely, the Ultras supported AS Roma as partially as possible — as partisans. The distance between them was so great that Nietzsche and his understanding of the pathos, or great sensation, of distance came to mind. Forms of life, he said, were distinguishable, all things considered, by morality and valuation. This was certainly true of the distance between the Ultra and bourgeois forms of life: one seeking extremes of emotion flowing from a small cohort, and the other a steady mild stream of emotion flowing from a universal cohort.

Linguist Philip Lieberman sought to explain the relationship between valuation and altruism by discovering from where the two entered the human experience. Resulting from the biological development of the brain and supralaryngeal tools needed to produce human speech, a new type of cognitive capacity evolved. This was the human ability to construct linguistically encoded behaviors such as those controlled by systems of morality and ethics.[18] 'These developments enabled us to induce the modes of altruism that bond us together as groups. In consequence, ... in place of the genetic programs that regulate the behaviors of all organic species, we developed ... culture-specific programs by which our human behaviors — cognizing, affective, and actional — came to be ... regulated.'[19]

Interestingly, this is the same conclusion reached by Nietzsche. After first exploring the link between language and consciousness, and concluding that conscious thought, that which takes the form of language, is the shallowest form of thought because it is designed only to connect one person to another, Nietzsche then seeks to understand how consciousness is connected to human social forms. 'Consciousness,' he says, 'belongs not to man's existence as an individual but rather to the community and herd-aspects of his nature; it developed only in relation to its usefulness to the herd. Consequently, we may only know ourselves through what is average and knowable from the herd's perspective. We know exactly as much as is useful to the human herd.'[20]

---

18   Lieberman, 1991, pp. 22–35.

19   Wynter, 1995, p. 7.

20   Nietzsche, 2001, pp. 211–214.

Lieberman continues his explication of the development of altruism to demonstrate how technology has allowed the human to burst outward from its small (pre-modern) communities to populate every continent and harness the forces of nature. We have done so, however, having surpassed the still operational altruistic models of previous centuries. While slavery, for example, was once a universal component of human forms of life, it is now 'universally outlawed' (thanks to our ever advancing moral and ethical systems). Race, the bane of one of its later variants, American racial slavery, is still 'unconquered.'[21]

In arguing thus, Lieberman demonstrates not only that ethico-behavioral systems were narratively driven, but also that they continue to be. For nowhere in his book on the evolution of altruistic behaviors and their relationship to morality does he feel the need to quantify his own moral positions — nor his use of these positions to justify the idea that the species is progressing because of its moral-ethical aversion to slavery. Nor, obviously, does he need to explain that 'racial prejudice' is abhorrent.

Indeed, language is not epiphenomenal to the social structures in which it acts, but a very part of those structures. Fernand Hallyn agrees, proposing that 'frames of signification' organize 'poetically,' that is, through language and grammar, to provide, among other things, the boundaries and boundary markers between 'us and them'. He terms this process the 'poetics of the *propter nos*' — the 'us' on whose behalf 'we' act.[22]

Utilizing a largely 'epistemic' version of culture (focusing on systems of representation), Sylvia Wynter explains the importance of the *propter nos* as the contextual basis of human altruism. She explains the history of various *propters nos*, showing how categorial models, such as those that came to be disciplines in the modern Academy — Geography, Anthropology, Psychology, Ecology, Economics, etc. — are often the barriers that must fall in order for altruistic advances to be made.[23]

---

21   Lieberman, 1991, p. 172.

22   Hallyn, 1990, p. 55.

23   Wynter, 1995.

What drives this form of human advancement is intellectual revolution or 'epistemic shifts.'[24] However, like Lieberman, Wynter assumes that progress is made only when our altruistic models become universalized, or universally inclusive. She proposes that the motivation of an epochal shift in human understanding (in our lifetime) should be the universality of our 'nos,' wherein all forms of life are equally valid and valued, thereby conceptually cancelling discrimination between human 'forms of life.'

Or, Progress Towards the Extremely Restricted

The Ultras represent instead another model of what we may call inter-altruistic co-identification — one that is exaggeratedly restricted. If the altruism of globalization is driven by a morality of total inclusion, wherein the universalization of women and men is made complete in a global market, the altruism of the Ultra is one of exclusion, exclusivity, and local particularity. These motivating forces will be made clear as the chapter progresses.

I have described *Curva Sud* as a 'kingdom of the word' because there, at the center of the Roman Ultra universe, I found a place where language, rhetoric, and ideology were paramount.[25] It is for this reason that I chose to use Sylvia Wynter and others who focus on the narrative element of human existence to explain the moral basis of altruistic behaviors. But where the moral thrust of the West is more and more associated with liberal civic and social principles like peace, stability, comfort, happiness, and equality, those of the Ultra can be identified in the words of Counter-Enlightenment thinkers like Nietzsche and Evola, for whom liberalism's values lead to cultural degeneration.[26]

'I brought a copy of *La Gaia Scienza* (*The Gay Science*, by Friedrich Nietzsche) to *Antichi Valori*,' I was told by Mario, a former member of the group. 'In that book is Nietzsche's greatest lesson to the Ultra *mentalità*:

---

24 Foucault, 1970, pp. xx-xxvi.

25 Koon, 1985, p. 4.

26 Sunic, 2004; Berezin, 2009.

that all good things come from oppositions. "*La guerra è la madre di tutte le buone cose*," (war is the mother of all good things) he said. Our *mentalità* was to practice this everyday — not through fighting but through understanding. By giving up aggression and rivalry we thought that the great and beautiful energy of life would wither away.' From Nietzsche, Mario went on to say, *Antichi Valori* learned to love hatred and have no fear of danger.

As if writing a description of the Ultra agonistic form of life, Evola explained that 'what is needed is a new radical front with clear boundaries between friend and foe. The future does not belong to those of crumbling and hybrid ideas but those of radicalism — the radicalism of absolute negations and majestic affirmations.'[27] The idea of embracing 'absolute negations and majestic affirmations' is accepted whole-heartedly by the leadership group of *Boys Roma*.

On a sweltering summer evening in late-July, 2007, I met this group of four, plus other members of *Boys*, to discuss Evola and the new government initiatives against the Ultras for the upcoming season. (Soccer season in Italy is from late-August to mid-May.) On this night, the topic of discussion was the opening section of Evola's *Imperialismo Pagano*, in which he dismisses the 'petty aims' of the liberal State and its economic, military, and industrial foundations but without embracing European Fascism as such. Instead he proposes Fascism based on the Roman Imperium, an ancient right to rule based on spiritual superiority. This *Imperium Romanum*, he says, 'can only be attained by those who have the power to transcend the petty lives of petty men and their petty appetites, national pride, values, nonvalues, and gods'[28] In a room of young, impressionable Ultras who considered themselves European-style Fascists, this was a bold choice of discussion. Fabio, second-in-command at *Boys*, explained to me beforehand that he hoped Evola would 'decenter' the group's understanding of Fascism and even its affiliation with neo-Fascists like *Forza Nuova*. 'We must put Rome at the center, not Fascism. I want our Ultras to be

---

27   Evola, 2002, p. 113.

28   Evola, 2004b, p. 62 (my translation).

critical of the world but in a way that puts them and their future in focus. Roberto Fiore [founder and leader of *Forza Nuova*] might be a good guy, but *Forza Nuova* will always do right by him, not Rome. No, it is up to us to look out for Rome,' he told me.

Looking back, I missed a perfect opportunity to discuss the absence of the State and nationalism in the worldview of a Roman Fascist. At the time, it just seemed obvious that Rome and the Romans would be the basis of the type of radicalization and political action the *Boys* Ultras were pursuing. As Michael Herzfeld described, Rome has a unique ability to (still) feel like the center of the world.[29] To the Romans, especially those thoroughly imbued with *Romanità*, there is very little of value in the world beyond Rome's walls. Ecumenicalism and the relativity of forms of life are 'recipes,' I was told, 'for living without pride' (see Chapters Three and Seven).

David Nugent describes the ways in which Peruvian peasants sought to diminish the racial categories imposed by colonialism in order to fully embrace, and be embraced by, the nation; as he says it, they 'erased race to make the nation.'[30] These Ultras were taking the opposite approach, openly embracing the idea of a Roman race, in order to disconnect themselves from the Italian nation and the 'empty promises of liberalism.' Indeed, it was not just *Boys Roma* that was pursuing such a course. Two small political groups, *Razza Romana* (Roman Race) and *Romulae Genti* (The Race of Romulus), invoked the same ideal of the Romans and what it means to carry such a marker of identity today.

The Ultras—Being Made Hard
A Mass Amongst Warriors

Earlier I explained that the Ultras use a conception of history that places high value on myth and tradition. Their history is a monumental history, not only because they live closer to heroism and memorialization than

---

29   Herzfeld, 2009, pp. 1–12.

30   Nugent, 2002, pp. 137–174.

other fans, but also because it is highly selective. As Nietzsche explained, monumentalism makes use of neither objectivity nor linear narratives but instead picks and chooses aspects of history to celebrate and diminish.[31]

How the Ultras use history is exemplified by their in-stadium activities like unfurling banners or devoting the act of fandom to the honor of fallen Ultras or Romans. One can observe it, too, in their actions beyond the stadium, such as the 2007 mass commemorating the most important *capo* (boss) in the history of *Boys Roma*, Paolo Zappavigna. At this mass, which took place in the *Basilica San Lorenzo Fuori le Mura*, it was clear that the level of respect for the Ultra being honored went far beyond compassion. It was true veneration by those who were witnesses to the life lost.

After the mass for Paolo, I sat in a dingy San Lorenzo café as a cold rain poured outside, speaking to Augusto of *Boys Roma* and Marcello of *Padroni di Casa*. These were two Ultras I did not know well at the time. They stayed to speak with me for two reasons. One, it was raining too hard for their journey home by scooter to be comfortably made; and two, because 'Duce', the boss of *Boys Roma* had encouraged them to do so.

I revisited, with them, the respect and commitment I felt I had witnessed earlier as approximately one hundred tattooed, t-shirt and jean clad Ultras performed the mass. The ceremony had been mundane until the priest said something about the excesses of youth which had misled Zappavigna into a dark period of violence—words that provoked the congregation to 'erupt' with hushed whistles and looks of derision, just as a stadium might explode at a hard foul by an opposing player. The shocked look on my face was met with a shrug of the shoulders and a '*pezzo di merda*' (piece of shit) murmured by Filippo the long-time *Fedayn* member whose flags I waved in Parma and Milano.

After the mass the leadership of *Boys Roma* stood next to a photo of Zappavigna, accepting the hugs, kisses, laughs, and condolences of all who approached them. Fabio, my main contact in the group, introduced me to Signora Zappavigna, Paolo's mother. She thanked me for being there to honor her son. I asked her why she had not spoken about her son, or stood

---

31 Nietzsche, 1997, pp. 59–123.

with the Ultras after the mass. 'These were his brothers,' she said. 'They built something special together; so much that they organized this mass for Paolo to honor him — just like they do every Sunday' (the traditional game day for soccer).

Even to a relative outsider — although had I been a stranger I would never have been allowed in the church — the afternoon was emotional. In the ritually and emotionally charged environments of the stadiums, I knew them to be eager to sacrifice and suffer. But to see them come to mass to honor one of their own with the same passionate commitment that they show at the games somehow seemed more important. I was beginning to understand that being Ultra was not something to be experienced only on weekends.

Upon telling the Ultras at the café how impressed I had been with the mass, they explained to me that the Ultras are not normal people. They are given to extremes of emotion, being at home with both great love and hatred. These extremes alone, I suggested, did not fully explain the hushed outburst during the mass. 'Certainly,' Marcello, a thirty-four-year-old baker and member of *Padroni di Casa* said, 'each of us in the church today had either been in battle with Paolo, or grew up in an Ultras group hearing stories about him and his courage. He was fearless and never turned his back. When you went into battle with Paolo there was no chance of being left behind.' '*Restare indietro* [being left behind]?' I asked for clarification. 'To be taken advantage of — by enemy Ultras or the police,' he continued. 'We are warriors steeled by war. Therefore, we understand the importance of the war. Otherwise, what the hell are we to do?'

The talk of war surprised me and they could tell. Augusto, a recently married thirty-one-year-old waiter at a nice pizzeria off Via Veneto and a member of *Boys* broke in, 'Five years in the *Curva* made me hard, especially at the end of the 1990s [when fights were a regular part of the Ultras experience].' 'We have done and seen things that normal people would cower against,' he said. 'As such there is an incredible distance between us and those outside the Ultras.' I asked if there was difficulty relating to those outside the Ultras. 'Those who live that way are already dead,' answered Marcello. I asked if theirs was an extreme position. 'Absolutely,' said Augusto, 'we are perhaps most extreme, but all Ultras are extreme. That is why they are Ultras.'

'*Per esempio* (for example),' said Marcello, a phrase that I would come to identify with him, 'we in *Padroni di Casa* understand that the war of the Ultras is not one for the politics of the State, nor completely for the honor and security of the city or the Ultra movement. In a much bigger way it is ultimately for liberation from [bourgeois moralism]. We cannot be at the stadium everyday but our experiences there prepare us for when we are not. *I padroni* (members of *Padroni di Casa*) are Ultras in all aspects of life.'

Marcello and Augusto went on to explain that the Ultra, the true Ultra that is, those like Paolo Zappavigna who devoted their lives to *Curva Sud*, demand 'unconditional sacrifice' from one another. In return the Ultra is united in confraternity with others who can be counted on in any situation. For many hundreds of Ultras, what happened at the mass was the culmination of times spent in defense of their brothers and sisters and in the protection of Paolo.

In exchanges like this, it was again made clear that I needed a way of understanding the Ultras that went beyond their merely being a subculture with its own values or characteristics. I wanted to find a way to understand how experiences in *Curva Sud*, the various cage-like structures comprising guest sections, and in Ultra dominated social settings, came to create and transform the ethics of many (Ultra) men and women (the few women who were, primarily as girlfriends, involved). The idea that oppositions are the driving force of the Ultra phenomenon was already clear. However, what I added to this as time went on was the idea that war played a crucial role. Not only does warfare need warriors, it also needs an ethical approach to conflict. The Ultras have both.

The Ultras: An Ethic Against Bourgeois Ideals

During my time with them, particularly the periods immediately following the 2007 deaths of police officer Filippo Raciti at the hands of Catania's
Ultras and Gabriele Sandri, Roma-born Ultra of SS Lazio, at the hands
of Arezzo police officer Luigi Spaccarotella, the Ultras made it clear to
me that they hated and were a direct contrast to '*il modo di vivere della
borghesia*,' or the bourgeois form of life. From Evola and Nietzsche, as
well as the contemporary Far Right, many Ultras have been given, in their
minds, a clear understanding of the forces at work within the bourgeois
phenomenon. *Nota bene*, however: The Ultra critique is hardly 'class-
based,' focusing instead — as does their critique of globalization — on
'spiritual' issues.

The Emptiness of the Universal and Bourgeois

The Ultras' use of Nietzsche ultimately focuses on his critique of the forces
of modernity, through which he demonstrated the 'emptiness' of universal
values and concepts such as equality and democracy. I found Nietzsche
useful in thinking through the distance between universal and particular
values and specifically how such a distance is maintained by the Ultras'
critique of globalization.

Although the Ultras are against the economic and political aspects of
globalization, at least those which impact upon soccer (in the form of
Calcio Moderno), their revolt against this form of modernity is primarily against its 'spiritual' or intellectual aspects, which they understood to
be hedonism, multiculturalism, rights-based movements like Gay Pride,
and universalist assumptions of culture based on the market.[32] It might
be more clear to discuss these things under the rubric of postmodernity,
as does Baudrillard, who explains postmodernity as a 'glandular corpse'
that celebrates 'handicaps, weirdos, degenerates, and asocial persons' at
the expense of the 'heroes' of previous forms of life.[33] In the language of

---

32   Sunic, 2007, p. 155.

33   Baudrillard, 2008, p. 79.

the Ultras, however, postmodernity hardly figures, although globalization is a big concern.

Instead of dismissing their rhetoric, I suggest that the Ultras, by focusing on the intellectual or epistemic aspects of globalization, point to a different way of understanding the phenomenon and how it impacts, or is understood to impact, local cultures. What the flourishing of American fast food would mean for Roman cuisine and culture is more upsetting to them than merely the specter of a McDonald's on every Roman corner.

Additionally, how they understand the issues connected to immigration and 'minority rights' is not the vulgar racism, xenophobia, or sexism that many expect of them, but something closer to issues of sovereignty and counter-modern writings on the degeneration of culture. In other words, the Ultra rejection of the form of modernity promised by globalization is not motivated by saying 'No', as some who study such phenomena assume, deploying labels like 'parochialism', 'racism', and 'discrimination'.[34] Instead it is a 'Yes' that is put into action by preferring and loving their own form of life, even if that means refusing and even hating the life forms of others.

The Ultra are opposed to a bourgeois life — that is, a life devoted to concerns of the market at the expense of spirituality, values, and ethics. According to Evola, the bourgeois type lives a life dominated by concern for safety, wellbeing, and material wealth.[35] In the inter-Ultra discourse on *Calcio Moderno*, one continuously hears laments that soccer is being made the domain of those who are unwilling to fight for anything — those who seek to purchase a connection to AS Roma, rather than getting their hands dirty or putting themselves in danger.

It is this part of the crowd, the consumerist bourgeois fans, that is referred to as just 'fans' by the Italian media. According to Claudio of *Ultras Romani*, this 'manipulation of our understanding of who is and isn't a fan is another aspect of the game's coming to be considered in the American style, as mere entertainment [without any ludic or even affective value]. One need only have money to be worthy of taking part.' The

---

34 Cole, 1997, p. 11; Sniderman et al, 2000, pp. 34–39.

35 Evola, 2002, p. 193.

Ultras consistently speak of the normal fans, the bourgeois who live vicari-ously through the Ultras so long as there is no violence, and who castigate the Ultras at the first sign of unrest, as those 'without spirit.' As Claudio explained, 'these fans like the passion we bring to the stadium but they want us to have that passion only while the game is on and only in forms which conform to their morality. They want us to live *orizzontalmente* (horizontally) and *passivamente* (passively) as they do.' 'This is strange,' he continued, 'because certainly they understand that our courage is foreign to them.'

Living Dangerously and Heroically

Claudio made it clear that the normal bourgeois fans lack courage be-cause, from the Ultra perspective, they thrive only within an environment of neutrality. It could be said that they 'swim in a sea of moderation, dilut-ing their passion for life in the gently flowing current.'[36] 'If there is one thing we Ultras despise it is neutrality,' said Claudio, which they equate with a deficiency of conviction; or with a life devoid of what Evola called a 'transcendent reference point.'[37]

Months after we had originally spoken in the San Lorenzo café I met Augusto of *Boys Roma* outside the guests' section in Livorno. We hugged and complimented each other for coming to an away game of the highest seriousness and symbolism for many of AS Roma's Ultras. AS Livorno Calcio plays in the city of the same name. Their Ultras are fiercely of the Far Left, matching the political affiliation of many of the townspeople. The *Partito Comunista d'Italia* (PCI) was founded in Livorno in 1921 and the Left has been entrenched there ever since. Naturally, the political Right dominating *Curva Sud* intensifies the rivalry with AS Roma's Ultras. When the clubs meet, the chanting, flag waving, and banners often have less to do with soccer than with political affiliation.

---

36   Cate, 2002, p. 111.

37   Evola, 2004, p. 11.

Figure 12. AS Livorno banner, 'Our tricolor [Italian flag] has a red star,'
Livorno, 2007.

Indeed, without politics, the clubs have no relation whatsoever. AS Livorno
has played in *Serie A* for only three seasons since 1949. Many non-Ultra
fans of AS Roma know little of Livorno and care not for the rivalry, understanding it as an 'Ultras thing.' For the Ultras, it is a rivalry that defines
the Ultra phenomenon. To get to Livorno in 2007, AS Roma's Ultras filled
a special train, three charter buses, and numerous cars. Two thousand of
the most committed Ultras made the trip. Most of these, it seemed, went
to chant '*Duce! Duce! Duce!*' for ninety minutes and then return to Rome.
When AS Roma scored, the *Duce* chants rang out in place of their various
songs in devotion to Rome and AS Roma. There were several flags of the
Italian Social Republic and a few of Nazi Germany in the guests' section.
Additionally, Roman Salutes sometimes replaced clapping. These were
countered in the Livorno *Curva Nord* with raised fists, chants of '*Stalin
Vive!*', flags of the USSR and PCI, and a large banner announcing that *Il*

nostro tricolore è con la stella rossa (our tri-color [Italian flag] has a red star, in reference to the international symbol of Communism).

When I mentioned to Augusto that I never see him away from Rome and had not seen him since the mass for Paolo, he told me why. 'Livorno is all or nothing,' he said. 'For us Fascists there is nothing like this game. You will see. This has nothing to do with soccer, just pure hatred.' I told him that it was the away game I had most looked forward to experiencing.

'Games like this,' he told me, 'made Zappavigna the legend he is. He used to tell us '*Onore e nobilità vengono da odium et bellum*" (honor and nobility come from hatred and war — he used the Latin purposefully). Later he explained to me how, for many of the older members of *Boys*, this was a motto — something to keep in mind in violent and intense situations. I asked if he thought about it beyond his life as an Ultra. 'That's impossible,' he said. 'The Ultras' understanding of soccer is the Ultras' understanding of the world. It makes sense when you use 'strength, honor, rivalry, and *Romanità*' to see how to live.' Such values, he went on, had given him something for which to fight, and a willingness to do so, making him stronger and more 'Ultra' than other normal people.[38]

Those who willingly commit their lives to a form of life that frowns upon rivalry and discrimination are seen as weak-willed seekers of comfort and coddling. What is worse, to the Ultras this bourgeois form of life seeks the diminution of exaltedness. Whether the Ultras reach those states in stadiums following AS Roma, in violent encounters, or through organized action in their communities is less important than their ability and willingness to seek occasions rich with meaning and seriousness. These moments are part of the Ultras' commitment to live a life '*a rischia il tutto per tutto*' (all or nothing).

For the Ultras, danger, adventure, and even pain are the most valid parts of life, for they require a commitment and resolve that most people would not consider worthy of our modern liberal societies.[39] Just as the

---

38 Just as *mentalità* is ubiquitous amongst the Ultras for explaining why they act as they do, so is Ultras as a way of explaining what it means to be an Ultra.

39 Nietzsche, 2007, p. 66.

Futurists and Fascists of the early twentieth century heeded Nietzsche's call to 'live dangerously,' the Ultras of today are using the same ideas to place distance between themselves and the bourgeoisie.

In his *Gay Science*, Nietzsche suggested that by living dangerously one would expand the horizons, or conditions of possibility, of existence. The modern world had made of life a struggle only to avoid struggle, strife, danger, pain, and discomfort. Conversely, by living with contempt for safety, security, and caution, one could re-invigorate life with commitment, bravery, and nobility.[40] As Mario, formerly of *Antichi Valori* and now *Romulae Genti*, explained to me, the love of hatreds and lack of fear of dangerous situations have set the Ultras apart from non-Ultras. 'The days we live together, like going to a big game in Milan or going to Brescia (another of the political rivalries of Roma's Ultras), are deeply felt. None of us will ever forget these battles,' he said.

As many journalists point out, attending soccer games can be dangerous. However, it was my experience that they are not exceedingly dangerous, and not dangerous at all for the bourgeois fans. Nonetheless, in comparison to spectating live sports in the United States, the Ultras experience is downright frightening. While boarding a train, arriving at a 'hostile' city, entering their stadium, and exchanging insults and projectiles with the locals, there is an element of the unknown that keeps one alert and tensed for contact. Add to that the aggressive nature of all interaction with those outside the group of AS Roma fans and after a handful of away games one begins to feel like a warrior marching into battle. It certainly amounts to very little compared to actual wartime experience, but it still offers considerable distance from passing one's afternoon on Via del Corso (a popular shopping street in Rome).

---

40 Nietzsche, 2001, pp. 160, 184, 199–248.

Evolan Heroism

In this environment, where one sings 'songs in honor of hostility,' a feeling of heroism and virtue emerges.[41] Evola outlined the two foundations of heroism in *Men Among The Ruins*. The first is that 'the measure of what one can demand of others is dictated by the measure of what one can demand from oneself.' The second is that 'those who cannot be their own masters should find a master outside of themselves.'[42] Both principles are entrenched in the ideas of dedication, discipline, and sacrifice. Vittorio of *Boys Roma* presented them to me as we drove to witness the return game of the *Coppa Italia* final in Milan.

He explained that the groups that maintain themselves over time, such as *Boys* and *Fedayn* (both in existence since 1972), are aware that leadership is crucial. As a youngster in the group he had found a copy of Evola's synthesis of the revolt against modernity that someone had left behind on a special train. Parts of it became 'a Bible of Ultra life,' he said, 'especially those on Rome and the specialness of being Roman — and at war with this world. Look behind us,' he said, referring to the back of the bus, 'why is there only a handful of people on this bus? Why aren't we being mobbed in a sea of humanity? Because it cannot be so: these ideas, these fists, these hard eyes — they are only for the few. You meet a lot of people in your life, yes? But how many Ultras? How many men who can live beyond the comfort and safety of this [form of life]?'

For other Ultras, though, there seems to be an unthinking devotion to the first of Evola's foundations of heroism. Their amount of self-mastery is measured in unflinchingly defending themselves and their group (and whatever group of AS Roma fans they are standing with at any moment). The Ultras most respected by other Ultras are those who have been witnessed standing their ground when under attack. Violence and the Ultras' ethic of violence were explained in the two previous chapters. As we saw then, aggressive oppositions occur only with great sacrifice and sense of duty toward other Ultras.

---

41   Nietzsche, 2006, p. 79.

42   Evola, 2002, p. 141.

Nietzschean Distance and Ultras at Away Games

The heroic principles are supercharged with value in Evola's work because they oppose the strict utility with which the 'merchant class' approaches life. For Evola, the heroism of the warrior functions by way of deep inter-personal commitments and sacrifices, while the utility of the merchant functions only for vulgar self-preservation;[43] those who live with a code of honor act from a sense of duty, responsibility, and 'love of distance'.[44] It was often repeated to me that the essence of the Ultras' *mentalità* was the experience of the away game; that there one felt an intense brother-hood with fellow AS Roma fans and an undeniable hatred for the enemy. Importantly, one felt hated by the enemy in return. 'At away games, there is only aggression. We sing against them and them against us. The people in the *curva* or *tribuna* [sideline seats] seem so far away from us. Like this, it is difficult to imagine what they think of us or the game,' Fabio of *Boys* explained.

Distance was one of Nietzsche's favorite concepts, having used it to promote methodological clarity as well as separation of the noble form of life from that of the modern herd.[45] Within the noble form of life, lived with a feeling of distance from others, the duties and responsibilities spoken of above only apply to one's equals: in the case of the Ultras, one's group or other Ultras.[46] This is important for the Ultras, as their form of inter-group 'nobility' cannot be earned by shirking one's duties.

Nor can it be earned by avoiding conflict. This is where the distance between the Ultras and others is greatest. Their form of warfare, concep-tual (in the form of the culture of opposition) or literal (in the form of violent encounters), is explicitly non-utilitarian. It is always in defense of some cherished values, even if these are applied after-the-fact. In this way, their rivalries are always moral endeavors—always involving an

---

43 Evola, 2002, p. 142.

44 Ibid, p. 2.

45 Nietzsche, 2003, p. 68.

46 Cate, 2002, p. 464.

investment of moral energies.[47] Loyalty, courage, and commitment are the demands made of Ultra upon Ultra. These are never more on display than when AS Roma's Ultras are away from Rome.

It is away from Rome that the Ultras act in a particularly militaristic way; marching together, singing and gesturing menacingly, insultingly, and defiantly. There happens at these moments a form of cohesion built from the euphoria of fear, adrenaline, and pride. Away games unfold like 'an education of the will'.[48] After years spent traveling together and facing down rival Ultras and police, as well as their own fear, a transformation occurs of which many Ultras are aware but know little how to describe.

The *arditi* (assault infantry soldiers) and other soldiers of World War I became banded together in what Mussolini called a *trincerocrazia* (a union of the trenches). These were men bounded together by consciousness of war, not class. They were united by the experience of fighting, killing, and surviving together. Italy was divided, wrote Mussolini, 'between those who were there and those who were not there; those who fought and those who did not fight; those who produced and those who were parasites'.[49] This feeling, and the *arditi* legend, is well known by many Ultras of the Left and Right, and is reproduced when Ultras, away from Rome, distinguish themselves, in knowledge and identity, from those who remain outside.[50]

Brian Pronger updated the phenomenological understanding of embodiment by adding an ethical element in order to more fully explain not only the consequences of living within a form of life, but also the possibility of moving between forms. Using Deleuze and Guattari's explanation of how flows of desire are affected by the reterritorialization of human energy (puissance) under capitalism, Pronger explained that one becomes conscious of one's body through what Merleau-Ponty called 'means of representation.' But, he added, those representations are

---

47 Leed, 1979, p. 61.

48 Nietzsche, 2003, p. 200.

49 Farrell, 2003, p. 72.

50 Leed, 1979, p. 36.

actually creative of the body's reality, through not only description but also inscription.[51] Thus, representation is not a deep enough concept to explain how profoundly we are shaped by not only material culture but knowledge systems as well.

In this way, the ethical aspects of behavior discussed above make their mark on the body. The Ultras, like soldiers or warriors, learn war not only from language but from immersion into war(like) events. Thus, the language of war, and talk of contestation, opposition, commitment, and sacrifice, becomes the reality through which their acts come to be understood as aggressive, ironic, or worthy of feelings of honor.

This process is experienced as an ethical transformation. Many Ultras associate and socialize only with other Ultras. This is because non-Ultras have no idea what 'truly motivates or interests' them. With other Ultras, there is no need to explain the experience of being an Ultra; one just is Ultra. Thus, they feel themselves as having been initiated into a new life, with the aggressive actions taken as a group acting as a 'baptism of fire,' much like a moment of conversion or illumination.[52]

Victor Turner explained such feelings of non-material *confraternita* as '*communitas*,' a new existential community built from common passage through states of transition.[53] Gabriele, an unaffiliated Ultra formerly of *AS Roma Ultras*, explained to me the 'love of life' and exhilaration he felt every time he arrived in Milan's central train station with a large group of AS Roma fans. He said it was like going into a war knowing you were unlikely to be harmed, but for which you still had to prepare mentally.

'Milan is interesting, he said, 'because you arrive there with normal people who come to shop or whatever. And there we are, looking at the group of policemen advancing up the platform. Some of us would love to fight each and every one of them, but others just want to get to San Siro (the stadium). Regardless, we know that the police could attack us if they want, and, what usually happens, they could lead us to the *Milanisti* (the

---

51   Pronger, 2002, p. 233.

52   Griffin, 2007, p. 157.

53   Turner, 1995, p. 126.

enemy Ultras) so they can beat on us. But we always expect an attack from someone. So, when the train arrives, you have to be ready. We might sing when we get off the train, but otherwise we are usually quiet and intense.'

Later I asked Giorgio of *Padroni di Casa* about Gabriele's awareness of the distance between the Ultras and the non-Ultras on the platform. 'It's true,' he agreed. 'It's very easy to think to yourself, who are these people and what are they doing with their lives? They speak of freedom but they seem like slaves.' Why do they seem like slaves, I asked. 'Because,' he responded, 'if you only do what is expected of you then you are not free.' Because of the particularity and extreme nature of such experiences, they are difficult to reconcile with a non-Ultra form of life. As Eric Leed explained, 'the personality, once adapted to war, is incommensurate with civilian society.'[54]

Life as War

> Antagonism between peoples or a state of war between them is in itself not the cause of a civilization's collapse; on the contrary the imminent sense of danger, just like victory, can consolidate, even in a material way, the network of a unitary structure and heat up a people's spirit through external manifestations, while peace and well-being may lead to a state of reduced tension that favors the action of the deeper causes of a possible disintegration.[55]

The Ultras have chosen war as their normal mode of interaction with others. Through war, they feel a constant tension, or seeking of battles, and the thrill of engaging in hostilities with others — be they verbal and ironic, as is often the case with the Ultras mode of *tifare contro* (rooting against), or physical and violent.

Tifare contro (rooting against), as the preceding chapters have demonstrated, is the normalized mode of being a 'fan' for the Ultras. Giovanni Francesio used the concept to describe the Ultras' in-stadium behaviors.[56]

---

54 Leed, 1979, p. 2.

55 Evola, 1995, p. 56.

56 Francesio, 2008.

However, he stopped short of using the concept to understand what it is in the Ultra phenomenon that buttresses those behaviors. As is clear, I am arguing that the oppositions for the Ultras do not end at the stadium but are only most obvious there. It is in the spaces and activities of the Ultras that are far removed from the stadium lights that the depth of the commitment to their form of life becomes apparent.

Commitment and Organic Community

Just as Eric Leed explained the idea of war held by many veterans of World War I, the Ultras employ an understanding of war and society that is romantic and non-economic.[57] The romanticism of the Ultras' use of war is seen in two ways: their promotion of an organic community, and their devotion to honor, sacrifice, and suffering as markers of status and distinction.

The Ultras believe themselves to be an organic community. One particularity noticed by scholars of the Ultra phenomenon is its trans-class nature. As Roversi and Balestri explained, the Ultras have always welcomed the participation of all social classes, even in cities with large industrial workforces and working classes, like Turin or Bologna.[58] They explained this the way many do in Italian piazzas, by the overall level of passion for soccer that exists at all levels of society. My interactions with larger groups (with over a hundred members) like *Boys Roma* and *Ultras Romani* supported this claim. However, it was made clearer by *Padroni di Casa*, which, while sharing the Fascist ideologies of *Boys*, does not share their skinhead aesthetics.

I asked Daniele (a new member of *Padroni di Casa*) about the multi-class makeup of the group and the Ultras. 'Who gives a damn about class stratification,' he responded. 'We are Fascists and therefore the bourgeois is a question of mentality. I have a little money, I went to the university, but above all I believe in a Fascist life. We don't think about money for

---

57   Leed, 1979, p. 6.

58   Roversi and Balestri, 2002, pp. 131–142.

money's sake, no. Instead we think about a heroic and radical life.' Others in *Padroni di Casa* seconded Daniele's attitude about the class composition of the *Curva*. One need not be poor, they told me, to fight for Fascism or the Ultras. Instead one needed '*le palle*' ('the balls,' or commitment and determination) and '*coraggio*' (courage). Later, on a visit to *CasaPound*, a new initiative of the Roman Far Right that seeks to transcend the limitations of the liberal political order that has hamstrung radical politics since the war, I overheard an impassioned explanation of the critique of the bourgeois form of life at the initiative's core.

Blending Mussolini and Amilcar Cabral, the young Fascist told a group of ten men and women that 'if one discounts the historical nature of the critique of liberalism — if one ignores the fact that Nietzsche, Evola, Pound, Sorel, Spengler, and all the others were professional academics or thinkers — then it might appear a form of "class suicide" is necessary in order accept that capitalism is leading us to an abyss. Certainly, we can be seen to benefit greatly from American imperialism and global capitalism. But regardless of the destruction of other peoples, so that you may live in comfort, you too are being destroyed — turned soft and impotent.'

Padroni di Casa's political agenda is not to fight against socialism and capitalism but against 'what materialism and the marketplace do to humanity. The logic of profit and marketing destroy any community or culture that confronts them.' Instead of a class-based critique of the bourgeois form of life, then, the Ultras believe themselves committed to a spiritual or cultural struggle. Being committed to something greater than oneself and one's personal gain is important because it demonstrates a move beyond the individualism that is inherently bourgeois. Primarily limited to the Ultras, AS Roma, and Rome, their commitment is shown in the willingness to fight and to stand against the will of others. It can be argued, as did Bromberger, that the fighting and defending are merely symbolic or even rhetorical.[59] However, this critique would have to ignore the extraordinary value placed upon rhetoric and symbolism by the Ultras. To see the world through the eyes of an Ultra is to see 'us against them'

---

59 Bromberger, 1993.

at every turn. They use this value to create of themselves a community whose basis lies beyond the material—in the realm of will, sentiment, volition.[60] This is their *mentalità*.

Sacrifice and Struggle

Part of the romanticism of the Ultras is how they create and understand their community. Another is the basis of that community—the sanctity of honor earned through sacrifice and struggle. An extension of Evola's ethics of the warrior, the nexus between sacrifice and warfare is explained by Allen Frantzen as a dominant theme not only of traditional Indo-European knowledge of warfare but also of the narratives of World War I veterans. In these narratives, the invocation of self-sacrifice as a path toward redemption is common.[61] AS Roma's Ultras use these narratives to create their very community, but more so to create a hierarchy within that community. They are a community of people who are expected to defend and fight for the things that are dear to them. The more accountable one shows oneself to be, the more 'Ultra' one may be seen to be.

In other words, no one may buy his or her way to group leadership or to respect within the *Curva*. One must be worthy of these. It serves this model of 'cultural capital accumulation' to have one's actions be understood as sacrifice and struggle. As Fabrizio of *Romulae Genti* told me as he waited tables in a center-of-Rome restaurant, 'one has to be committed to be an Ultra. It is not something you can do once and then claim to be. The groups are too serious about this—if you come in as a tourist and then get caught talking about how hard you are, it can be trouble.' I asked how the groups might know. 'We are everywhere in this city and we know everyone,' he responded wryly.

I asked Mario about the constant references to sacrifice amongst AS Roma's Ultras and how this related to how much fun the Ultras seemed to have. 'Even though it is fun,' he told me, 'no one else will do it. [The

---

60   Leed, 1979, p. 92.

61   Frantzen, 2004, p. 261.

bourgeois fans] will not sing, follow AS Roma away from Rome, and would never fight. Even though it is fun, there are many times when it is not. Look at Manchester, he said, referring to a 2007 Champions League quarterfinal game in which AS Roma lost 7–1 to Manchester United. There, 'we had the humiliating defeat, hooligans seeking revenge on us for what happened in Rome [a number of English fans were stabbed before the first game between the clubs], and police on horseback that were more interested in beating us than protecting us. Singing that night was difficult, but by singing and supporting AS Roma we showed that we have honor. By standing up to the rushes of the hooligans we showed courage and that Romans are not to be trifled with.'

In terms of performance, the act of singing even when AS Roma is losing is seen as sacrifice because one is acting when the 'spirit' is unwilling. Traveling great distances is sacrifice because it takes considerable time and involves discomfort. Facing a group of *Carabinieri* with machine guns and a small tank is a sensation that other 'normal' fans are unwilling to feel. Certainly, facing another group of Ultras armed with bricks and bottles or police officers with night-sticks, and doing so with *coraggio* (courage) and in *sprezzo del pericolo* (defiance of danger), is beyond what others are willing to do in the name of Rome. Willingness to do these things is the root of honor. The unwillingness of others to do them is what creates the distance between Ultras and others.

Conclusion

The Ultras understand that warfare is redemptive. Nietzsche explained warfare as the 'father of all good things' because, as he said, it makes life poetic. It brings raw emotion and an affective sensibility to the fore.[62] The Ultras seem to understand the poetry of which Nietzsche spoke, as they experience so much of life in states of euphoria or raging disgust. The Ultras life is extreme, as is made evident by their rivalries. From their perspective, the bourgeois life of safety and security, in which thrills are

---

62   Nietzsche, 2007, p. 90.

provided by consumerism, is a life castrated of its passion. In the years they were active in *Curva Sud*, *Antichi Valori* unfurled many banners that spoke of these ideas. One of the most concise, *Contro Tutto e Tutti* (Against everyone and everything), explained the Ultra *mentalità* perfectly. This refusal to reconcile or compromise was seconded by *Boys Roma*. Their 2004 banner reading *Sempre Schierati Mai Omologati* (Always in [military] formation, never homogenized/standardized) is a declaration of war against *Calcio Moderno* and standardization. It can also be read as a life of war, danger, and confrontation in defiance of the 'homogenized form of life' that opposes the Ultras.

CHAPTER SIX

Romanità and the Ultras

This chapter examines the concept *Romanità*, an extreme identification with Rome and things Roman, and what Rome means to the Ultras. Through its history, culture, and cultural symbols, Rome is the main inspirational entity for the Ultras; it makes knowable their deep affection. Even in the 'nastier' elements of their politics, witnessed in the preceding chapters, the Ultras are not motivated by a narrow, or parochial, fearfulness, but instead an intensely positive and prideful feeling of connection to place. Their discursive understanding of themselves, the rest of Italy and the world are filtered through Rome, and their relationship to the city's past, present, and future glory and greatness. This chapter examines the theoretical aspects of *Romanità* and then turns to examples of how the Ultras use and present their own vision of the intense connection between themselves and the city.

Romanità

Romanità as *Campanilismo?*

Campanilismo, or localism, is understood as an excessive attachment to one's town or birthplace.[1] It can lead to a particular identification and

---

1   Barzini, 1996, p. 13.

process of differentiation that can ultimately result in fragmentation and conflict.[2] Although generally used to describe the process through which many Italians interact with nationalizing trends, it is perfectly incorporated into the *mentalità* of the Ultras.[3] Thus, *campanilismo* could be used as an introductory element of a general *mentalità* of Italian Ultras, as the phenomenon is deeply linked with strong associations between glory, team, and town throughout Italy.

Romanità is a highly-exaggerated version of *campanilismo*, for *Romanità* is at base a hyper-identification with Rome and things Roman that causes fragmentation and conflict. I have already explained how extremely limited is the altruistic inclusiveness, or *propter nos*, of the Ultras and how this impacts their political ideology and behavior.[4] Based on my experiences and the behaviors of Ultras that I have witnessed, it is clear that a strong attachment to their city exists. Indeed, the national movement-based *Movimento Ultras* highlights 'local particularity' as the primary aspect of soccer under attack by *Calcio Moderno*.[5]

However, as connected as they might be, there is more to *Romanità* than *campanilismo*; there is also Fascism. I demonstrated in previous chapters that the Ultras have an 'aristocratic' sense through which they relish the distance between themselves and others. This 'aristocratic' sense, I explained, also makes the Ultras improper Fascists, in that there is little desire for unity (even amongst the Ultras themselves) or sense of being part of a movement. In other words, most of the Ultras are lacking a feeling of responsibility that would allow the phenomenon a truly political function.

---

2   Poppi, 1992, p. 81; Allum, 2000, p. 43.

3   Putnam, 1993, p. 27.

4   Hallyn, 1990, pp. 55–56.

5   *Movimento Ultras* is a loose confederation of various Ultra groups across Italia. It was started in the mid-1990s after the death of Genoa Ultra Vincenzo Spagnolo at the hands of AC Milan Ultras. It released a manifesto and several press releases from 1996 to 2006 but has been quiet since. Federations of this type are unpopular amongst Roma's Ultras because they presuppose an amount of unity with enemy Ultras that is often impossible to achieve.

There is a similar tension between Ultras, *Romanità*, and Fascism among Leftist groups, which also have a strong association with *Romanità*. This is because the Leftist and self-described apolitical groups, themselves interacting with *Romanità*, acknowledge the role played by historical and current Fascism in keeping alive not only Roman political discourse but also Roman self-conception.

Manuele, a member of *Fedayn*, explained *Romanità* to me in simple terms. '*Romanità*,' he said, 'is the thing that makes AS Roma's Ultras different from and superior to any others. It links the Ultras with the past and future of the city, and our city is more steeped in glory and conquest, in veneration and honor, than any city in the world. Other Ultras love their cities, as they should, but when looking for glory, they have no choice but to envy us.' I suggested to Manuele how similar was his understanding of *Romanità* to that of Ultras on the Right.

Like the Ultras, Fascism sought to link itself with the past and future of the city through *Romanità*. It also understood Rome as a city of glory and conquest, as well as of honor and veneration — ideals that drove Mussolini's project to transform, aggrandize, and render more fascist the center of Rome.[6] Indeed, Rome, as home to both the unification of Europe through imperial conquest and Catholicism, was for Fascism a universal symbol.[7]

Manuele responded with brevity: 'It's true because Fascism is also Roman,' an attitude that will be explained in the next chapter. However, there is an important distinction between the *Romanità* of the Ultras and that of Fascism. Fascism utilized *Romanità* not only to lend itself legitimacy by linking its rule with Imperial Rome, but also to undermine the power of *campanilismo* in the provinces. *Romanità* was to be the unifying narrative of the Italian Fascist State. Thus, its universal aspects were highlighted.[8]

---

6   Painter, Jr., 2005, pp. 1–5.

7   Falasca-Zamponi, 1997, pp. 90–91; Koon, 1995, p. 7.

8   Falasca-Zamponi, 1997, p. 90.

Romanità motivates an inversion of the universal mission of Rome for the Ultras, being reserved, rather, as the rarified domain of Romans. It is not a universal phenomenon or mission, but what separates them from someone in Milan, for example, who can no better understand Rome than a foreign tourist. Nor is it a will to unity as part of Italian nationalism. Instead, Fascist Ultras of AS Roma seek to make little more than the *Curva Sud* Fascist. I will now turn to a deeper explanation of the differences between the Ultra and other uses of *Romanità*.

Understanding *Romanità*
Liberal and Fascist Italy

Romanità is primarily studied and theorized by scholars of Fascism and the unification of Italy. The study of the uses of Rome by Fascism parallels that of the uses of Rome by the Ultras inasmuch as the Ultras understand themselves as a continuation of the Fascist project of creating a Third Rome.[9] While this will be discussed in Chapter Seven, it is important to note that the political project of AS Roma's Ultras is an attempt to replace the liberal bourgeois order of the present day with a recreation of the largely mythologized values of the warrior society of Ancient Rome.

Romanità was defined by Piergiorgio Zunino as a pre-modern and mythical (as opposed to historical) form of collective mentality best expressed in nostalgia for ancient Rome.[10] Claudio Fugo found this definition useful as he attempted to explain how an idea of Rome operated in the fascist understanding of history. Fascist history, he says, was structurally dependent upon a break with the past. He argued that Fascism did not seek a continuation of Classical Roman identity within a Fascist context. Instead, Fascism sought to use Rome, through *Romanità*, to lessen the influence of a modern, linear view of history amongst Italians. In other words, Fascism used a concept of history that aimed at diminishing the

---

9   Farrell, 2003, p. 222.

10   Fugo, 2003, p. 23.

conceptual import of the meta-narratives creative of modern political subjects.[11]

Tracy Koon, meanwhile, is less concerned about the functioning of history and historiography during the Fascist era. Instead, he linked *Romanità* first with liberal *Risorgimento* thinkers and their desire to find a unifying discourse for all peoples of the peninsula. Secondly, he pursued *Romanità* through to the Fascist period to show how then, as well, the greatness of Rome's imperial power was glorified as a unifying discourse.

Thus, he presents *Romanità* as a discourse that, contrary to Fugo, created links between the Classical and modern periods. By focusing more upon Mussolini's speeches and the symbolic finery of Fascism, Koon understood *Romanità* as a powerful tool in Mussolini's drive to create (via Fascism) a Third Rome (after the Classical and the Papal). Indeed, part of the power *Romanità* was that it (as a discourse) demonstrated the supposed Classical origins of Fascism.[12]

By presenting identification with the past as a fundamental element of the creation of a new civilization, itself based on the values and historical successes of Classical Rome, Fascism not only desired to universalize amongst Italians the celebration of their Classical origins, but also to make all actions, not matter how banal, historical. According to Koon, children in classrooms and *Balilla* (or, *Opera Nazionale Balilla*, the after-school and weekend youth groups which were intended to increase physical fitness and understanding of Fascism) organizations learnt the proper moral and spiritual value of their Roman heritage. Through the *Balilla*, the children were not only to learn valor and military discipline, but also that 'Rome is alive' through each of them.[13]

---

11   Ibid, pp. 20–23.

12   Koon, 1985, p. 19.

13   Koon, 1985, p. 20–21.

Evola

Unsurprisingly, given his own uses of Rome as an idealized entity, Evola had much to say about *Romanità*. In *Men Among the Ruins*, he demonstrates that Rome is unique among cities because it can be used as a forceful affect.[14] Rome, he explained, as might the Ultras, is an ideal. As such it demonstrates the fallacy of the political Left's reduction of life and politics (one and the same for Evola) to the interests of economic class. Rome must be part of a form of life (and State) seeking to transcend the vulgar economic determinism of materialism. That the previous generations of 'conservatives' sought to defend their economic interests at all costs, even at the expense of 'a higher right, dignity, and... legacy of values, ideas, and principles,' made them unworthy of being revered by the generation of 'revolutionary conservatives' which Evola hoped to mold. Instead, it would be the traditions and principles of Classical Rome that would guide their war.[15]

Evola was influenced by Nietzsche's distinction between 'acting unhistorically and suprahistorically' against the power of linear 'modern' history to destroy one's 'will to life as art'.[16] Acting unhistorically allowed one to forget history by enclosing oneself within a bounded temporal horizon. Acting suprahistorically was, by contrast, a more powerful option and one that inclined practitioners toward the greatness achieved in all periods. The suprahistorical bestowed 'the eternal' unto the actions and existence of the mortal.[17]

For Evola, *Romanità* was a suprahistorical agent. He acknowledged that the radical Left perpetuated an idea that *Romanità* was 'antihistorical' in that it motivated attachment to ideology at the expense of commitment to class conflict and was thus an example of irrational reaction to historical dialectical processes.[18] Even as he used the concept 'antihistorical' to

---

14   Evola, 2002, p. 115.

15   Ibid, p. 114.

16   Nietzsche, 1997, p. 115.

17   Ibid, pp. 115–116.

18   Evola, 2002, p. 181.

attack the liberalization of the world, however, he described Rome and *Romanità* in Nietzsche's terms. There are immutable principles, he said, that have been useful in creating ascending cultural forms. These principles can only be found by looking toward the past, toward tradition. 'Tradition,' he said, 'is neither servile conformity to what has been, nor a sluggish perpetuation of the past into the present. [It] is something simultaneously meta-historical and dynamic: it is an overall ordering force, in the service of principles that have the chrism of a superior legitimacy'.[19]

Figure 13. Typical view of a game in *Curva Sud*,
always full of Roman imagery, 2006.

Romanità has value, then, for Evola, because it does not seek to re-establish the institutions of Classical Rome, but the principles of which such institutions were expressions. Some of the principles to which Evola gave so much power were visible in the Roman cultural and psychological

---

19 Ibid, p. 115.

characteristics to be striven for in the present. These were self-control, an enlightened boldness, a concise speech and determined and coherent conduct, a cold and dominating attitude; *virtus* (virile spirit and courage, not moralism); *fortitudo* and *constantia* (spiritual strength); *sapientia* (thoughtfulness and awareness); *disciplina* (love for self-given law and form); *fides* (loyalty and faithfulness); *dignitas* (studied and moderated seriousness); *religio* and *pietas* (respect and veneration for the gods); deliberate actions; realism as love for the essential, not the material; the ideal of clarity; inner equilibrium and suspicion of confused mysticism; love of boundaries; and unity in pursuit of higher goals.[20]

In remembering, and desiring, all of these, one does not seek a teleological and transcendental law in which the past mechanically determines the present. Instead, one would seek only to properly distinguish subversive and degenerative cultural elements from those capable of sustaining greatness.[21] Evola's highly Nietzschean model was itself also highly modern. Emilio Gentile explains that the form of modernity sought by Fascism was a mythologized modernity, in which a symbiosis between 'art and life, culture and politics' would be made possible by adherence to an 'activist conception of life'.[22] Fascist modernity's focus on vitalism, daring, faith, mythic thought — and its disaffection with reality — was designed to promote a moving forward while carrying a slightly heavier load than that demanded by other, more liberal forms of modernity. It also became the basis of its use of *Romanità*, but in the form of myth dramatically celebrated by Sorel as a 'spur' to courage and faith.[23]

---

20   Evola, 2002, p. 259.

21   Ibid, p. 181; Evola, 2003, pp. 107–109.

22   Gentile, 2003, p. 59.

23   Ibid, p. 60.

Ultra Uses of *Romanità*

Romanità as Counter-Modern Discourse

Having just stated that *Romanità*, and its uses by Evola and Fascism, is a form political modernism, I must make clear why I continue to call it counter-modern. As I explained in the Introduction, Fascism is a complex mixture of political modernism and counter-modern, or Counter-Enlightenment, philosophy. In other words, it seeks to actualize a way of living that is an aggrandizement of the radical edge of modernity, with its fetishes for change, movement, industrialization, and efficiency,[24] while at the same time constructing a cultural core around a scathing critique of the intellectual bases of such social change, namely egalitarianism, marketization, and individualism.[25] *Romanità* might be useful as a means of motivating the 'actualization' of modern life, in the guise of political and social change, but in its championing of selected elements of Rome's intellectual heritage, demonstrated above by Evola, it is essentially counter-modern.

To take the matter further, Evola explained his use of *Romanità* in terms that countered the metaphors of collective human aggregates found not only in the origins of liberalism (the people, the nation) but in Hegel (the State). Instead of these concepts, which subsume the individual human will to a system that counter-balances the potential for individual greatness, Evola proposed the Roman and Nordic systems of Tradition. These, he felt, 'do not recognize the voice of the leveled multitudes, but instead beat down and mock these idols of clay, these modern ideologies, and organize themselves on the ... recognition of the irreducible differences among men, which define themselves in the natural and dynamic relation of their intensity'.[26] The idealized elements of Roman character, then, are not attainable for the multitude. As we have seen, the Ultras

---

24 Gentile, 2003, p. 60.

25 Sternhell, 1994, p. 3.

26 Evola, 2007, p. 62.

conceive of themselves in the same terms, as an elite element that is separated from the bourgeois masses by their own devotion to Evola's ideals.

It was suggested in previous chapters that the Ultras' *mentalità*, while containing aspects common to all Ultra groups in Italy, is better developed in AS Roma's Ultras than in other *curvas*. It is, perhaps, no accident that the founders of *Commando Ultra Curva Sud* coined the phrase '*mentalità Ultras*' in 1977. This is because of the extraordinary depth of feeling they have for the city of Rome as well as the depth of historical and mythical narratives to be found in the city. Rome, its history and symbolic universe, confer upon Ultra thought and action a sense of 'the eternal' or extreme importance.

In 2004 Vincenzo Patanè Garsia interviewed Etore, one of the leaders of *AS Roma Ultras*. He spoke of AS Roma's Ultras as '*rappresentati di Roma città, e di tutto ciò che vi sta dietro ... millenni di Storia e di cultura*' (representatives of the city and all which that entails ... millennia of history and culture). He continued to explain the pride and responsibility this conferred on the Ultras. '*Come eredi di un Impero, come figli della Lupa, come gente Romana, fieri e orgogliosi andiamo in giro* [...] *a sostenere i colori della nostra squadra e sopratutto della nostra città, la più bella del mondo*' (like heirs of an emperor, or children of the *Lupa* [*Capitolina*], or the Roman people fierce and proud, we go on tour to support the colors of our team, but above all the colors of our city — the most beautiful in the world).[27]

While I was unable to interview Etore for this project I met others who know him well. One of these was Federico, founding member of *Antichi Valori*, and former member of *AS Roma Ultras*. He described Etore as a '*bravo ragazzo*,' (good guy, one of us) one of those always present and one who never turned his back to the enemy. I asked about his statement, quoted by Garsia, hoping to understand the rarity of his love of Rome. Federico shrugged his shoulders and told me, 'we all feel this way — it is normal — if someone is this way they are an Ultra.' Sensing my next question, he interrupted, 'even if one does not go to the stadium.' In other

---

27   Garsia, 2004, p. 209.

words, not only is Etore's feeling for Rome and what it means to be Roman not unique, but it is enough to agree with him in order to be considered an Ultra by those who see themselves as the 'keepers of the faith,' the most proud and fierce of the Ultras. Federico's analysis points to an interesting question. If one may be an Ultra without going to a stadium, what is the purpose of the game of soccer within the Ultra phenomenon? And this raises the prior question of why soccer is important to the Ultras.

Why a sport is popular in a particular time and place is often impossible to answer. Soccer holds a special place in any debate on the subject, as the United States, the tastemaker of the vast majority of popular culture in the West, is virtually bereft of passion for the game. Avoiding the psychological aspects of aesthetics or fandom, Markovits and Hellerman provide a social/material explanation for the popularity of sports in time and place. The main factor they identify is the presence of a sport for a long period, and crucially, at the moment of industrialization and the creation of mass society. Another factor is that a sport must be played, and not just watched, by a large percentage of the population. Finally, a sport should have enough media coverage that it becomes part of the 'hegemonic sports culture' of the nation. It should be discussed long after the games are finished.[28]

The popularity of soccer tends to be a given in countries where it is hegemonic. That it is hegemonic is demonstrated by the connection of national character with the playing style found in each nation. For instance, the Brazilians connect 'beauty and art' with the ways their professional and national teams play.[29] Similarly, the Dutch want their teams to play beautifully rather than 'doing anything' to win.[30] The Italians, instead, seem to have always associated soccer with warfare. Simon Martin reports on the failure of *Serie A* to unite the peninsula, as Mussolini had intended, because of the extreme partisanship of local fans.[31] Similarly John Foot

---

28 Markovits and Hellerman, 2001, pp. 10–12.

29 Williams, 2006, p. xiv.

30 Winner, 2000, p. 60.

31 Martin, 2004, p. 27.

summarizes the origins of Italian soccer by explaining the exacerbation of civic rivalries by the game.[32]

The Ultras and their understanding of soccer fit nicely within this understanding of soccer. The game was imported to Italy in the 1880s and became nationalized in the 1920s, meeting Markovits's and Hellerman's criteria. Likewise, Italians obsess over the game in midweek and it is no doubt the dominant sport in the country from a media point of view, and every Ultra of AS Roma and every fan of soccer I met in Italy played the game in some form. Turning to the national character of the Italian game, the element of warfare and rivalry, as I have shown, is absolutely central to the Ultras as fans and as a unique social phenomenon.

But if soccer is important and available enough to be the sport of choice for the Ultras, what purpose do they see it serving? Following Allen Guttman's research of Ancient Roman spectators, the Ultras are perfectly consistent with the purpose of Roman sports for their most passionate fans: as an opportunity for partisanship. Guttman uses ancient sources to explain that Roman spectators were extremely partisan, to the point that partisanship seems to have been the point, or at least the draw, of spectating sports in the ancient city. Pliny the Younger, Guttman tells us, had difficulty understanding the passions of the masses for sports. If the masses had a genuine appreciation for the skills one needs to properly control a speeding chariot, perhaps he would have been more sympathetic to their passions. Instead, Pliny said, 'it is the racing colors they really support and care about, and if the colors were to be exchanged in mid-course ... they would transfer their favor and enthusiasm. Such is the popularity and importance of a worthless shirt.'[33] Guttman continues, explaining that team loyalties were so deep that often a man's funerary inscription would mention his partisanship.[34]

So deep were the passions for chariot teams that violence between sets of fans was common, with certain rivalries being so inflamed that the rival

---

32 Foot, 2006, pp. 1–41.

33 Guttman, 1981, p. 11.

34 Ibid, p. 12.

cities were prohibited from hosting games.[35] Further, identification as a fan of a certain team bound one to a common body that had political clout. Certain colors, as teams were divided by color, were historically affiliated to certain parties. This was true regardless of social rank. 'Whatever differences in behavior and even social class there may have been,' Guttman explains, 'partisans of both colors moved in much the same world.'[36]

In Rome, it never occurred to me to ask the Ultras why they liked soccer. I never even asked myself why I like it, which for me, as an American male raised in a family of athletes of American football and baseball, was far less likely than Italian males who grew up playing the game. Later, however, when the research demanded an answer to the question, I contacted Federico of *Antichi Valori*. Predictably, he was stumped when I asked why he liked soccer. He had no answer, as if I asked him why he liked oxygen. When I explained what Markovits and Hellerman proposed, he seemed mildly interested but ultimately just said, 'it makes sense.' However, when I told him about Guttman's portrayal of Roman spectators, he was dumbfounded that he 'had never known this deep connection between [the Ultras] and the Romans.' He asked for Guttman's sources so that he could find them in Latin, excitedly telling me 'Rome amazes me almost every day, even after thirty-seven years.' Sociological theory was one thing, in other words, but Rome, and an Ultra's connection to Rome, was something else entirely.

Sorel distinguishes between the 'mere observation of facts' and the 'inner reason of things' which is found in the myths that motivate 'the will to act.'[37] *Romanità* is attached to the latter. These types of myths, Sorel argues, are strong enough to safeguard utopias that have no just reason to survive, such as the French Republic.[38] Interestingly, Sorel also explains that myths are even capable of guarding against the 'invasion of ideas and morals' of

---

35 Ibid.

36 Ibid.

37 Sorel, 1999, pp. 24–28.

38 Ibid, p. 29.

the 'hostile' bourgeois class.[39] *Romanità* is certainly used by the Ultras as a bulwark against the bourgeois form of life.

Through Federico I was introduced to other former members of *Antichi Valori*. As I explained in Chapter One, Antichi *Valori* are amongst the most dedicated of the Ultras — they are neither completely Left nor Right but are dedicated instead to Rome. Unlike the imposing and rather menacing skinheads and ideologues of *Boys Roma* and *Padroni di Casa*, to be re-visited below, the four former leaders of *Antichi Valori* are 'clean-cut' professionals and students. Their backgrounds are similar: they are well educated (each having achieved the *baccalaureato*, or bachelor's degree), have steady jobs, steady girlfriends or wives, and live at home or nearby their working parents. They spend as many hours together as possible during the week, often dining out or going to bars to play *calcio balilla* (table soccer). On summer weekends, they go to the beaches near Rome, where table soccer is also widely played. In August, they travel abroad or in Trentino.

What separates these young men from others (outside the Ultras phenomenon) is *Romanità*. Integral to each of the activities that they undertake together is a sense of pride in being Roman and a sense of duty or responsibility to 'defend her honor.' I knew from the history of *Antichi Valori* that they were extremely steeped in the history of Rome, but through passing time with them away from the stadium I learned just how deeply being an Ultra and living according to its *mentalità*` can impact one's life.

For instance, discussing *Romanità* with Federico and Fabrizio (another of the founders of the group) in a Monteverde bar the day after AS Roma won the 2006–7 *Coppa Italia*, Fabrizio made it clear that it was only *Romanità* that made them different. I had begun by suggesting that willingness to fight was quite important in placing distance between them and non-Ultras. He explained to me that fighting was not a random exercise for the Ultras. Sure, he said, there are some who are *'fatto da*

---

39   Ibid, p. 32.

ferro' (made of iron) and just enjoy fighting but a true Ultra does not fight without cause (for more on this see Chapter Four).

'We only fight because of *Romanità*,' he said. 'Fight as Ultras?' I asked. 'Yes, fight as Ultras,' he replied. Federico interjected something I found most interesting. 'We are sons of a *vecchia mentalità* [old/ancient worldview],' he said. 'Fighting is a big part of being an Ultra because we seek a glory that is not provided by the modern world. Instead, we seek an old glory, one made with *virtu*` [virtue like Nietzsche described virtue free of 'priggish morality']; a virtue that leads to the strength necessary to do difficult things.'[40] Again, Federico, as had Etore (of *AS Roma Ultras*) and Manuele (of *Fedayn*) invoked a *Romanità* that was prone to violence, a vision distinctly at odds with the Rome of neoliberal Italy.

Because of its unique history, *Romanità* is perfectly suited to sustain the Ultra *mentalità*. As a fascist discourse, *Romanità* was replete with a model of glory and tradition that made both of these a function of aggression and conquest. The *Terza Roma* (Third Rome) of Mussolini was to be an imperial Rome, beginning with colonies in Libya, Ethiopia, and Eritrea. This Rome was an ideal to be made real by way of controlling the Mediterranean, or *Mare Nostrum*.

The Ultras have been more influenced by this form of *Romanità* than the Liberal nationalist form explained by Fugo. For AS Roma's Ultras, Italy matters very little, except as a terrain of Roman conquest. From Rome, the Ultras are able to feel themselves heir to a culture and a system of traits (such as those described by Evola — see above).

Returning to Federico's statement that the Ultras were 'sons of an old worldview,' it must not be understated how *Romanità* in this form acts to motivate behaviors. Even as the Ultras' love for Rome is often made known through creative acts such as choreographies and articles in fanzines, these are but the outward manifestations of a *mentalità* that coincides with the list of Roman traits given by Evola. Those traits were designed to celebrate a virile form of life that has been destroyed by the

---

40 Nietzsche, 2003, p. 182; Nietzsche, 2003, p. 176.

'effeminacy of modernity,' and they are made natural to the Ultras through the Roman qualities appreciated by Evola and even Mussolini.

Choreographies and banners arise from the same energies and desires as do the fights and acts of aggression or disrespect derided by the Italian press. Maurizio of *Padroni di Casa* explained this best. 'We are men who remember well the words of the *Duce*. For us Rome is the reference point of a victorious life, the myth that gives us hope for a life that is strong and wise [he is paraphrasing a Mussolini speech popular among Roman Fascists for its discussion of Rome as the vision of a Fascist Italy]. It would be impossible, then, to live in fear of fights or of the police. Our Rome is that of the true Romans.' In upholding aggression, honor, discipline, and the idea of glory through violence, the Ultras feel themselves upholding the *true spirit* of Rome.

One sees here a process similar to the theatrical politics analyzed by Kertzer. Theatrical and cultish politics, he explained, are functioning in modern societies just as they did in what were assumed to be 'traditional' societies. These political forms are based on ritual practices and liturgies that attach great meaning to action. They are also based on mythical or ideational discourses, like *Romanità*, which 'give meaning to the world around us' and provide the fabric of order in the face of chaos. Far from lulling their audiences to sleep, these discourses and narratives transform ideas into a lived reality.[41] Or, as Mussolini said, 'for us ideas are not abstractions but physical forces. When the idea seeks to become reified in the world it does so through manifestations that are nervous, muscular, and physical'.[42]

Returning to Sorel, who was one of Mussolini's main intellectual influences, the value of an idea or myth is singular — in its ability to motivate action.[43] The provocation of thought is a function of which both knowledge and myth are capable. However, it is the domain of the latter to provoke

---

41   Kertzer, 1988, p. 13.

42   Duggan, 2007, p. 350.

43   Farrell, 2003, p. 30.

action in the form of violence.[44] And, because of the bourgeois aversion to violence, when one acts violently (more clearly in a revolutionarily violent way), one is able to move beyond the form of life defined by liberalism. In thinking this way, Sorel revealed the influence of Nietzsche, whose own *Übermensch* was to be born from a thorough rejection of modernity and its values.

Romanità as Inhibitor of Universal Altruism

Romanità is useful for the Ultras as a discourse that limits the scope of altrusitic inclusiveness. It is apparent that the Ultras celebration of themselves as Romans is done at the expense of feelings of inclusiveness with others. Although many scholars, and what Luca of *Boys Roma* called '*giornalisti morali*' (journalists of morality), lament the Italian tendency to identify with narrow altruistic scopes (hence the concept *campanilismo*), the Ultras understand this part of their *mentalità* to be entirely positive.

Luca, a thirty-three-year-old member of both *Boys Roma* and *Forza Nuova* (the neo-Fascist party led by Roberto Fiore) works for Ryanair, a low-cost airline with routes between Ireland and the continent. As such he speaks English with great enthusiasm, smiling while discussing topics that would make others grimace. He learned English at *La Sapienza* University (neither of his parents speak anything but the Roman dialect) and enjoys reading certain titles in English literature. His favorites? '[Burgess'] *A Clockwork Orange*, [Easton-Ellis'] *American Psycho*, and [Palahniuk's] *Fight Club*.'

'Almost too perfect,' I say. 'Yes, it is,' he says, 'knowing [English] allows me to know the subtleties of what is being said. For example, all three books understand that the prohibition against violence is just a [bourgeois] moral phenomenon.' Returning to the point, I asked, 'just like the prohibition against *Romanità* and extreme rivalry in soccer?' 'Exactly!' he replied. 'Why would anyone have a problem with our love of Rome? Only if they feared being excluded.' I asked him to explain. 'There are many

44   Sorel, 1999, p. 46.

people who believe that the world belongs to them *del tutto* [full stop] and that anywhere people build a wall against them is a sign of ignorance.' 'And not pride or protection,' I interject. 'We are not allowed pride. Our pride is what you [Americans] call racism.'

Having befriended a handful of *Forzanovisti* (members of *Forza Nuova*) and many Rightist Ultras, I was prepared for his understanding of the cultural politics of neo-liberal globalization. However, for the first time I asked, 'do you find more *Romanità* in *Forza Nuova* or *Boys Roma*?' Without hesitation he replied, 'In the Ultras there is far more *Romanità*. Fascists are mostly nationalists — they want a pure Italy while [AS Roma's] Ultras want a pure stadium or a Roman life that, for us, is much deeper than the American life.' We spoke for a few more minutes on the topic but finally he said something monumental. 'At *Boys Roma,* we talk about the Coliseum and how it was built. Do you know where the money came from to build it?' he asked before continuing. 'Discover this and you will know why it is beloved by "true Romans." [The Coliseum was built by the Flavian imperial dynasty with riches taken from the sacked city of Jerusalem. As such it is perhaps the ultimate symbol of Rome being enriched at the expense of its enemies.] Anyway, with the Fascists we do not discuss this so much. Fascism is important because without political struggle we are only consumers. But the Ultras are important because I am Roman,' he said, touching his heart.

Many Ultras share an active love, piety, and fidelity toward Rome. It's past and present, every wall, *porta* (door/gate), *via* (street), *vicolo* (small street), and piazza are venerated and revered. To be considered a '*figlio della Lupa*' (son of the she-wolf) is an honor that many celebrate like a working title.[45] It is not conferred upon them, but something they feel. For some groups that are well versed in the history, culture, and traditions of the city, like *Antichi Valori*, to be *figlio dell Lupa, un vero Romano* (a true Roma), or *un legionario* (legionnaire), was a particularly extreme mark

---

45   The *Figli della Lupa* were elite Fascist youth groups as part of the *Opera Nazionale Balilla*, the afterschool indoctrination and exercise camps of the Italian Fascist State. The Ultras use the term in the same way, to distinguish themselves from others less aware of the history and traditions of the city (or of Fascism).

of distinction — almost liminal. A young Ultra called a 'true Roman' by a group leader was in essence being called legitimate and someone to be respected and regarded.

In this way, *Romanità* may be understood as a positive force. If it acts as a bulwark against the outside world, it is doing so to protect valued traditions. If it stems the influence of foreign peoples, it does so to prohibit cultural degeneration. Thus, for AS Roma's Ultras, *Romanità* is a title for their mode of altruism. This is why the Ultra consider so much at stake when they protest against *Calcio Moderno* or a *Roma omologata* (Rome standardized, or brought within the sphere of globalization/multiculturalism). Their community is composed of and defined by their commitment to understanding Rome as the greatest accomplishment in human history.

Fabrizio, a longtime Ultra who has been in both *Monteverde* and *Tradizione Distinzione Roma*, lives in Monteverde. I saw him every morning at the Pulcini pastry shop, a neighborhood institution. Fabrizio sells small machinery to farmers just outside Rome. As such, his job takes him in the opposite direction of the many commuters who come into Rome's center for work. I wouldn't have it any other way. I can't stand to be around the tourists who take our city to be a big playground or some kind of joke, he told me. The first week that we lived in Rome, my wife and I entered Pulcini during the morning rush. Fabrizio was there and made a nasty comment about tourists invading even their neighborhood. He muttered 'pieces of shit' in our direction as he left.

It took another three months for us to go back to Pulcini. When we did, however, it was every morning; often enough for us to be considered locals by the owners and other regulars. We were embraced by the local pharmacist, herbalist, shoe store owner, sunglass store owner, and so on. Eventually word reached Fabrizio that I was someone he should meet. After a cagey introduction by Luca, Pulcini's manager, Fabrizio and I met and talked every morning for one year. He admitted to being hostile to my presence in Monteverde and to assuming I was 'just some tourist who was coming to treat [his] city as a toilet.' His aversion to tourists and tourism allowed me to work this aspect of localism into our discussions on the

Ultras. 'Tourism,' he told me, 'is the most vulgar thing a person can do. These people come to Rome knowing nothing and they leave knowing nothing.'

I spoke to him about tourism's impact on the Greek island of Skyros, which has seen tourism become the basis for what is presented as 'traditional' in style of housing and products sold as artisanal and has upset the traditional hierarchical relations with the land. To combat this, the local population of the island began to treat tourism as a necessary evil, whereas before tourists were treated as guests and 'part of the family'.[46] 'Rome has always been a tourist destination, even for the ancients. So, it is hard to know what is ours and what is just a facade created to make tourists happy. The historic center [of Rome] is largely of the latter variety for us. We [he began speaking for *Monteverde*] want to walk our streets and hear our language, not the hysterical cackling of Americans and Germans.' I asked him about the monetary influence of tourism in Rome, and the way the city caters to tourism. 'When drunken Poles swim in the *Trevi* [fountain], or American students destroy Trastevere, the city is enslaved by them.'

'There is nothing else for the Romans to do but open a shop or work in a restaurant selling horrible food to people who know no better,' he continued. 'Is this the equivalent of what happened on Skyros?' I asked. 'It must be,' he responded, 'as we would never eat pizza for lunch or drink cappuccino in the evening. Yet, this is what passes for our food now. At least,' he added, 'the [Roman] Forum is still ours. It is too abstract for the tourists so they do not spoil it for us. The rest of the center they can have, as it is just a shopping district now. All the history and *Romanità* have been stripped away.'

Fabrizio's comments were clearly examples of tourism creating distance between the local populations of tourist destinations and the tourists who visit them. For an Ultra, though, this distance acted to increase the sense that Rome was under siege. Tourists have a high impact on the lives of locals, from overcrowding infrastructure to higher prices for food

---

46   Zarkia, 1996, pp. 87–109.

and housing, and Fabrizio lumped them in with immigrants as well.[47] 'The economy can fail. I will have no problems when it does. What I worry about, and what *Monteverde* worried about, was the destruction of culture under the weight of these people,' he told me. I asked if he thought Roman culture was not strong enough to withstand a few immigrants and a lot of tourists. 'Fair enough,' he said, 'I should have more faith in my culture. It is just that we have seen so much of it change. Romans used to be proud but happy, even my parents were like this until recently. Now, we are proud and angry. We are defensive because we see that in a few more generations, the city might be more immigrant than Roman and more commercial than cultural. We've already lost political autonomy [because of the European Union] and the right to keep our city ours.'

I asked about his parents' influence on his activities in *Monteverde*. 'They loved *Monteverde*,' he responded enthusiastically, 'for we were doing something they wanted to do but could not because of responsibilities. Truly, we were never violent; we just kept our neighborhood as we wanted it. Now, had there been tourists we would have spilled blood!' Fabrizio's parents, he went on, were part of a generation that saw Rome flourish as a tourist destination and that likewise flourished itself. However, his parents, like other Ultras' parents I encountered, became disillusioned with the price of the changes tourism brought. Especially given Monteverde's proximity to Trastevere, his parents often lamented that small restaurants and Roman butchers had closed shop to make way for 'Indians selling postcards and gaudy t-shirts.' Their desperation fed Fabrizio's passion for the Ultras, which he, like many others, saw as a way to connect with something Roman that was not tainted by the bourgeois form of life and to keep soccer from befalling the same fate as the tourist areas of the city.

The parents' desperation points as well to a process of 'cultural dispossession,' wherein the economic and political system is aligned with foreign interests that ultimately eliminate the options for local people to live in a locally meaningful way.[48] The sense of dispossession is strong among

---

47 Pedregal, 1996, pp. 45–62.

48 Creed, 2011, pp. 1–27.

Romans, as Herzfeld (2009) has also discovered. Whereas the celebration of self-hood amongst Europeans is often unacknowledged before it is irrevocably under attack,[49] there are other possibilities — most notably the experiences of post-colonial peoples who actually achieved peoplehood as a result of a struggle for cultural survival.[50] Romans resemble the latter, in some ways, having long been keenly aware of not only their patrimony but also how their inheritance entitles them to feelings of distinction.[51] There is a birthright to Rome that Romans often feel is undermined by the city also being a world capital. Instead of turning their backs on the intellectual and material heritage that comes to define being Roman, the many Ultras I met embrace it to the point of rejecting what Rome may mean to anyone else.

Neither their *propter nos* (the 'us' on whose behalf 'we' act) nor their ambitions are indeterminate.[52] Like the Greek youths described by Nietzsche in 'Homer's Contest,' the Ultras act for the good of their city. They seek to aggrandize Rome through the means at their disposal: singing, choreography, colors, and violent encounters. The contest between cities may have changed but the *mentalità* that fueled their rivalries is maintained by the Ultras. For the Ultra, then, *Romanità* is an inspiration not to dwell in an enervating dead history but to be active in the present.[53] What *Calcio Moderno* threatens is not only the Ultra form of life, but the Roman form of life as well. By seeking to extinguish the Ultras, the 'keepers of the faith,' it threatens the eternal timelessness of Rome.

The Ultras and Rome
Roman and/or Fascist Symbols

In the nervous and uncertain days between the death of Gabriele Sandri on November 11, 2007 and the beginning of the Ultra protest on December

---

49   Southgate, 2010, pp. 124–131.

50   Said, 1993, pp. 97–111.

51   Herzfeld, 2009, p. 3.

52   Hallyn, 1990, pp. 55–56.

53   Griffin, 2007, p. 222.

2, 2007, there was news that brought other conversations to a halt in Ultra circles. On November 20, archaeologists found what they assumed to be the fabled *Lupercale*. The next day's *Il Romanista*, screamed from the front page, 'Romolo, Remo, e la Lupa: Trovata la Grotta' and inside pages two and three were entirely devoted to the discovery.[54] The *Lupercale* was the cave believed to be the spot on which the *Lupa* (she-wolf) fed Remus and Romulus. It was found sixteen meters below the ground near the house of Augustus on the Palatine.

At dinner with a group of Ultras and their girlfriends and wives the conversation was about the cave. I proposed that the cave was more a shrine to the narrative of the *Lupa* than the actual cave in which the twins were saved and reared, adding that the shrine (obviously) had a long history but probably served a more public purpose in Augustinian Rome than before. To which someone added, 'Just as Augustus served a bigger purpose in Fascist Rome than in other of Rome's periods.' The Romans then began discussing the merits of the Richard Meier museum at the Ara Pacis, as well as the complexity of the Piazza Augusto Imperatore where it is found — the most fascist spot in Italy, I was told. Eventually the conversation turned toward Mussolini's transformation of the city, including Monteverde — where the dinner and conversation took place.

La Lupa Capitolina (The Capitoline She-Wolf)

The three most common uses of Roman history by the Ultra each have Fascist associations. The first is the *Lupa Capitolina*. *La Lupa*, as she is affectionately known, along with the twins Remus and Romulus whom she suckled, is the symbol of the city. It represents an origin narrative that has been popular in Rome at least since the fifth century BC. The story of Remus and Romulus has approximately sixty variations, all of which conclude with Romulus founding the city upon the Palatine hill in 753 BC.[55] The symbol can be found all over the city, on statues, garbage bins, lamp

---

54 *Il Romanista*, Anno IV, Numero 321, 21 November 2007, pp. 1–3.

55 Forsythe, 2005, pp. 59–74.

posts, drainage grates, bridges, buildings, etc. It can also be found upon the shield (or crest) of AS Roma. The placing of the yellow and red shield 'over the heart' on the AS Roma jersey signifies for the Ultras loyalty and dedication not just to AS Roma but also to Rome. The *Lupa* was placed on many of the buildings, bridges, drainage grates, and statues by the Fascist government. As part of Mussolini's *Romanità* campaign, it became a crucial symbol linking the Fascist era with Classical Rome. Through the *Lupa*, Romans and other Italians were transported to a period when the eternal ideals and values of Rome were the guiding forces of life. Thus, it was celebrated as a sacred symbol.[56]

For the Ultras, the nurturing *Lupa* is the essence of the city. This is because of the historiography the *Lupa* promotes. As Fabrizio of *Antichi Valori* explained, 'The gods established the city, true? Anyway, who the hell knows. It seems beautiful to me to believe the city is divine.' In other words, it is impossible to maintain the mystical and mythical bases of life when ecology is the narrative used to explain the city's origins. The *Lupa*, though, is the product of a monumental history — one that has ebbed and flowed in the city's long duration, and one that does not fail to understand the power of narrative in human behavior.

Coincidentally, SS Lazio's symbol is the imperial eagle, another Classical Roman symbol — this time of military aggression, as the eagle standard was more popular amongst the legions than the *Lupa*. Likewise, it too was a symbol put to great use by Fascism, leaving both sets of Ultras to revere symbols which link them with Classical and Fascist Rome.

XXI Aprile 753 aC

The 'mystery of Roman continuity' is embedded in the second of the three Ultra symbols: the 21st of April. This date, *XXI Aprile 753 aC*, records the moment when Romulus founded the city. As noted in the second chapter, one of the longest running groups in *Curva Sud* (although today the group meets in the *Tevere* Grandstand) was *XXI Aprile 753 aC*. Each season, the

---

56   Gentile, 1996, p. 76.

game played in Rome nearest April 21st is celebrated like a birthday in *Curva Sud*. Banners from many or all of the groups are displayed, each with its own message of best wishes for the city. In 2006, the occasion was marked on April 22nd when AS Roma hosted UC Sampdoria from Genova. Messages like *'Buon natale Urbe Immortale'* (Happy Birthday Immortal City) dotted the *Curva*. In the *Tevere* Grandstand, *XXI Aprile* laid a long banner for the duration of the game which read '*2759 Anni di Storia, Auguri Mamma Roma*' (2759 Years of History, Best Wishes Mother Rome).

April 21st was made an official holiday in Italy by Mussolini beginning in 1926. It was the first Fascist holiday, intended to replace May Day. April 21st was meant to symbolize the power of 'work and discipline'.[57] It was also meant to be a point of transition from the Italian (liberal) past of pacifism, cowardice, comfort, and peace to a future of aggression, heroism, conquest, and struggle.[58] The postwar period witnessed the re-establishment of May 1st as a national labor holiday and April 21st is mentioned only amongst the Romans as a day of celebration. For the Ultras, it is better this way. 'For other Italians,' Giorgio of *Ultras Romani* explained to me, 'the day is only an abstraction if they are even aware of its significance. If they do not live the greatness of Rome everyday then they are undeserving of joining a celebration in its honor,' he said.

Giallo e Rosso (Yellow and Red)

The third most common use of Roman history by the Ultra are the colors yellow and red. The two connote oil and wine, blood and gold, and the sun and the heart. In any case, they were the state colors of Classical Rome and are still the official colors of the city. And they are the colors of AS Roma. For the Ultras, they are sacred because of all three connotations.

When AS Roma was founded in 1927, it was as an act of *Romanità*. Mussolini desired another squad, besides SS Lazio, to represent the city

---

57 Falasca-Zamponi, 1997, p. 92.

58 Ibid, p. 91.

in the Italian championship. The name AS Roma and the *Lupa Capitolina* were chosen, as were the yellow and red colors, in order to deliberately invoke the links between Fascist and Classical Rome.[59]

Romanità and *Curva Sud Roma*
www.asromaultras.org

It was no surprise for me to be confronted with Ultras impassioned by some aspect of the city's history. The website for *AS Roma Ultras* made it clear to all who visited it that the Ultras are benefactors of the glory of Rome. In the section titled '*Roma e Romani,*' (Rome and Romans) the history of the city is presented from the particular *mentalità* of the Ultras. One is greeted by a quote from Stendhal's *Voyages en Italie* (1826):

'*Il Romano mi sembra superiore sotto tutti gli aspetti alle altre popolazioni d'Italia. Ha più forza di carattere, più semplicità, e, incomparabilmente, più spirito. Dategli un Napoleone per venti anni e Romani saranno sicuramente il primo popolo d'Europa*' (The Roman seems to me superior by all accounts to the other peoples of Italy. [He] has more strength of character, more simplicity, and incomparably more spirit. Give them a Napoleon for twenty years and the Romans will absolutely be the finest people of Europe).

One then proceeds through the 2761 years of Roman history, beginning with various versions of the city's origin narrative; the aggressive expansion of the city and civilization throughout Italy, Europe, and the Mediterranean; explanations of *SPQR*; and the uncertain origins of the *Lupa Capitolina*. The architectural wonders of the city are explained, from the Coliseum to the Pantheon.

The Classical period ends with an account of the Roman passion for sport that mirrors the analysis of Guttman (1981). The section is entitled '*gli Ultras dell'antica Roma*' (the Ultras in Classical Roma). Unsurprisingly, sport is presented as an extremely partisan affair, with the various zones and political factions determining for whom one was a fan. This

---

59   Martin, 2004, p. 170.

interpretation is continued to explain the relations between Romans and other Italians from the Renaissance to today. Vignettes and quotes are provided which proclaim the superiority of Romans to all other peoples, and Rome as superior to all other cities.

Lorenzo, author of the website, including the section described above, left *Curva Sud* when *AS Roma Ultras* collapsed. He now attends each home game in the *Tevere* Grandstand, where he uses his camera to capture the activities of the *Curva*. Even though he is not *'della Curva'* (in the Curva) he is still an intensively devoted Ultra. His life consists of family (he is married and has a newborn daughter) and the Ultras.

Professionally Lorenzo is an attorney who specializes in helping Ultras who are arrested as a result of Ultra-related activities. In years past — he began practicing law in 2003 — this involved advising Italian Ultras arrested for fighting and, especially, those arrested in foreign countries. These days, however, due to the crackdown on Ultra behaviors that followed the death of Raciti in February 2007, he strives to be a leading advocate of freedom of expression in Italian legal circles.

Fanzines and Choreographies
Vecchie Maniere (Old Ways) and History Lessons

This approach to the history of the city was extended to *Vecchie Maniere*, the 'fanzine' of *AS Roma Ultras* as well. Each month this group published a small periodical for distribution within the Curva. In addition to information on upcoming AS Roma games and travel options to away games, there was a feature called 'Roma Vrbs Nostra' (Our City Rome) which detailed some aspect of the city's 'art, history and civilization.'[60] Federico, one of the founding members of *Antichi Valori* wrote the articles. Without irony, he explained to me that the *Vrbs Nostra* feature was 'just a part of being Ultra and Roman. They were not written to demonstrate our

---

60 AS Roma Ultras, *Vecchie Maniere*, Tuesday 18 February 2003, pp. 8–9.

intelligence to those who did not know us, but because '*Roma è la luce*" (Rome is the light).[61]

Among Fascist Ultras, it was common to find some, especially the group leaders of *Boys Roma* and *Padroni di Casa*, who spoke of Fascism in the same emotive terms as they did Rome. It was common to hear these Ultras say that 'Mussolini loved Rome,' or that 'Mussolini built Rome.' This was explained to me during a bus ride to Milan with *Boys*. The acting '*capo*' (boss) sat next to me and explained that Fascism was Roman and therefore to be cherished and respected.

Named Maurizio but called '*Duce*' by the *Boys* Ultras, not only because of his association with Fascism but also his uncanny similarity in appearance to Mussolini, he is the most imposing and menacing Ultra I encountered. He looks as if he could walk through a wall, having a thick muscular body and a large bald head. I never saw him without large aviator sunglasses and a t-shirt with a Fascist-inspired message (All Blacks and 1934 World Cup being two examples). Conversely, he is generous with his time and resources, always making sure that his Ultras act with proper dignity and discipline.

Upon being told by Fabio (the second-in-command at *Boys* and one of my most informative contacts) that I was knowledgeable about the history of Fascism and Rome, *Duce* struck up numerous conversations with me during our eight-hour trip to Milan. He explained to me that Classical Rome as we recognize it today is only thanks to Mussolini and Fascism, which sought to re-establish the greatness of *Roma Antica*. I talked to him as best as I could, considering he spoke only Roman dialect, about Mussolini's destruction of the medieval quarter that stood around Piazza Venezia and covered parts of the forums.[62] 'He destroyed what was weak and decadent in our history,' he added.

---

61 The saying comes from the film The Gladiator. Maximus, the main character, is asked what Rome means to him. He replies that, having seen that most of the world is brutal, crude, and dark, Rome, for him, is 'the light.' The saying is popular amongst AS Roma's Ultras.

62 Painter, Jr., 2005; Herzfeld, 2009.

Choreographies and the Use of *Romanità*

In Chapter Three I explained that the Ultras employ a monumental form of history, in which linear history is less important than the myths and narratives of greatness that can be generated by history. The *Boys Roma* leader's explanation of Mussolini's Rome was an example of this approach. Vast stretches of Roman history are dismissed by the Ultras; Medieval, Baroque, Renaissance, and Liberal periods pale in relation to the Classical and Fascist periods as sources of 'their Rome.' Augustus, Julius Caesar, and Horatius Cocles have all made appearances in *Curva Sud* in recent years.

Horatius Cocles

Horatius Cocles was the subject of a choreography created by *Boys Roma* for a game against SS Lazio in 2002. Horatius was a hero of early Republican Rome. He singlehandedly saved the city from an invading Etruscan army by defending and then setting fire to a wooden bridge across the Tiber. The Etruscans had already captured the Gianicolo hill and were making their way down toward the bridge to advance into Rome. As Roman soldiers deserted their positions, he took up his shield and sword, crossed alone to the far side of the river, and ordered the deserters to destroy the bridge. Alone, he faced the Etruscan forces, 'one man against an army.' After killing many of the enemy, he jumped into the Tiber and swam to safety.[63]

Boys depicted Horatius as a marble statue with the shield/symbol of AS Roma carved over his heart. Horatius was bathed in red and yellow as Ultras throughout the *Curva* held small cards with the colors aloft. Below the painting depicting Horatius were the words '*Oltre la Morte*,' (beyond the grave).[64] In other words, *Curva Sud*, acting in the name of Horatius, was ready to defend the city from foreign invasion. In doing so, the Ultras

---

63   Livy, 2002, pp. 118–120.

64   Cacciari, 2004, p. 15.

conflated themselves with Horatius, as heroes who were destined to sacrifice themselves in service to Rome.

For that 2002 derby (as games between local rivals are called), AS Roma's Ultras were determined to make it understood that they shared the city with no one; hence, the reference to Horatius defending the city from foreigners. Since the 1999–2000 season, when SS Lazio won the Italian championship, SS Lazio fans had an increased presence in the city, or so it seemed. It became popular to speak of 'the two *Capitoline* (Roman) teams' much to the chagrin of *Curva Sud*. There were many banners in the *Curva* that night which questioned the right of the Lazio fans to call themselves Roman. For instance, one read (in Roman dialect) '*Lazzià guardate la carta d'identità poi ce parli de Romanità*' (Lazio fans, check your identification cards and then speak to us about *Romanità*).

Roma ai Romani (Rome for the Romans)

In 2000, SS Lazio was the defending champion of Italy. When they matched up against AS Roma, *Curva Sud* made a choreography depicting the seal of the city — a crowned red shield emblazoned with SPQR in gold flanked by the flags of Italy and Rome.[65] Below was written '*Nome, Colori, Tradizione, Roma Resta Giallorosso*' (name, colors, tradition, Rome remains yellow-red).

Regardless of SS Lazio's success, the city remained the property of AS Roma fans. The Ultras demonstrated this not from spite but because they believed that SS Lazio had no claim to the city. They were formed in 1900 as a regional team, twenty-seven years before AS Roma, and had willingly chosen to ignore the colors and history of Rome when deciding on their own name. And anyone whose loyalty lies with the region or any other abstraction at the expense of Rome is considered a foreigner. The name, colors, and traditions of Rome were coterminous with those of AS Roma and *Curva Sud*.

Still another year earlier in 1999, *AS Roma Ultras* presented another choreography that conflated *Curva Sud* with the Classical history of the

---

65   Nini, 2007, p. 42.

city. With the *Curva* bathed from side to side in yellow, red, and white cards, the center section held aloft a painting of a centurion and ten legionaries marching behind shields adorned with 'ASR' and under a standard of the *Lupa Capitolina*. In the sky overhead, evoking the cross envisioned by Constantine, was the shield/symbol of AS Roma.[66] Below this scene was written '*Tu Non Vedrai Nessuna Cosa al Mondo Maggior di Roma*' (You will never see anything in the world greater than Rome). Not greater than AS Roma, but Rome. The choreography was the best example of the Ultra connection of city, team, Ultra, and glory.

But it was not the only one. The 1995 derby fell on April 23rd, and to celebrate Rome's birthday *Curva Sud* was again a sea of yellow and red cards. Instead of a centralized image, however, the main elements of the choreography were spread across the entire bottom of the *curva*. Supported by a length of aqueduct were the arch of Constantine, the Pantheon, the dome of San Pietro, the Coliseum, Piazza Navona, and the temple of Hercules.[67] Below this image was written '*Quanto Sei Bella Roma*' (Rome, how beautiful you are).

In December 2000, *Curva Sud* presented a monumental choreography of hundreds of red and yellow *vessilli*, or standards. Group leaders held aloft *vessilli* bearing the name and symbol of the group. Other members held aloft either yellow cards or red standards with SPQR, the *Lupa Capitolina*, or '*Ave Roma*' (Hail Roma). The central image was set below a large *striscione* reading '*Urbs Nostra*' (Our City). It was of a large *vessillo* featuring the *Lupa Capitolina* in front of a red and yellow shield. Written below the *Lupa* were the words '*Gens Julia*,' or Julian people, in reference to the descendants of Julius Caesar.[68] Below the *Curva* ran a banner saying '*Nel Nome di Roma si Innalzano i Vessilli dell'Impero*' (In the name of Rome, the standards of the emperor are raised). It was another opportunity to remind the SS Lazio fans that only *Romanisti* (AS Roma fans) were Caesar's people. More importantly, it demonstrated that the

---

66 Ibid, p. 43.

67 Cacciari, 2004, p. 31.

68 Ibid, p. 35.

Ultras understand themselves in those terms: as descendants of Classical Romans.

On another occasion, *Curva Sud* chose to connect the eternal (Roman) law which guided the rise to dominance of Rome over all other Mediterranean cultures to the victory of AS Roma in the Italian championship of 2000–2001. During that season's game against AC Milan, the *Curva* held aloft the crowned SPQR shield that acts as the crest of Rome.[69] Below, the *Curva* announced '*Legge Eterna di Roma Eterna...la Vittoria!*' (Eternal law of eternal Rome ... to victory!).

In case any *Milanisti* (AC Milan fans) might miss the point, *AS Roma Ultras* unfurled a banner just after the game started which read '*Siamo Noi Romani, Siete Voi Schiavi*' (We Are Romans, You Are Slaves). There is no contradiction or contradistinction between Rome, AS Roma, and the *Curva*. There is no level of abstraction that the Ultras justify by presenting the crest of the city as their own. Nor is there a contradiction in their having signed the anti-immigrant graffiti on Via della Lupa with the words *AS Roma Ultras* (to be discussed in Chapter Seven).

The *mentalità* of AS Roma's Ultras was perfectly summarized in a banner displayed by *Tradizione Distinzione Roma* during an unknown game. It connected the good of the Ultra and AS Roma with the good of the city. It enmeshed the classical glory of Rome with its own. It reveled in the agonistic form of life maintained by the Ultras, and connected it with the good of Rome, past and future.[70] It read simply '*Contro Tutto e Tutti. Gloria a Roma*' (Against Everything and Everyone, Glory to Rome); again, not AS Roma, but Rome. The Ultras rarely, if ever, feel the need to distinguish between the two.

Conclusion

In this chapter, it was shown how *Romanità* resembles and is distinguishable from *campanilismo* (extreme localism). Although it too is a discourse of localism, *Romanità* also has a history as a concept meant to unite the

---

69   Ibid, p. 16.

70   Garsia, 2004, p. 1.

Italian nation, in both liberal and Fascist contexts. For the Ultras, it is, instead, a discourse of localism, but one that incorporates the Fascist period of the city's history while promoting a critique of the universal values of liberalism. More important than its discursive uses, though, are the ways in which *Romanità* is a salient feature of the Ultras' general worldview. Not only is it prominently displayed in the choreographies of *Curva Sud Roma* but also in its use of Roman symbols like the *Lupa Capitolina*. These symbols are designed to promote 'Roman values' in a way that distinguishes the Romans from all other peoples. In this light, their politics are given meaning as the positions and actions of a population who understands itself as under siege from forces that seek to diminish the value of Rome and being Roman.

Coda: Three Songs of *Curva Sud Roma*

The most common means of expression for the Ultras is through song. Each *Curva* in Italy has its own songbook, featuring songs of devotion, insult, threat, irony, and scorn. *Curva Sud* Roma is no different. During any game the Ultras may perform between twenty and thirty songs, with the higher number usually being reached by songs that insult specific teams. For reasons already made clear, AS Roma's Ultras sing many songs which insult SS Lazio, AC Milan, FC Juventus, and SC Napoli; but sing very few against smaller provincial teams and cities. Overall, the majority of songs performed by AS Roma's Ultras are of their devotion to the squad and city.

There are three songs created by *Curva Sud Roma* in recent years that demonstrate their understanding of Rome, *Romanità*, and themselves. In each of them the Ultras are above all else defenders of the city — either the actual city or its honor. The songs demonstrate how aware, and prideful, of the city's history and traditions are the Ultras, who, in addition, present themselves as a line of defense against those who would reduce its value to that of a marketplace.

Dai rioni, dai quartieri	From the districts and neighborhoods
siamo venuti fino qua,	to here we have come
siamo gli ultras della Roma	we are the Ultras of AS Roma
onoriamo la città	and we honor the city

Siamo gli ultras della Roma e fieri	We are the Ultras of AS Roma and fierce
centurioni e cavalieri, a difendere la città	centurions and knights, to defend the city
orgoglio della nostra storia	proud of our history
Ave Roma, Roma vittoriosa,	Hail Rome, Victorious Rome
com'è scritto nella storia	as it is written in history
il vento gelido del Nord	the cold wind of the north
non ci potrà fermare	cannot stop us

Semo romani trasteverini,	We are Romans from Trastevere
semo signori senza quatrini;	we are gentlemen without money
er core nostro è 'na capanna	our heart is a mere hut
core sincero che nun te 'nganna	an honest heart that does not seek to fool you
si stai in bolletta noi t'aiutamo	if you are without money we will help you
però da micchi nun ce passamo	but we are not to be considered stupid
noi semo magnatori de spaghetti	we are spaghetti eaters
de le trasteverine li bulletti	the cocks of Trastevere girls
Roma bella, Roma mia	beautiful Rome, my Rome
te se vonno portà via	they want to take you away
Campidojo co' S. Pietro se vorebbero comprà	they'd like to buy Campidoglio and St Peter's

qui se vonno comprà tutto,	and everything else besides
pure er sole e l'aria fresca	even the sun and the fresh air
ma la fava romanesca je potemo arigalà	but we can present them instead with a Roman fava

CHAPTER SEVEN

Globalization and Local Particularity

In the previous chapter I demonstrated how *Romanità* motivates the Ultras to celebrate the rich history, culture, and cultural symbols of Rome. It explained that the Ultras' self-understanding, as well as their understanding of the world-at-large, is filtered through Rome, producing an aggressive awareness of discourses of glory and greatness. This chapter continues these ideas but applies them to the political narratives and actions of Ultras belonging to groups of the Far Right.

While I was unable to witness the most extreme political actions of some Ultras, like the raiding of Roma gypsy camps or the storming of RAI's studios, instead, I witnessed Ultras talking about them. Because of this, much of what follows is rhetorical. I am not suggesting that discourse is apolitical, however; on the contrary, in the pages to follow, there are acts of thinking and speaking that accentuate the derelict potential of discourses and philosophies that undermine the bourgeois form of life. In instances where I was present, such as the MTV Day protest, Family Day, and the Gay Pride parade, what the Ultras had to say about what they were doing seemed more important than what they, in fact, did. By focusing on discourse, though, I was able to get a clear sense of how localism was used by the Ultras — not as a discourse, per se, but as a framework for inter-personal relationships and for understanding the contemporary world's right to expect, or demand, change in and to Rome. In other words, the Ultras' 'local' was so glaring, and, as I will demonstrate, so permeated with ideas of Classical and Fascist glory, that liberal change was understood as something that had to come from outside — something imposed upon the city by the forces of liberalism that they associated with globalization.

The chapter begins by demonstrating how *Romanità* operates as a discourse, inculcating the Ultras with a critique of modernity that aims above all at protecting Rome from the influences of the postmodern State and globalization. I then discuss the impact of the organized Far Right on *Curva Sud Roma* before examining the political interests of the Ultras. To do so I detail Ultra protests against MTV, a Gay Pride parade, African immigration, and the presence of Roma gypsies in Rome.

Postmodernity and Globalization

One of the reasons that the Ultras are such an important aspect of the Western peoples' struggle for autonomy and self-determination in the face of the unthinking servility that capitalism and the State demand of our lives, is that they are situated at the nodal point at which so many of these demands intersect with our bodies; and at these intersections, the Ultras willfully complicate the exchanges at hand: morality and truth, the State and passivity, minority and majority, consumption and happiness, security and prosperity, radicalism and the Left, and conservatism and the Right.

For example, the Ultras undoubtedly stand and fight against the form of economic and moral postmodernity that the contemporary State uses to effectively control its subject populations, at once proclaiming an embrace of the Third World, multiculturalism, and ecumenical visions of globalization as well as demanding a concomitant intellectual and social duty to reject the stifling contours of 'traditional European values.' These are now understood, without irony, not as core aspects of a collection of distinct 'local cultures' (as non-Western, previously Other, cultures would be celebrated), but as racist and exclusionary albatrosses weighing down the efforts to make Europe and the world one free market.[1] The discourse and ethical content of *No al Calcio Moderno*, as we will see, demonstrate the Ultras' awareness of the links that can be made between moralities of altruism and the State-sponsored capitalist marketization of human life.

The Ultras allow us to see that this process involves a mediation of government, governance, and media control of information and, in effect, evaluational technologies and techniques, on the one hand, and the options given a Western individual as 'a life' on the other: from the understanding of one's very subjectivity to the administration of finances and the vast array of boredom management strategies, all the way to the creation of domains of knowledge and how these come to police our access to what anthropology once dichotomized as the sacred and the profane. The postmodernization of State administration has certainly made clearer the essential functions of the effective State outlined by Mussolini: the soldier, the policeman, the tax-collector, and the judge,[2] but it has done so by enmeshing this bare assemblage of force and exploitation with the regime of moral castigation and legally enforced altruistic expansionism and intellectual disarmament that has become the Ultras most powerful enemy.

And it is in engaging this enemy that the Ultras effectively expose the intolerance laying at the heart of the new morality of multiculturalism and the universal human; while pointing out how it is wielded by the State and capitalism as a type of physiological pedagogy to undermine dissent. The rest of this chapter seeks to explain, perhaps by a circuitous route, how the State's outlawing of the most dangerous kinds of particularity in the name of universalizing the bourgeois human, works hand in hand with its drive to include 'racial minorities, gays and lesbians, immigrants,'[3] and

---

1   O'Meara, 2004, pp. 20–22.

2   Lyttleton, 2004, p. 51.

3   O'Meara, 2004, p. 23.

any other loyal subculture whose inclusion makes affordable the exclusion of the becoming ever more defiant 'native population.'[4]

With this perspective in mind, one may begin to understand the conditions that guide the political interests and choices of the Ultras. Simply put, the Ultras come to know and interact with the political world through the intense narratives of the Ultra *mentalità*. Strength, honor, discipline, virtue, sacrifice, and loyalty are just a few of the themes contained in this worldview that I have described. These lead not only to a highly Fascist interpretation of politics but also one that is moralized. In the *Curva*, the Ultras create a tableau of local gestures and performances that directly challenge the homogenizing tendencies of *Calcio Moderno*. They give greater value to local particularity than to multi-national corporate interests and the understanding of the game as a televisual product. Beyond the *Curva* this same commitment to local particularity dominates, but here they are also able to expose the moral bases of the forces that they believe are aligned against them.

The Ultras and Politics

While the Ultras are intensely, aggressively, and radically political, the 'political behaviors' to which they commit are largely extra-parliamentary. In other words, organizing, voting, holding office and campaigning for political parties is not what they have in mind when thinking or acting politically. Instead, Ultra politics is largely about putting the Ultra *mentalità* into action in a larger context than the *Curva*. In this, the Ultras' use of politics mirrors the 'ritual and cultish' aspects of other forms of Italian politics (namely the Radical Left and Italian Communist Party). As David Kerzer explains, politics of this kind are not solely interested in transforming society, but also with acting strictly within the terms of the cosmological myths that buttress the movement in question.[5]

---

4   Ibid.

5   Kertzer, 1988, p. 13.

The Ultras and the Presence of the Far Right in the *Curva*

Nonetheless, the Ultras have contacts with, and are influenced by Italian political parties and movements. At this moment in *Curva Sud Roma*'s history, the Far Right is the most important of these, as the *Curva* shifted from a mix of political ideologies at its inception to being dominated by the Far Right in the early-1990s. This shift coincided with the general shift in the Italian working class from the Left to the Right, making it consistent with larger trends in Italian society.[6] The Far Right still dominates today — especially amongst the large groups, yet it is difficult to ascertain why this is so from the Ultras.

According to Ultras from both the Left and Right, there is no mystery as to why Fascism took over the *Curva*. 'The Right,' said Massimiliano, an Ultra of *Fedayn* who grew up in a family committed to Leftist parties and concerns, 'is the more powerful force in Rome's history. If one looks at history, Rome has almost always been in their hands. The only *Curva Sud* I've ever known has been in their hands too.' I asked how his family resisted the Rightist persuasion. 'My father is from a small town in Campania between Rome and Campobasso,' he answered, 'where everyone is Communist. I was born in Rome in 1979 and would hear many things in school about Communism and Fascism. But for me it was just normal to follow my family's understandings.'

'And in *Curva Sud*?' I asked. '*Fedayn* was the only strong Leftist group when I began going to the Curva in 1996,' he said, 'and I knew some of the guys from school. It was natural to go to *Fedayn*, even beyond politics in the *Curva*.' Like many of the Leftist Ultras, Massimiliano is convinced that politics should have no place amongst the Ultras. 'Ultras is a commitment to AS Roma, not to politics. The beauty of being an Ultra is the purity and focus it gives — there is only AS Roma!' he said with a smile.

Conversely, those on the Right feel that politics is the central thrust of the Ultras. 'To be a Roman is basically to be a Fascist,' Stefano, a former

---

6   Ginsborg, 2003b, pp. 17–35.

member of the disbanded *Monteverde* explained. 'But to be a proud Roman is absolutely to be a Fascist. We Ultras did the same things that Fascism is doing today. We had an office, we cleaned our streets (referring to the neighborhood cleansing of drug dealers, illegal street vendors, and Roma panhandlers mentioned in Chapter One for which *Monteverde* was notorious amongst the Ultras), and we fought Communists in school and in the piazzas. *Curva Sud* was just an extension of that because it was our advertising. We could support AS Roma but also demonstrate the joy of being a proud Fascist and proud Roman."

Similar to Massimiliano, Stefano's household had a political outlook, but this time of the Far Right, 'just as was the entire Monteverde neighborhood,' he said. And, similar to Stefano I had to prompt Massimiliano to discuss the place of the Right in the *Curva*. 'I found *Monteverde* here on my street,' he said, 'so coming into the *Curva* as a Fascist was something I never decided. I was an AS Roma fan and Fascist just like my friends [in the group].'

It is unclear if anyone besides the Ultras and the fascists has made *Romanità* such an integral part of their politics or general worldview. That the Ultras of the Right equate Fascism and *Romanità* begs the question whether an intermediate source of inspiration for their passions is available. In the years between the fall of Fascism and the rise of the Right amongst the Ultras, was there any movement or cultural element keeping the two alive? Certainly, Julius Evola comes to mind, as do scholars of Fascism like Emilio Gentile, professor of history at Rome's *La Sapienza* University. I have already demonstrated the prevalence of Evolan thought amongst the Rightist Ultras but cannot do so for Gentile. However, his model of how Fascism used *Romanità* is perhaps the most useful for fully explicating how the politics of the Ultras evolves from a love of, and desire to protect, Rome to a will to act violently in this regard.

Romanità, Ultras, and Fascism

According to Gentile, the Fascist State was implemented with the idea that the human character is malleable, 'as an expression of a historical tradition, of the customs, beliefs, and ethic of a whole people'.[7] The State, then, felt it could create the content of its subjects' character. *Romanità* was central to this project. Fascism taught of a Rome that was 'grounded in virtue, knowledge, and discipline, the secret of greatness' with the expectation that modern Italians would become worthy heirs of their Roman forefathers by embracing these same ideals.[8] The *metanoia*, or change of feeling, amongst the Romanizing Italians would demonstrate that *Romanità* was an active agent in modern Fascist Italy. 'This was no idea petrified in this or that traditional form, but alive and in action — belonging to our own current awareness of politics and history'.[9] *Romanità* was a part of the mythologizing impetus of Fascism, which saw no limits to the power of ideas and ideals to motivate behaviors. And it is this affective power that the Ultras have put to use. But, just as with the teachings of Evola, Nietzsche, and Sorel, and the legacy of Fascism, the Ultras have made use of *Romanità* in a way that uniquely serves their purposes.

If Ultras on the Left and Right seemed to agree that Fascism was just a normal part of their experiences of Rome and the Ultras, why was this so? The Ultras never adequately answered the question. However, Stefano (above) had alerted me to the correlation between Roman pride and Fascism. I asked Federico, formerly of *Antichi Valori*, if he agreed with Stefano's formula. 'Absolutely,' he said, 'but only because the Fascists have always used *Romanità* as a way to legitimize Fascism. And today, look at how *Forza Nuova* uses Rome and its imagery. It is no accident that the *Forzanovisti* [members of *Forza Nuova*] use the *Lupa* [Capitoline She-Wolf] and *Stadio dei Marmi* [stadium of marbles — created by the PNF for parades, sporting events, and other public displays, it is a small oval surrounded by hyper-masculine neo-Classical statues] in their publications, as well as celebrating April 21st [as noted above, the birthday of Rome]. Aside from us [AS Roma's Ultras] the Fascists make the most use of *Romanità*.'

---

7   Gentile, 1996, p. 96.

8   Ibid, p. 76.

9   Ibid, p. 77.

Figure 14. Mosaic celebrating the Blackshirts, *Stadio Olimpico*, Rome, 2006.

'Is that why the Fascists dominate the *Curva*?' I asked. 'I think so,' he said, 'but also because when I and others of my generation became active in the *Curva*, the Left was discredited after the Berlin Wall fell. At school the Fascists had the only critique of capitalism that we felt had not been discredited. It may have been defeated in war, but it was not discredited as ideology. Plus,' he continued, '*Boys Roma* and *Opposta Fazione* were the best Ultras and they were the best Fascists. When we looked for the one, we saw the other.'

It was most interesting that when the Ultras discussed Fascism they did so in ways that mirrored their political consciousness as Ultras — in terms of ideology, history, and *mentalità*. Conversely, when the media discuss Fascism in the Italian *curvas* it is normally a discussion of parties. Interestingly, of all the Ultras in today's *Curva Sud* who openly discuss Fascism, the two most important and influential groups — *Boys Roma* and *Padroni di Casa* — have deep connections to Fascist political parties.

More importantly, though, they demonstrate how Fascism preexisted the Fascist political parties in the *Curva*.

Boys Roma has been a fascist-based Ultra group since 1972, although for long periods, with no official links to parties. *Padroni di Casa* has only been in *Curva Sud* since 2007, but their pedigree reaches back to the rightist-oriented *Opposta Fazione* and then *Tradizione Distinzione Roma*. Here too this was without any outward connection to political parties. Today, however, both have open connections to the two dominant parties of the Italian Far Right: *Forza Nuova* and *Fiamma Tricolore* (and later, *CasaPound*).

The Parties of the Far Right and Today's *Curva Sud*

Even though these parties, both of which understand themselves as movements, are of the Right and share a similar critique of communism and liberalism, they each consider themselves an enemy of the other. Those from *Forza Nuova* speak of those in *Fiamma Tricolore* as something akin to *zingari* (slur for gypsy) who are compromising the spirit of Fascism — and vice versa. *Fiamma Tricolore* was started in 1995 by members of *Movimento Sociale Italiano* (MSI) who refused to compromise their radical credentials by participating in the move of the more moderate successor party, *Alleanza Nazionale*, toward the center. *Fiamma Tricolore* is active at the community level in most of Rome's working-class neighborhoods, and through its leader Luca Romagnoli it also seeks parliamentary legitimacy and influence.

Forza Nuova, by contrast, seeks no parliamentary power. Its actions are movement-like in that they focus on community presence and local organization via a series of offices. *Forza Nuova* was founded as an organic extension of Roberto Fiore's *Terza Posizione* organization that was outlawed in Italy after being associated with the 1980 bombing of the Bologna Central railway station. Its Roman members understand themselves entirely as radical activists and many seek opportunities to confront others, whether in '*la piazza*' (dialogue and outreach) or in '*la strada*' (violent attack).

Of the two, it is *Forza Nuova* that has the most influence in today's *Curva Sud*. This is difficult to ascertain, however, because both *Forza Nuova* and *Fiamma Tricolore* have members in the various *Curva Sud* groups. When *Tradizione Distinzione Roma* disbanded in 2007 it was because some members, including its founder Gianluca Iannone, desired to spend more time outside the *Curva*. The new group they founded, *Padroni di Casa*, was immediately associated with the political Right, specifically *Fiamma Tricolore*.

On the day that *Padroni di Casa* introduced itself to *Curva Sud*, I was with *Boys Roma*. The leadership of *Boys* was comprised of three men at the time; two of who are actively involved in *Forza Nuova*, while the other is of *Fiamma Tricolore*. Some within the group speculate that the current inability of *Boys* to prosper as in the days of Paolo Zappavigna is due to this crucial rift. That day in the *Curva*, one of the leaders affiliated with *Forza Nuova* watched derisively as *Padroni di Casa* entered the *curva* as a group just after the game had begun. He leaned into me and said only, '*sono da Fiamma*' (they are [members] of *Fiamma Tricolore*).

Since that day in February 2007, *Padroni di Casa* have twice switched their party allegiance — first to *Forza Nuova*, and then, several months later, to start the now nationwide movement *CasaPound Italia*. Named in honor of the Fascistic American poet Ezra Pound, *CasaPound Italia* seeks to be a new type of Fascist movement — one that is just as active in acculturating as in activism. At *Padroni di Casa's* office *CasaPound*, the original office of the nationwide movement, weekly lecture, film, and cultural events are held. They have affiliations with Roman Futurist artists and poets, Evolan and Nietzschean students, and a host of Fascist Romans of various professions.

The movement's ultimate goal, according to its leader Gianluca Iannone, is to become an autonomous voice of 'truly radical Fascism in a way that the post-war Fascists have been unable to maintain.' *CasaPound's* Fascism takes the beauty and passion of the Ultras and applies them to the piazza. On 3 November, 2008, three gentlemen identified as members of *CasaPound* stormed the studio of RAI 3, Italy's main Left wing television network, as the program *Chi l'ha Visto* was preparing to air a video of the previous day's violent encounter between activists on the Far Right and Left in Piazza Navona. The fight was related to ongoing polemics and street battles due to the Left's protests of proposed school reforms. *CasaPound Italia* released a statement saying it would no longer tolerate the violence against Fascist activists by their Leftist counterparts. Two days later *Il Messaggero* linked *CasaPound Italia* to *Padroni di Casa*, as Iannone was among those arrested for the assault on RAI 3.

Neither representatives of *Fiamma Tricolore* nor *Forza Nuova* admitted to using the Ultras as a site for recruiting. During a brief conversation with a *Fiamma Tricolore* contact (provided to me by the third member of *Boys'* leadership), it was explained that *Fiamma Tricolore* does not officially enter the Italian *curvas*. Any shared membership between the two, Ultras and Fascism, is coincidental, he explained. 'In the past, though, the *curvas* were fertile ground for the organized Right, and many Ultras became involved in *Fiamma Tricolore* through being Ultras — myself included,' he told me.

A longer conversation at the Piazza Vescovio office of *Forza Nuova* was similarly dismissive of the Ultras. I was told by Martin Alvaro, a well-known *Forza Nuova* activist, that the Ultras are of no interest whatsoever to their movement. Even though some members of *Forza Nuova* hailed from both SS Lazio's *Curva Nord* and AS Roma's *Curva Sud*, the Ultras, he said, had never been a large part of *Forza Nuova's* recruitment scheme. When asked why, he explained that, 'The *curvas* were unreliable, being fuller of hedonists than Fascists.' Whatever the position of *Forza Nuova* on the Ultras, my research pointed to deep crossovers between their form of political activism and that of the Ultras. These connections will be explained in the following two sections.

In contrast to what Martin Alvaro told me, that there are only coincidental members of both the Ultras and *Forza Nuova*, I can attest to there being a number of *AS Roma Ultras* who follow the actions of *Forza*

Nuova closely. While these persons did not speak of Fiore or other national leaders of *Forza Nuova*, they all knew of those who were attached
to '*Piazza Vescovio*,' as *Forza Nuova* was called (because of the location
of their Rome office). On the rare occasions when I was with Ultras and
Forza Nuova members away from a strictly Ultra related activity (such as
an AS Roma game or an office of one of the groups), neither the Ultras
nor soccer were discussed. For the Ultras this is rare, as it would be hard
to converse with an Ultra for five minutes without the discussion turning
to either the *Curva* or AS Roma.

One can conclude, therefore, that the parties of the Far Right and the
Ultras of *Curva Sud* Roma are two overlapping constituents that intersect
without necessarily uniting. While the issues that concern these parties
are certainly important to the Ultras, from alleged immigrant crime to the
national trade deficit with China, it is most likely that the large majority
of Ultras have become devoted to these concerns without the intervention
of the organized Far Right. There are certainly Ultras who are active in
organized Fascism, as will be made clear below, but there seemed to be
many more who consider themselves Fascist without being dedicated to
the Fascist parties. As I said above, it was common to speak with Ultras
like Federico, Mario, or Gabriele of *Romulae Genti* who knew Martin
Alvaro of *Forza Nuova* and the goings on of that party but who otherwise
never made serious contact with organized Fascism.

That Ultras like them were dedicated to the ideology of Fascism and
were familiar with leading Roman Fascists but never committed themselves to *Forza Nuova*, for instance, might play a role in the ways my contacts in the Extreme Rightist parties disparaged the Ultras. Meanwhile,
odd as it seems, the Ultras in the post-Raciti/Sandri era are castigated in
the media more severely than the Fascists. It could be that the fascist parties have chosen to distance themselves from the Ultras given their present conflict with the State. Nevertheless, even without formal connections
to the parties, the Rightist Ultra groups operate with Fascism in mind,
adopting *squadrismo* (action in the form of Fascist paramilitary squads),
an ethic of violence that celebrates engagement and aggression, pageantry

as a form of political action, and a critique of modernity. It could be said, then, that the Ultras are another form of Fascism.

The Ultras as Political Actors
MTV Day

In the early Fall of each year, MTV holds a one-day festival in Rome called MTV Day. In 2007, it was held in Piazza di Porta San Giovanni and was attended by a group of twenty Ultras belonging to *Padroni di Casa*. They were there along with a sizable contingent of Roman university students belonging to *Forza Nuova's* student wing, *Lotta Studentesca*. The purpose was not to enjoy the festivities but to protest them. They marched into the piazza behind a banner reading *'Boicotta MTV'* (Boycott MTV). Behind the banner the Ultras distributed handbills explaining their presence:

> MTV completes ten years? Ten years of brainwashing millions of children. Ten years of dishonor, relativism, materialism, and hedonism! In the media society that shapes how we think, MTV has for years influenced the ideas and style of life of the young, promoting a process of homogenization that annuls particularity and identity. *Lotta Studentesca* retains the right to our own characteristics and the differences between these and a society that is becoming more Americanized by the day. For this we have entered the piazza today, to contest the ever-present Americanized media, and to stimulate a desire amongst the youth to desire and hold dear our true identity and traditions of our people. To be revolutionary today is to love Tradition.

The terms of the protest were typical of the Ultras' understanding of globalization and what is at stake in its triumph. MTV is perhaps the greatest purveyor of American values on Italian television. It is a twenty-four hour-a-day promoter of what the Ultras call leisure, avarice, and vulgarity. As in the US, its shows like 'Cribs,' 'Pimp My Ride,' and 'The Fabulous Life Of ...' present a constant stream of, as said the *Lotta Studentesca* leaflet, 'relativism, materialism, and hedonism.' Through its original shows like 'Buzzin'' and 'Nabari,' MTV Italia promotes the idea that Italy is a multi-cultural and multiracial society in which all groups share friendship and understanding despite their differences. Black Africans, burkha wearing

Muslim girls, and Italian teens share experiences and interests. On other shows, like 'A Shot at Love with Tila Tequila,' Italians learn of the thrills of bisexuality and sexual promiscuity. The Rightists' banner and handbills expressed outrage at this cluster of messages.

Family Day and Gay Pride

The Ultras' protest against MTV Day showed a highly-moralized understanding of the terms of globalization. The protection of institutions and traditions, however they are defined — in this case as the bulwark of 'particularity' against 'homogenization' — is not a goal for the sake of the Italian State, but instead is part of a local fight against multicultural-and-globalization-based change — change imposed either from without or from the perspective of liberal or modern 'progress.' In either case, the Ultras understand both as a shameful flight from their own culture. These were also the terms with which they engaged Family Day and the annual Roman Gay Pride parade.

Family Day was the Church-organized day to protest DICO — Rights and Obligations of Permanently Cohabiting Persons, the bill proposed by members of the 2006–2007 Prodi government, which sought rights for cohabiting couples, including homosexuals. Held on a warm May day in Piazza di Porta San Giovanni, the rally brought together hundreds of Catholic organizations from all around Italy. The Far Right parties were there as well, with *Alleanza Nazionale* urging all parties to carry no colors so as not to risk making the family seem a 'political object.'

Concurrently in Piazza Navona there was a rally in support of purely secular government. Here, demonstrators sought to keep the church from being involved in political issues. At the time of these demonstrations 'Ratzinger' (as most Ultras called Pope Benedict XVI) was in Brazil proclaiming the need of the church to be unconcerned with the political issues of the day. The irony was not lost on Federico, the former member of *Antichi Valori* with whom I attended Family Day. Even though he grew up in the shadow of the Vatican, worked in its museums as a tour guide, supported Family Day, and approved of Ratzinger, he noted that it made sense for the Pope to say this in Latin America, as the conservative elements in the church had struggled to eradicate that continent's Liberation Theology since the 1960s. For Federico, the Church was and is extremely political. It is not always that he, and other Romans, agrees with the Church's politics, but on this occasion, he said, he and many others did.

The Ultras who attended Family Day did so for much the same reasons other Ultras had attended MTV Day. At the latter, they were protesting a celebration of turbo-capitalism, hedonism, and hyper-materialism; at the former they joined a celebration of tradition, idealism, and protectionism. Thus, the events were two sides of the same coin. The Ultras talked about Family Day not as an anti-gay statement, but as an opportunity to show the Prodi government that his will to make of Italy one grand market, as the US and UK are understood, is opposed by Italians. It was explained to me that the problem of the Italian Left is that it is always too ready to undermine Italian traditions in order to please the international community. 'They attack proud and strong Italians on behalf of immigrants and silly pleasure seekers,' Federico told me.

The Pope pronounced on the issue in the week before Family Day. Where the Ultras spoke of tradition, he spoke of sin. Nonetheless, there was little distinction between their arguments. The materialist philosophies, Capitalism and Marxism, had torn away our ability to be more than vulgar matter, he said.[10] When secularism is embraced, a wholly abstract human follows. Ratzinger did not continue in this way for long, but I mentioned it to the Ultras for a reaction. I was told by Mario, now of *Ultras Primavalle* but formerly of *Monteverde*, '[not to] worry about traditions collapsing in Rome. The rest of the world lives without tradition because their history, culture — existence itself — are not real. But here in Rome, the past is so important that you cannot even live in it. We have a perpetual present [*il presente permanente*] that stretches back 2700 years.'

Mario's statement demonstrates the depth of the Ultras' commitments to Rome as a place in which history, culture, and existence (to use his

---

10   For information on the Pope's lecture see http://www.catholicsocialscientists.org/ CSSR/Archival/2009/Burke%20-%20Article.pdf, accessed January 2010.

words) operate differently than elsewhere in the world. *Romanità* is more than just a weekend-only ideological dalliance for the Ultras. Instead, it acts as the basis for their understanding of cultural and historical processes. It ensures that culture and history form a visible and knowable 'web of significance' through which the mundane everyday is made knowable. As he said, the past is important in Rome because there really is no past — all is lived presently and immediately. Mario assumes that this does not happen elsewhere in the world, because beyond Rome, culture and history are not real — playing no true role in how people live.

I was reminded of Michael Polanyi's struggle to justify the forms of knowledge generated by zealotry, through which violence and terror are given fuel. Borrowing from Hannah Arendt, he explains that revolutionary education is designed to abolish the line between truth and fiction, thereby making every knowable thing a 'statement of purpose.'[11] Leaving aside his epistemology (and political aversion to extremism), his understanding of knowledge serving a purpose but also being pliable is reflected in Mario's statement. And, there is no mistaking that this devotion to Rome is a form of extremism. Rome's visibly multi-layered history makes the city's historical importance a constant reminder of what is 'at stake' for the Ultras. In effect, their feelings of proprietorship are manifested in every evening stroll they take.

The Church was less at issue on Family Day than was taking a stand against the liberalization of Italian society. The media coverage of Family Day made it an issue of 'gay rights' and the '*grettezza*' (close-mindedness) the 'traditional Italian' that keeps Italy from 'making progress.' For the Ultras, Family Day was less about these immediate concerns than with an opportunity to take exception to the very idea of the liberal, rights-based human to begin with. Nietzsche wrote about 'breeding strength' as an ideal for his radical aristocratic nobility. Strength, like nobility itself, was to be achieved through struggle and hardship. It was to oppose the very

---

11   Polanyi, 1974, p. 242.

idea that 'man' is given value by virtue of his ability to participate equally in a marketplace (what Nietzsche called 'mechanical virtue').[12]

Strength, instead, was to be created through isolation.[13] Elsewhere, Nietzsche explained that one can only maintain what is one's own by maintaining adequate distance from one's neighbors.[14] The Ultras have used this formula to great effect against other Ultras and fan bases, but it also motivates their oppositions to globalization. The adoption of more liberal and secular understandings of the human is not a problem unless it is being imposed or being popularized due to the influence of what they see as degrading elements within society. Certainly, MTV Day, and MTV in general, was singled out as an insidious influence on Italians. In seeking distance from the form of life being promoted by MTV the Ultras also make arguments for an organic understanding of society.

The idea that the State is an organism that thrives and declines in conjunction with its population is central to Counter-Enlightenment thought. Although the Fascists saw in this a material rationale, and thus promoted the general health of the population, Sorel, following Nietzsche, was more concerned with how the weakness of a political class — one ashamed of ruling — leads to a toleration of weakness that ultimately effects the policy decisions of a State.[15] Michael O'Meara has discussed the implications of such an idea amongst those who are opposed to liberalism today. Far from the biological justifications for nation-or-people-hood, the organic State idea hinges upon 'common heritage and tradition' for relevance and survival.[16] Tradition, he proposes, functions as a skeleton upon which peoples constitute themselves. While modernity and rationalism propose that traditions are contextual and are thus fluid and less valuable as markers of human behavior, O'Meara counters by explaining that tradition, like history, is more about the present than the past. Thus,

---

12 Nietzsche, 2003, p. 176.

13 Ibid, p. 166.

14 Nietzsche, 2006, p. 42.

15 Sorel, 1999, p. 182.

16 O'Meara, 2004, p. 104.

one can act through a market-driven, homogenizing liberalism or one can act through something else. That something else, the Ultras believe, is their 'own Roman culture.' I asked a group of five *Ultras Romani* Ultras if the State or the Church could be considered part of this culture. They responded, only the Church.

The Church was also at the center of discourse surrounding the Gay Pride parade. And, like DICO and Family Day, the issue was around 'rights,' pitting the Prodi government against the Pope. It was not surprising that this was so. Along with the family, scholars and journalists often present the Church as the reason for Italy's notoriously weak State.[17] Because of its ability to act as a political sovereign, the Church was historically able to control understanding of the issues that, in the summer of 2007, were in danger of becoming the domain of liberal 'rights.'

It seemed Italy was struggling to accept that the State was actually to be responsible for defining the family. The family as a legal and material entity was something different from the family as the basis of human life. The sanctity of the family, said the Church, came from God; the impositions of a secular State were out of place in relation to an institution given the species by its creator.

The days leading up to the June parade were contentious. On June 15, the *Northern League* continued to agitate against Prodi, as their twenty-two MPs stormed the Lower House, demanding the government clear out. This was part of Fini, Bossi, and Berlusconi's new initiative against Prodi in the wake of vast Rightist victories in regional elections, as well as the consequence of uninterrupted bickering, disunity, and indecision within the Prodi coalition. The latest flare up was caused by the government's decision to allow various ministers to march in the Gay Pride parade. Catholics within the government were outraged as the parade was set to embrace calls for rights of gay marriage, adoption, and even assisted fertility.

The Right was quick to expect a full assault on the Church's control of public discourse on the family (an issue that had been debated since

---

17   Ginsborg, 2003b, pp. 129–134.

DICO was unveiled in February 2007), while the Left said it must support any demonstration calling for greater secularization and bans against discrimination. Leftist MP's had even called for more rights for Chinese immigrants, after a number of them attacked police in Milan upon being ticketed for illegally unloading trucks in a public street.

Saturday morning, in Piazza Bologna, Piazza Vescovio, and Piazza Dalmazia (near Mussolini's former residence at Villa Torlonia), were found fascist graffiti against the march (and gays as well): 'Gays, Rome does not want you,' 'Italy needs children, not gays,' 'Gays, no rights for you,' and the particularly nasty, 'Gays to the ovens.'

The parade was more disputatious than had been Family Day and its counter demonstration in Piazza Navona. The paraders aggressively condemned the Church and the Pope. They rode on floats laden with men in drag, transsexuals, and nudity. They called for an end to discrimination against gays. Commentators noted that Italy was far behind other Western countries in its attitudes toward homosexuality and in addressing equal protection issues.

This time with a small group of Rightist Ultras, I witnessed only a few minutes of the parade. The group of Ultras met with a large group from *Forza Nuova* on Via Cavour. Aside from occasional slurs against gays, the meeting was mostly to complain against Prodi and the 'rights seekers' who were attempting, it was argued, 'to hold Italy and its history, honor, and traditions hostage for their own benefit.' The Left, they said, had, as usual, aligned itself against anything of value or tradition, anything Italian, in order to shame the country into 'keeping up with some universally defined progress.'

The Ultras attacked the paraders within the terms of their general attack on liberalism and globalization. 'Who were these people,' asked Luca, a thirty-eight-year-old veteran of *Tradizione Distinzione Roma* who now was well respected in *Padroni di Casa*, 'to make demands on the Pope? What had they done to be worthy of insulting a Roman institution? On whose behalf, and to whose benefit, did they expect Italy to change? If things were better for them in other parts of Europe, why not leave?' he asked.

The other Ultras answered angrily, showing their disgust that Italy now had 'minority' issues. Luca spoke of 'spineless weaklings who made demands without having made themselves worthy of demand.' They complained bitterly that Italy had not been like this before the European Union. But now, it was changing life for the worse. Two things were especially interesting about their complaints: their continual questioning why policy makers were dismissing what Italians wanted; and their anger at the assumptions driving 'minorities' to demand 'their rights.'

When I proposed to them that plurality is demonstrative of progress in liberal societies, Luca told me in response that '*gli Ultras sono i veri subalterni*' (the Ultras are the true subalterns). 'It seems that one can be anything in Italy except an Ultra. And you are telling me that these people bring more to Italy than us? We want Italy to be strong, virile, and proud but instead we get an Italy determined to be a cesspool,' he said. Poetically, on the same day as the Gay Pride parade it was announced that soccer-related violence had fallen dramatically after Raciti's death, showing the value of the crackdown on the Ultras. As already noted, attacks on police were down 93%, while violent encounters between fans were down 44%.[18]

Luca insisted upon driving me back to Monteverde as evening fell. While driving, he identified three crucial 'political enemies' of the Ultras: American-based popular culture, 'which celebrated above all vulgar materialism and ignorance;' the Italian State, 'which, in the hands of the Left was intent on making Italy a melting-pot, diminishing the value of Italian culture and history at every turn;' and the European Union, 'which debilitated culture for the sake of a free market that demanded consumerism and inclusiveness from all.' The EU would be center stage in the true bane of Ultra politics, immigration and the Roma.

---

18   *Il Romanista*, Anno IV, Numero 136, 16 June, 2007, p. 2.

Immigration and the Roma
Perspectives on Rome and Immigration

In November 2007, Massimo D'Alema, then Minister of Foreign Affairs, was in Turkey to demonstrate the Italian government's support for that country's entrance into the European Union. When asked in a press conference about his position on the issue, he did not use a cultural-historical argument. Instead, he chose multiculturalism as rationale for Turkey being a part of Europe. While others in Europe were debating Turkey's cultural and historical connections to Europe, D'Alema chose to put the onus on Europe itself to be worthy of Turkey. As he put it, Turkey must be admitted, 'out of a commitment to creating a Europe based on inclusion and tolerance.'

His words stung the ears of *Curva Sud*'s Ultras, for again, the idea of tolerance and inclusiveness were being wielded against those who saw in Europe something worth protecting from dilution. That same week, I walked in the neighborhood south of The Vatican called Borgo, but which the Ultras who live there call 'Gregorio Settimo'. The area, like other established Roman neighborhoods, is a self-contained universe. It has a fresh market, wine bars, small restaurants, cafés, clothing stores for men, women, and children, pastry shops, *gelato* shops, banks, and insurance offices. Almost every corner is covered in Ultra graffiti and the area's Ultras walk the streets with a sense of pride. Most of them know everyone, from the merchants to the men and boys standing in front of each café or mechanics shop. In two hours, one might only walk two blocks, as the Ultras stop and converse with their neighbors.

The neighborhood is also home to a recent addition, a kebab stand. Typically associated with Turks, kebab stands are opening throughout Rome. The owners of this particular stand are not Turks but Indians. The first time I encountered the stand with Ultras there was derision and a dismissive silence. The only comment made was that 'a few years ago there were no kebab stands in Rome. Now they are everywhere.' I asked if anyone had eaten kebab and they acted as if I had suggested cannibalism.

A few weeks later I received a call from Danillo, one of the dismissive Ultras. Danillo, a twenty-nine-year-old waiter in a restaurant near Campo dei Fiori, lives in Gregorio Settimo with his mother and father. His aunt lives in the same building several floors below. His girlfriend lives on the next block and they are usually inseparable. They met when she was a student in need of a Latin tutor. (Being in the same neighborhood both sets of parents knew of the other; thus, hers were aware that Danillo might help their daughter learn Latin.) Now they work together in her family's small restaurant. She even occasionally attends games with him now that he is no longer affiliated with *Fedayn* but attends games in the *Tevere* Grandstand. According to Danillo, 'the *Curva* is no place for women because it is dangerous.' He often chastised me for taking my wife to games.

He was never a member of *Fedayn* because he didn't live in the *Quadraro* neighborhood, but was close friends with many in that group, and thus stood behind their banner. Danillo is not a Fascist, per se, but is well versed in the history of Fascism, especially as it pertains to Rome. He is interesting for his proximity to *Fedayn* (a formerly Leftist group but now only mildly political) and for his less-than-zealous ideological commitment to Fascism. Like Federico of *Antichi Valori*, Danillo's parents are extremely proud Romans, even going so far as to show me their modest collection of antique espresso cups adorned with images of Rome at the turn-of-the-century.

Danillo told me that he had eaten kebab from the stand after a recent game (as no restaurants were open at the hour on a Sunday night). He had enjoyed the kebab and said the people were friendly. He was quick to add, though, that this did not signal a change in his negative attitude toward the proliferation of kebab stands in Rome.

'Rome,' he said, 'is opening up to foreigners because the government and the EU are forcing it to do so. [The Roman people] are left to lament the changes in their neighborhoods and an influx of people who neither speak our language nor take an interest in our culture. How do these people have the right to come here and do very little to be accepted,' he asked, 'and those who have been here for generations, who can trace their Roman heritage seven generations [as he could, his mother proudly told me] have no right to defend the form of life that we have created in that time?' He went on to say that Rome was his city, not theirs. He would never dream of going to another country to set up shop. Such a move would be 'the most vulgar [form] of materialism.' I asked him what he feared in the presence of the Indians. 'The eventual destruction of Roman culture,' he said.

Danillo, like Luca and so many others, was exaggeratedly aware of the sanctity of Roman culture. He had been given a responsibility toward Rome as a birthright from his parents and family, but also from the Ultras. The most common mode of discussing Rome amongst the Ultras with whom I had the most contact was in terms of pride, protection, honor, and sacrifice. From Ultras of various ages and numbers of years of involvement with *Curva Sud*, as well as from various neighborhoods, I heard self-descriptions as '*cavalieri*' (knights). Lorenzo of *AS Roma Ultras* explained that it comes from an old *CUCS*-era (1972–92) song that speaks about proud knights in defense of Rome's honor. The Ultras seemed to have taken to heart this message and earnestly see themselves in these terms. Danillo made clear his commitment. 'It would be an honor to die serving Rome, but I don't give a damn about Italy,' he said.

Regardless of the effect this kind of sentiment has on the Italian military, Danillo's comment points to the ongoing predominance of *campanilismo* in the Italian worldview. In fact, it would be difficult to find anything more 'Italian' in that worldview than an extremely local, or at best regional, focus. Allum and Diamanti point out that the anti-Italian views of those involved in the *Northern League* are barely enough to unify that party across the regions of the north. Instead, there is the sense that, while Italy is bad for the people of the north, the *Northern League* might be too broadly focused to truly promote the best interests of all northern peoples.[19]

Although not to the same extreme, one even senses regionalism amongst the chapters of *Forza Nuova*. Despite a missive from Roberto

---

19   Allum and Diamanti, 1996, pp. 152–154.

Fiore, national leader of the party, proclaiming the solidarity of
'*Forzanovisti*' (members of the party) and explaining the lack of need,
therefore, for regional or local chapter websites (as all news could be coordinated through the main *Forza Nuova* site), members have still created
local websites devoted to their activities. These, such as the members of
'*Forza Nuova Roma*,' often use blog sites that operate free of charge and
slightly under the radar of the party bosses.[20] Even amongst the nationalists, then, there is a strong undercurrent of regionalism and localism.

Anthropological studies on prejudice against immigrants in Italy
rarely present the justifications of natives in terms that would be coherent
to those natives. Sniderman and Peri, for example, explain that refugees
are struggling for acceptance in Italy because of 'skinhead violence' and
the 'extreme prejudice' of marginalized Italians.[21] They spend considerable
time redefining 'prejudice,' taking it from a psychological model to one
that incorporates the creation and dissemination of discourses of difference. They wanted to know, in the end, what made otherwise intelligent
people succumb to the idea that immigrants are somehow different from
them.[22] In the end, the issue was more about intolerance than prejudice.
Some Italians, they argue, were being made intolerant of others because
they were manipulated to be so by the media and Far Right parties. Those
parties had used manipulated statistics to fan flames of fear against immigrant crime and a specious argument against cultural dilution to rally
honest Italians to their cause.[23]

Elsewhere, Jeffrey Cole studied the attitudes of Sicilians toward
African 'new immigrants' in the 1990s. Like the Sniderman and Peri study,
Cole views the intolerance of 'new racists' on the Far Right as evidence
of ignorance and manipulation. However, he presents a more accurate
model of Sicilian interaction with immigrants and immigration than

---

20 Blog sites have been rendered less common since Facebook has cornered the market
    on most discourse in the West. See https://facebook.com/forzanuovaroma.

21 Sniderman et al, 2000, p. 4.

22 Ibid, pp. 8–11.

23 Ibid, pp. 91–119.

do Sniderman and Peri, for he explains how attitudes change depending on place and economy — showing that bourgeois merchants and college students think most favorably about immigrants, both being influenced by 'market rationality'.[24] Unfortunately, neither of these studies leave space for attitudes toward immigration such as those of the Ultras.

The Roman Ultras I met showed no signs of being xenophobic. In fact, their justifications for desiring stability in cultural form showed the emptiness of xenophobia as a concept. They had no fear of outsiders, others, or foreign cultural traditions. Their fear, instead, was that Rome was to become a cosmopolitan multicultural '*guazzabuglio*' (mishmash). Even as a great number of the Ultras of *Curva Sud* could be assumed to be children of a previous generation of migrants, more than likely from the Italian south, there is, interestingly, no discursive awareness of the fact in their self-understandings. While the city was not an industrial center, as were Milan, Genoa, and Turin, there was enough money (in tourism, service employment and shop keeping) and cultural allure (in *La Dolce Vita*) to make Rome a viable option to Southern provincial life.[25] Throughout the 1950s and 1960s Rome's population swelled by one-third with migrants from around Lazio (the region of which Rome is capital) and other Southern regions.[26]

Nonetheless, the overwhelming cultural identifier for AS Roma's Ultras is Rome and 'being Roman.' While there could be a process of 'national invention' here, whereby an artificial community is created through narratives that promote the cohesion of disparate groups,[27] I suspect it is the 'truth' of *Romanità* that renders the ideology of Roman greatness and 'the Rome of the Ultras' nearly isomorphic — so much so that one's pre-Roman genealogy is less relevant than one's current commitment to Rome and *Curva Sud*. The 'inventedness' of memory (see Chapters Three, Four, and Five), or, its metaphorical and monumental form, often allows for

24 Cole, 1997, p. 92.

25 Zamagni, 2000, pp. 55–61.

26 Ginsborg, 2003a, p. 220.

27 Hobsbawm and Ranger, 1992, pp. 1–12.

omission and invisibility in specific areas (usually associated with some form of moralism — as in truth and reconciliation).[28] Just as the Ultras discriminate between the various strata of Roman history, they often willingly ignore their personal sundry backgrounds.

Romanità is a feeling, another *mentalità* to be sure, but it is also something material and recognizable in the physiology of the Ultras. These are often men of the hardest order, with muscles, tattoos, and extreme self-discipline, who will shed tears while gazing upon Rome from the Gianicolo Hill. As a caveat, however, I must say that having a deep Roman pedigree is extremely important to those who have it. The Ultra with the longest Roman genealogy I met, Danillo of *Antichi Valori*, boasted seven-generations, but only through his mother's line. His father is a migrant from Campagna. Even so, Danillo stakes his claim to Romanness on his *Romanità* and years of service in *Curva Sud*, as he says, '*per difendere l'onore di Roma*' (in defense of the honor of Rome).

With regard to the Ultras' militarism, explained in Chapter Five, their actions 'in defense of Rome' are more determinant of Romanness than their respective backgrounds. To sacrifice and, potentially, suffer for Rome's honor, is considered heroic, and, as will be demonstrated in the next chapter, the conferring of 'Roman' status is of the highest seriousness. That being said, Ultras must demonstrate their willingness to 'be an Ultra' for an extended period before being honored thus.

The 'Ultra' honored with 'Romanness' was myself. My being American was an issue in that it gave my new status even more *gravitas* (seriousness, weight). But the Ultras used my Americanness to make points to me that might not otherwise ring true. One was their use of 'melting pot' to explain the distance between their Rome and the Rome of the rest of the modern world. With no melting pot ideology of their own, the Ultras wondered why the liberal world expected them to open their arms to anyone who wanted to set up shop in Rome. Their identification with Rome was something to be admired, they said. Their identification with Rome was their model for how other peoples should interact with their cities.

---

28   Crapanzano, 2004, pp. 156–157.

Luca (introduced above) and a group of sixteen Ultras at *Padroni di Casa* were dumbfounded when I explained that it was not part of being American to have strong connections to where we were born or lived. On their behalf (metaphorically), Luca asked, '*come si puo vivere così, a testa in giù*' (how can one live like this, with one's head down). For them, to live was a matter of pride; so much so that it seemed never to have occurred to them that others might not feel about their place of residence the way they do about Rome. Further, the idea of 'hanging one's head' conjures images of shame, weakness, and defeat — the antithesis of what the Ultras' form of life is about.

For them, the issue of immigrants had little to do with rejection of others through ignorance but of protecting something they cherish from diminution. Again, they wanted to know 'how many immigrants came to Rome because of their undying passion for Rome and to become Roman.' I relayed numerous stories about American students proudly displaying their ignorance of Rome, its history and topography, on the 8 tram from Trastevere. The Ultras were not surprised. 'Trastevere is ruined. It's no longer Roman but full of foreigners,' I was told dismissively.

On other occasions I was also told what Trastevere was like as little as twenty years ago. Needless to say, their understanding of Trastevere, even if driven by nostalgia, mirrored their understanding of the rest of the city. Romans who still lived in the neighborhood suffered every day at the hands of unfeeling and mobbish tourists and immigrants, Daniele of *Giovinezza* said, as we walked the area on a summer evening. Again, with my being an American a focal point of conversation, he wanted me to 'tell the world' that the grandparents and elders who were the nobility of Roman society were now just victims of rowdy American students and vulgar immigrant merchants.

African Immigrants

The two types of immigration of most concern to the Ultras are the arrival of African illegal immigrants to Lampedusa and the legal immigration of Roma gypsies from Eastern Europe. While they are ambivalent about the

Africans, they are downright hostile to the Roma. Despite having ample opportunities to witness Ultra hostilities to African immigrants, I saw none, aside from the instance described in the Introduction. Migrants from Africa were most commonly encountered in Rome as sidewalk salesmen of counterfeit purses, CDs, and DVDs. Perhaps because they tended to be seen in Rome's historical center and not in other neighborhoods, the Ultras had little to say to them. That being said, they often wondered aloud why they had come to Rome. The only answer they knew of was 'da fare soldi' (to make money). To make money was the worst answer they could have come up with. For the Ultras ask of each and all the same that they ask of themselves — not to diminish ourselves by reducing life to a series of opportunities to make or spend money. This critique of life as a marketplace was clearly consistent with their critique of *Calcio Moderno*.

For all of the ambivalence of how the Ultras interacted with African immigration in Rome, there was little sympathy for those arriving in Lampedusa, an island off the southwestern coast of Sicily. From early Spring to late Fall, it was normal to read daily in the morning papers or to see on television that a boat or raft carrying Africans had made its way to Lampedusa. According to ANSA and Istat, 20,450 Africans made their way to Lampedusa in 2007. Through 9 October, 27,417 had arrived there in 2008 (since 1998, roughly 265,000 Africans had arrived in Italy by boat). Coming in from twenty-five to 450 at a time, the Africans were seen literally as a flood by the Ultras. And, with each arrival, the Left and Right politicians argued publicly about how to properly handle the situation. Predictably, the Left sought the more compassionate approach, saying that not only would denying the Africans entrance be inhumane, it would be illegal. In March 2007, Romano Prodi even went so far as to commend his government for having 'an open-door policy on immigration.' Immigrants, he explained, were 'a true blessing for businesses, for less skilled workers and in helping care for the elderly and disabled.'

Even as it was illegal to deny asylum seekers the right to a hearing, the Paris-based Organization for Economic Cooperation and Development announced that, while legal aliens were arriving in Italy and Europe in record numbers — 31,000 in Italy in 2005 alone — those applying for asylum had dropped to 15% of total arrivals.

The most extreme gesture in support of the Africans was reported by the German newspaper *Der Spiegel*, which covered the plans of *Amani*, an Italian nonprofit, to erect a monument in Lampedusa commemorating those Africans who died at sea attempting to illegally enter Italy. According to officials at *Amani*, the thousands of Africans who seek to reach Lampedusa and other European ports each year are 'victims of unscrupulous human traffickers who pocket hundreds of euros to take them on rickety boats unfit for the journey.'

The Right rejected the economic and humanitarian discourses, choosing instead to focus upon the cultural and social effects of immigration. Jole Santeli of *Forza Italia* accused Prodi of ignoring the feelings of Italians on the issue. He explained that the presence of immigrants was causing tension in Italian cities, as even few immigrants give the impression that the country is changing beyond recognition. TNT Sofres, a French research institute, found that the majority of Italians feared immigration because of the cultural change it must entail. While they were less concerned about the economic impact of immigration, 50% of 4900 respondents saw immigration as a threat to the country's cultural identity. According to the same survey, 75% saw illegal immigration as an important problem, 57% said that there were too many foreigners living in Italy, and 53% said failure to assimilate was the fault of the immigrants.

In response, Interior Minister Giuliano Amato, author of the Amato Decree (see Chapters Two and Three), said that it would be dangerous to put limits on immigrants. Thanks to an extremely low birthrate (1.23 children per woman), Italy's population was in steady decline, and immigrants were an important source of labor. The real worry, he said, was 'ideological prejudices' against immigration, as had been witnessed in Holland, where the native population demanded that immigrants speak Dutch and show knowledge of Dutch culture and history. The Ultras were as incensed over these comments as they had been over the Amato Decree.

'How,' I was asked by Giulio, a twenty-eight-year-old Monte Testaccio nightclub bartender and unaffiliated Ultra formerly of *AS Roma Ultras*, 'could someone feel no unease about selling-out his culture and history in order to appease multinational businesses and mercenary foreigners who only want to exploit our country?' According to Mabel Berezin, when exogenous threats to national or cultural identity arise, most people will turn to the State or to 'law and order' as allies against the *xenos* (stranger).[29] The Ultras and others on the Right had no such ally in the Center-Left government of Romano Prodi. This was not only because of policy decisions that aimed at more fully connecting Italy to the global marketplace, but because the Prodi government readily adopted the neo-liberal language of immigration justification couched solely in terms of demographic decline and economic benefit.[30]

The European Union, Immigration, and the Roma

In the summer of 2007, the European Parliament consistently utilized a neoliberal understanding of the world as a marketplace, saying that it would be tantamount to suicide if Europe closed its doors to immigrants. Being chaired by the Italian Socialist Lili Gruber, the European Parliament urged the European Union to make immigration easier, rather than more difficult. Romano Prodi made similar comments soon after, arguing that 'protectionism' of any kind was suicidal. 'Italy is not afraid to open its borders,' he said.

Speaking about successful cuts to Italy's 18.6-billion-euro trade deficit, Prodi explained that it was only due to embracing globalization that the country was re-establishing itself as an economic power. Being competitive was the biggest challenge and biggest responsibility, he said. This came weeks after the European Union lamented Italy's budget deficits. With Stability Pact budget limits set at 3%, the European Parliament urged the Prodi government to make drastic cuts to services and to make the bureaucracy more efficient. Despite having debts totaling 105% of GDP, Italy

---

29   Berezin, 2009, p. 34.

30   Ibid, pp. 30–31.

was expected to have zero deficits by 2010. The only way to achieve that goal was by cutting expenditure on services and applying tax revenues to the debt.

It was particularly galling for the Rightist Ultras to hear Prodi and representatives of the European Union speaking to Italians about globalization and immigration. 'It is the will of these forces,' Fabio of *Boys Roma* told me, 'that Africans and Muslims praying in mosques be the face of Italy.' Of Prodi, little more was expected, despite his being Italian. 'He is a Communist,' he said, despite Prodi having been a former member of the Center-Left and Right Christian Democrats. The European Union, though, had become an enemy in ways that few expected. Many in Italy had expected the economic hardships of membership. As a country that had historically used currency devaluation to stem the onset of inflation, Italy was now at the mercy of the powerful French and German economies. Inflation figures were reported each evening on RAI's TG1. 2.4% was the norm for late-2007 (a three-year high). Pasta and bread prices had increased 300% in one year.

While waiting for a table in a Monteverde pizzeria, Luca of *Padroni di Casa* and I glanced at the news on the pizzeria's bar area TV. It was the week before Christmas, 2007. The only news, it seemed, was bad news. The Ultras were still on strike following the Circo Massimo protest (see Chapter Eight), Italian soldiers were dying in Afghanistan, and the Roma crimes were prompting popular cries for their deportation to Romania. At that, Luca sneered, 'That will never happen.' I agreed that it would be difficult, assuming they were Romanian in origin, given Romania's member status in the European Union. 'Exactly,' he told me, 'we have lost our sovereignty to these people.' 'Which people — the European Union or the Roma?' I asked. 'Well, the European Union,' he laughed, 'although I guess one could say both. Anyway, we have lost the right to defend ourselves.'

In 2007, four high-profile crimes committed by Roma captured the public's attention. The first was the April 2007 murder of Vanessa Russo by two Roma prostitutes. The second was the murder of four Roma children by their parents near Livorno in August 2007. The third was the brutal October 2007 rape and murder by beating of Giovanna Reggiani by a Roma with a history of violent crime. And the fourth was the rape of a Roman woman in December 2007. The response to each was similar. Romans, not just Ultras, were outraged. They wanted the gypsies out of Rome and without delay.

The government's responses were less uniform, with there being little it could do initially. There was no legal precedent for expelling the Roma, it was said, now that Romania, home country to most of the gypsies in Italy, was a member of the European Union. A hastily drawn decree after the Reggiani rape and murder was held up to the public as proof that the government was aware of public demands that something be done to rid the country of Roma. But, because the authors of the decree had also included measures to decrease crimes against homosexuals, President Napolitano refused to sign it into law. After the rape and knifing in December, a new version of the bill was drafted which allowed for the deportation of violent immigrants, even if they had come from European Union countries.

Walter Veltroni, then mayor of Rome (before leaving the post to form the American-style Democratic Party in 2008), addressed public outrage by claiming that 'in the first seven months of 2007, 75% of arrests for murder, rape and robbery [had] been Romanian Roma.' 'Roma committed seventy-six murders in the last year and a half — a record which surpassed the forty-eight committed in a similar time-frame by Albanians a decade ago. In the same period, from January 2006 to June 2007,' Veltroni explained, 'almost half of rapes were committed by Roma. They also topped the statistics for people trafficking and forcing women and girls into prostitution — while they were second to Senegalese nationals for robberies.' Police began sweeping *campi nomadi* (Roma camps) nationwide soon after. Arrests were made of Roma without proper identification or proven criminal records either in Romania or Italy.

On November 1, two days after Giovanna Reggiani had been found clinging to life in a ditch near a gypsy camp along the Tiber, six to eight men (and perhaps one woman) with metal bars, knives, and chains attacked a Roma camp near Tor Bella Monaca, a suburb on the eastern outskirts of Rome. The same camp had been the target of a *Forza Nuova* manifestation in October.

Even earlier there were raids against other Roma camps in Rome. On consecutive nights in late September 2007 young Italians attacked a camp near Ponte Mammolo with not only knives and metal bars but also Molotov cocktails. The camp was burned but no one was injured. One arrest was made.[31] It was revealed by *La Repubblica* five months later that the arrested youth was an AS Roma Ultra. Raids of camps in Milan and Naples also occurred.

The extreme action of the raiders was condemned by the media, the government, and by charitable organizations. *La Repubblica* a Center-Left newspaper based in Rome, published a series of appeals for reason and tolerance as well as condemnations of hatred and violence. Representatives of Veltroni's government expressed solidarity with the victims of the raids, saying that peace and tolerance was the true face of Rome, not violence and xenophobia. A *Rifondazione Comunista* party member, Massimiliano Smeriglio, was horrified that 'racist Romans' were attempting to eradicate from their communities '*rom, migranti, lavavetri, e prostitute*' (Roma, migrants, squeegee men, and prostitutes).

An immigrant rights group called EveryOne said that, as usual, Roma were the victims of racism, while only one man had been guilty of murdering Reggiani. In December Linda Laura Sabbadini, the head of Istat, addressed the Global Forum on Gender Statistics. Speaking on the issue of Roma crime in Italy, she explained that the perception of Roma as criminals was due more to stereotype than fact. In fact, Roma only committed 10% of the rapes in Italy, she said. She failed to relate that number to their percentage of the population, however, which, according to *Il Messaggero*, a Center-Right Roman newspaper, was 0.3% in 2007.

Not only were the Ultras not impressed by the discourse of tolerance and peaceful coexistence; they were, in some cases, openly committed to ridding their communities of Roma, prostitutes, squeegee men, and migrant workers, as Smeriglio had said. From the perspective of the Ultras,

---

31 *Il Romanista*. Anno IV Numero 260. Venerdi 21 Settembre 2007, p. 11.

it is difficult to interpret the responses to Roma crime as being motivated by prejudice, xenophobia, or racism. They desired to maintain strong connections with their communities, with their narrowly defined altruistic co-identifiers. A failure to do so seemed a form of self-abasement in the name of a multiculturalism that could promise them nothing but the diminishment of their form of life.

Conclusion

AS Roma's Ultras are a political phenomenon. Within the *Curva*, the themes and scenes of their aesthetic displays often invoke the Fascist and ancient past of Rome. Beyond the *Curva*, they are sometimes involved with the leading neo-Fascist parties in Italy. Even when unaligned with these parties, however, the Ultras make use of a critique of the contemporary world that puts them at odds with the political issues of neoliberal globalization as well as the concurrent morality of pluralism and inclusion that globalization promotes.

In this chapter, I demonstrated that the Ultras are politically active. More importantly, I explained that these activities are buttressed by a worldview that links *Romanità* with protectionism, a will to violence, and a vision of society based upon the narrow confines of their altruism.

The deep affection for Rome carried by AS Roma's Ultras links them with Fascism and the uses to which it put *Romanità*. According to members of both Ultra groups and neo-Fascist parties, it is the former that promote a use of *Romanità* in the present. As such, the political concerns and actions of the Ultras are given meaning by the devotion to Rome. Their protest against MTV, their presence at Family Day, and their opposition to Rome's Gay Pride parade each showed a concern more for the modernization of Rome in neoliberal terms than an aversion to the constituents whose rights were being advanced.

Likewise, the Ultras take an oppositional stance to immigration. Clandestine Africans arriving in Lampedusa are the most visible examples in the Italian media. More locally, it is the Roma that have become the symbol of anti-immigrant feeling. However, as I demonstrated above, it is less the xenophobic aversion to the Roma that drives Ultra opposition but a sense of helplessness in the face of systemic obstacles to removing the Roma from Rome.

This chapter is a critique of anthropologists who assume that prejudice, xenophobia, and resource competition fully explain the interaction between locals and immigrants. Moralistic assumptions about the local benefits of immigrants are, I suggest, often connected to an unquestioned belief in the neoliberal economic model that promotes flexible cheap labor and hyper-consumption. In place of these assumptions, I allowed the Ultras to speak for themselves, using the terms that are coherent in their local context.

CHAPTER EIGHT

Circo Massimo and the Ultra War Against *Calcio Moderno*

I n the third and fourth chapters I described responses by the State and the Ultras to the deaths of Fillipo Raciti and Gabriele Sandri. The government, riding a wave of popular outrage at the violent outbursts of the Ultras, implemented policing measures that seem more suited to ending the Ultra phenomenon than the violence associated with soccer. The Ultras, for their part, acted to protect themselves, their movement, soccer, and the honor of their cohort from the repression of the State and from incursions of *Calcio Moderno*.

This chapter continues the discussion of Chapter Three, as well as those in-between, acting as a crescendo of the various aspects of the Ultras, from *mentalità* to their political commitments and actions. The chapter focuses on the *Circo Massimo* protest of December 2, 2007, which was a protest not only against the killing of Gabriele Sandri but also the highly-moralized war against the Ultras that had been escalating since the killing of Raciti in February 2007. It then discusses the changes to the game and to fandom that have occurred in Italy and other European countries as a result of the explosion of the televising and marketing of soccer.

Il Perchè di Una Protesta (Why We Protest)

Lorenzo Contucci's *AS Roma Ultras* website announced a *sciopero* (strike) by *Curva Sud*'s Ultras on the morning of November 29, 2007. Instead of attending the upcoming game against Udinese Calcio, the Ultras would gather at Rome's fabled *Circo Massimo*. The notice reflected their dedication to a form of life at odds with the bourgeois ideals of the Italian State which, as the protest unfolded, came to be talked about as an '*avvento vuota della vita Italiana*' (a coming emptiness of modern Italian life). In it we see how the Ultras understand the interstices between justice (and injustice), the media, and the new interests in soccer that are moving the game away from its attachments to local populations and cultural forms.

> Fan of AS Roma, Ultras of *Curva Sud*, simple customer of this industry of *calcio*, or deluded and romantic supporter of an ideal (and style) of life, to you we write this notice in order to explain why next Sunday, when AS Roma hosts Udinese, *Curva Sud* will remain empty of people and passion. The death of Gabriele Sandri is already being forgotten, exceeded by and buried under a system which safeguards its own interests and disregards those of others. All that happens will be distorted, destroyed, or reconstructed with the objective of being made instruments for the powerful. This is what is happening, now as always.

> In a country where "the law is equal for all," but all are not equal before the law, we are once again spectators of a new injustice. We see ourselves for the umpteenth time the targets of a public opinion manipulated by the press, the mass media, and the instruments of power. The Ultras are being destroyed because the *curve* are oases of free thinking and spaces counter to the increasing homogeneity of a lobotomized society devoid of values. They are lands not yet standardized and directed by the usual binaries of the interested — lands not made comfortable with those in control.

> Once upon a time, there were choreographies, colors, flags, and banners. These are characteristics of how the *curve* had always been. But because of today's repression they will become only faded memories.

At this moment, in light of our reflections and above all our consciences, we must leave and remain outside the *Curva* but also this state of affairs. We ask each of you to reflect, to remember, and to begin to behave more justly, in these decidedly delicate times.

You will not find us outside the gates of *Curva Sud* this Sunday because then others would be able to say that it is only our bullying that has kept the *Curva* empty. The only possibility we have of saving our dignity and rights is that each of us, as both accomplices and victims of this situation, chooses to leave behind that which is designed to ensure our extinction.

The appointment is for Sunday [December 2, 2007] at 14:00 in the *Circo Massimo*. Come with scarves and flags united with the thoughts, passions, and ideals of being *Ultras della nostra Roma*.

The spectacle has begun, but without us.[1]

The Groups of *Curva Sud*

The document was signed in deference to the spectacle that would take place on the field, referring to the feeling of sacrifice being made by those who would choose to attend the protest instead of supporting *their* team. Indeed, the proprietorship of soccer was the main issue of the protest. Was it to be the soccer of the fans and locales where it was played or the soccer of television and global capitalism?

In the days between Sandri's death and the decision by the *Curva* to protest, the Ultras had learned that they were banned until further notice from travel to away games. The Observatory (National Observatory of Sporting Events) would announce each week which games would be available for guests. Given the media's incessant speculation on the matter, there was no surprise. On the radio and television, journalists and private individuals directed rhetorical questions at the Observatory. There seemed to be a campaign against allowing the Ultras to continue to be a part of the game. Unsurprisingly, the Ultras wondered aloud at the rationale of the decision.

---

1   Translated from an original document in the collection of the author.

At the *Boys Roma* office as the group decided on participating in the protest, I was surrounded not only by Ultras of varying ages, members of the leadership of *Boys* and *Ultras Romani*, members of *Fiamma Tricolore*, but also the widow and son of Paolo Zappavigna. Conversations were focused on how exactly the Ultras could defend themselves against the press and the police. What purpose did banning away-travel serve? How were away games related to the actual killing of Sandri? 'Do the police blame us to the point that they cannot help themselves killing us if we travel to see a game?' Simone, an animated and outspoken *Boys* Ultra asked. Fabio answered, 'The riots were not because of away games — they were because the State killed an innocent person and then did nothing to honor the victim.' 'Therefore, why not close rest-stop restaurants or keep the police from having guns?' Flaminio of *Ultras Romani* added. They decided that banning away-travel was irrelevant — unless the real crime was that Gabriele was where he was when the bullet was fired because he was an Ultra.

Fabrizio, a well-respected *Boys* Ultra — and, at thirty-eight, the oldest Ultra in the room — who had once proudly shown me his *Fiamma Tricolore* membership card, stressed that they analyze how the media was operating to bend public opinion. 'On the same day that we learned of the elevated charges we also learned that the group of SS Lazio Ultras were armed and that away games were banned,' he said. He was referring to the news of November 15, 2007, on which it was announced that the charge against Luigi Spaccatorella (police officer who shot and killed Gabriele Sandri) had been elevated to voluntary manslaughter, and that knives were found in the possession of the SS Lazio Ultras amongst whom 'Gabbo' was traveling.

'The media want so desperately to blame Gabriele's death on Gabriele and the Ultras,' Fabrizio explained, 'that they shamed themselves in front of the entire nation with the claim [on November 17, 2007] that Sandri was found with rocks in his pocket.' Sandri's brother held a press conference to say that the accusation was 'insane' and that what was found was the type of limestone pebbles and residue used for aging denim. Fabrizio finished with a copy of *Il Romanista* in his hand. 'The media,' he announced while rifling through the pages, 'had even succeeded in making martyrs of themselves and the 'civil mass of true fans who are the true victims of the actions of the Ultras'.'[2]

As the leaders decided what action to take regarding the proposed protest, many reiterated Fabrizio's idea that the media were making criminals of the victims, and martyrs of the criminals. Even as there is incredible distance between the Ultras and those beyond the realm of their narrow altruistic bonds, it did not take a zealot to understand that words like *rabbia* (rage), *compassione* (compassion), *impegno* (commitment), and *onore* (honor), that play such a large role in how the Ultras explain the world, have less value for the general public. 'In getting the games stopped and attacking the police, we and the Atalanta Ultras acted with [these things], while the teams and the league acted only to benefit SKY and its advertisers,' Fabio said.

After the meeting, a few Ultras walked to a bar for a beer. Among them were Fabio of *Boys* and Adriano of *Ultras Romani*, both of whom I knew were present near the Olympic Stadium the night of Sandri's death. Both were model Ultras — always present away from Rome, always ready to confront any opponent, always generous to fellow *AS Roma Ultras*. In other words, they acted in accord with the *mentalità*, were therefore widely respected, and could speak for their groups (and really the entire *Curva Sud*) without fear of reprisal.

As I have already demonstrated, the Ultras are serious about, and protective of, their *mentalità*, the various components of which have been outlined above. Most of these can be summed up in a short statement that graced the shirt of an unknown *AS Roma Ultra* at a game in Empoli. 'Our *mentalità* knows only hatred and rivalry,' it said. Another aspect of the *mentalità*, especially applicable to the point I was making about Fabio and Adriano, is summarized in a piece of *Monteverde* graffiti: 'Our *mentalità* is called silence. Death to spies.' One acts with hatred and rivalry, and then keeps quiet about it so as to keep the State from obtaining evidence. A

---

2   *Il Romanista*. Anno IV, n. 301. 16 November 2007, pp. 1, 3.

short explanation of 'acting in accord with the *mentalità*,' is somewhere between these two sentiments.

I asked Fabio and Adriano — given the State's argument that Gabriele was killed without his identity as an Ultra being known, and that, therefore, it was an incident unrelated to soccer (which, moreover, did not warrant the cancelling of the day's games) — whether there was any action the league or State could have taken that would have prevented the uprising in Rome. 'Nothing,' Adriano said. Certainly, I added, those making the decisions knew how the Ultras would react. 'They know us because they are experts on the Ultras,' Adriano said sarcastically. 'They know us as criminals, vandals, or mindless Fascists made so by the infiltration and goading of political extremists. One would think that having us together, physically and emotionally, all over the country, would be the last thing they wanted.' Was he suggesting that the State wanted a violent reaction from the Ultras? 'The State should have cancelled all games immediately and pleaded hat in hand for peace.'

I asked about the targets of the Ultras during the fighting. 'To attack police stations and the offices of CONI [the Italian Olympic Committee, a standing body which has authority over all organized sport in Italy] showed that they knew what they were doing. They were not hooligans,' answered Fabio, slyly distancing himself from the perpetrators. Finally, I asked, half in jest, if the Ultras were terrorists. An unnamed Roman prosecutor had been quoted by ANSA saying that the Ultras, by 'attacking three police stations, were trying to wrest control from the State.' 'We cannot even buy tickets, travel to and stay in a different city, or go in a stadium to sing for ninety minutes, yet the world is at our command?' Fabio bellowed. 'Now the Atalanta Ultras are banned from their own stadium for four months, only for protesting the 'vergogna dello stato,' [shame of the State] and we are attempting to take over? No! We are not terrorists but neither do we feel shame for our honorable actions.' He continued talking about the Ultras in Bergamo. 'Because there is one thing for certain: the only people in Bergamo who acted with dignity, honor, compassion, respect, and anything else the opposite of shame were the Ultras who got the game stopped. The players and the *Lega* [*Calcio*] acted with absolute shame, and the country now follows their lead, blaming this whole affair on us.'

December 2, 2007: *Circo Massimo Roma*

The idea behind the protest was to give the authorities what they wanted: soccer without the Ultras. Organizers thought that if they showed the country what 'modern soccer,' without the passion and pageantry of the Ultras, looked like, Italians would be more cautious in demanding their removal from the game. Because the Ultras live in a world dominated by other Ultras and all things Ultra, it struck me on numerous occasions that they were at once incredibly aware, and also unaware of the distance between themselves and other people and fans. In this case, their intended audience was the mass who have chosen to watch games on television rather than at stadiums: that mass of 'good fans' who are perfectly suited to *Calcio Moderno* because they consume, rather than participate in, the game.

The *tifosi buoni* (good fans) as they are often called in the media, are the consumerist bourgeois fans that see the game as an entertainment, who cheer politely for the home team, who value sportsmanship over partisanship, who disavow racism in all its forms, who accept what happens on the field with humility, who experience the joy of fandom minus the aggression, and who cheer only in a way that displays education and bearing. In other words, the 'model fan' is as far removed as possible from the Ultras.

The Ultras, in being denied the right to travel to support AS Roma, decided in meetings like the one at *Boys Roma*, that if they could not be a part of an AS Roma game, they would martyr themselves and not watch it at all. At least that way SKY and its advertisers would not benefit by their absence from stadiums. It was almost romantic, then, that the Ultras thought they could gain a measure of public acceptance by removing their voices and colors from the stadium.

Approximately 200 Ultras representing various groups amassed near the Ostiense Station in Testaccio before heading together to the *Circo*

Massimo. The leader of this group, 'Spadino' of *Ultras Romani*, spoke about what could be expected during the day, as well as what protocol was expected from the protest's organizers. 'Under no circumstances,' he said, 'are we to engage the police. We will sing and gesture against them, but that is all.' Someone asked what would happen if the police invaded the *Circo*. 'They will not do so,' he said, relaying to us what he had learned from a police source. We were told to expect many journalists and photographers. Again, the directions were to have no contact with them. We were free to insult them in song, but action against them would not be tolerated.

'The *Circo* is a public space, so the public will be present: police, media, tourists, and Romans. It is up to us to show who we are. We will give them nothing, but the media will *strumentalizzare* [exploit] our actions to suit their needs. There will be many Ultras there, even from rival groups and from groups long dead. However, the day is about unity,' he said, 'and any group choosing to participate will be honored in return. Because,' he concluded, 'the protest is also an opportunity to show how great *Curva Sud Roma* can be.'

We entered the *Circo* around 1 PM. There was little going on except greetings and eating. Some group members climbed the Aventine-side wall of the *Circo* in order to place their banners on the ground. Within an hour, the central core of the *Circo* was full of Ultras. There were few, if any, normal fans present, but only the most committed and hardened Ultras, like one would see at a risky away game (like Juventus, Fiorentina, or Livorno). These numbered approximately 6,000. Instead of the agitated state in which one finds these characters away from Rome, there were only hugs, smiles, and well wishes.

Figure 15. Journalists watch the protest. Note the banners on the Aventine wall of the *Circo Massimo*, Rome, December 2, 2007.

Some of the Ultras brought their children to the *Circo*. They could be seen standing with their battle-hardened fathers carrying and waving flags of *Boys*, *Fedayn*, and even the disbanded Fascist group *Tradizione Distinzione Roma*. Later in the day, the *Fedayn* child 'representative,' a girl of approximately seven years, waved the group's flag as the current members encircled her and sang the *Fedayn* anthem. Given the group's 'silence' I dared not ask who she was. Frankly, I felt that taking her photograph was the most dangerous thing I ever did amongst the Ultras.

Ten minutes before game-time, *Ultras Romani* called everyone together, using one of the megaphones now banned from stadiums. The Ultras began singing, and a long banner was unfurled at the base of the Aventine wall, but only after a series of bombs exploded and smoke candles and emergency flares were lit to announce to all that the day's activities (and festivities) were beginning. The banner was held aloft for the gathered media and Ultras with cameras and cell phones to plainly see and capture.

'*Questa è l'ora de mostra' quanto valemo*,' (This is the time to show how much we are worth) it read. Not only was it part of the chorus to famous Roman singer Lando Fiorini's beloved song *Forza Roma*, which celebrated AS Roma's Championship of 1983–1984, but it was also a perfect encapsulation of the goal of the protest.

The list of current groups participating in the protest was a who's who of *Curva Sud Roma*: *Arditi, Ultras Romani, Tor Bella Monaca, Razza Romana, Ultras San Lorenzo-Primavalle, Fedayn, Boys Roma, Giovinezza, LVPI, Casa Albertone, Padroni di Casa, Roma Casual Firm, Irish Clan Roma*, and a dozen smaller groups all placed banners on the Aventine or held flags with the intent that their contribution be noted by those present.

As game-time approached, groups began forming around those with portable radios and cell phones (with radio service) so as to follow the action. As if on cue, the sky turned dark and rain began to fall. Only a few Ultras had been prescient enough to bring umbrellas. A few of them, along with the media, sought cover under the trees on the Palatine side of the *Circo*. Most just ignored the rain and kept following the game. And they sang. Just as if at the stadium, the Ultras began singing at the kick-off and continued to do so until the first half ended.

Throughout the first half I walked around the *Circo*, getting a sense of who was there and who was not. Some in the *Curva*, who call themselves Ultras, were against the protest because they were against the participating groups. Because the Far Right is ubiquitous in today's Curva, the primary distinction between most groups is whether or not a group sells merchandise.

For *Fedayn*, the selling of merchandise is tantamount to practicing *Calcio Moderno*. It is a betrayal of the Ultra *mentalità* and the expressly written manifestoes of almost every group in the *Curva*. There is righteousness in the voice of those who speak against merchandise (bearing a group's name and/or logo for sale to the general public) in the *Curva* that one does not witness when discussing any other topic. Not only does the selling of merchandise reduce the Ultra to vulgar capitalists, say *Fedayn* members, but it also cheapens the experience of being an Ultra.

If a stadium of 60,000 can all hold aloft a *Boys Roma* scarf, what is the value of committing oneself to the group and sacrificing oneself for the honor of wearing one? Without this honor, according to some, the Ultras are decadent.

The crux of the issue, though, is found in the metaphor most used to describe the practice: *si mangia dalla Curva* (one eats from the *Curva*). To be seen as eating, or desiring to eat, from the money of other Ultras is to be seen, as Gianluca, a longtime *Fedayn* member explained during a game with bombs and flares alight all around us, as 'reducing the *Curva* to a marketplace and the Ultras to vulgar consumers.' Upon asking members of one Ultra group about another in *Curva Sud* or even elsewhere in Italy, frequently one is told before anything else, 'they eat from the *curva.*' Of course, for those groups who sell merchandise, the practice is understood as a means toward self-sufficiency.

From the perspective of *Ultras Romani*, they are not a group seeking enrichment from *Curva Sud*, but merely a new way of being Ultra. Adriano, one of the most energetic and committed Ultras I have met, explained to me that the group was not as far removed from Ultra traditions as other groups think, despite their being the only group in the history of *Curva Sud* that one pays a membership fee to join. In response to charges of 'eating from the curva,' he told me that *Ultras Romani* is more involved with charity and fund-raising initiatives (such as money for imprisoned Ultras, memorials for deceased Ultras, helping children's hospitals in Rome, and helping sick and needy AS Roma fans) than any other group in Italy.

These types of benevolence are commonplace in *Curva Sud* and other Italian *curvas*, but because *Ultras Romani* maintains relationships with the club and players, theirs are given more attention than other efforts. Federico of *Giovinezza* (Youth, but also the title of the Italian national anthem under Fascism), one of the purist (and most Fascist) groups, countered by reminding me that all the groups work in their communities, and do so without commercializing being an Ultra.

While many of AS Roma's Ultras point to *Calcio Moderno* and the reduction of the *Curva* to just another space within the global market-place as the reason why merchandising is largely frowned upon, the issue points to another fault line within the *Curva*. Along with politics and merchandising there exists a question about what type of space *Curva Sud* should be. Those on the Left envision a *Curva* that is non-political and thus unspoiled by the mundane issues of society. The Right, conversely, envisions a *Curva* that is highly political, organized, and hierarchical.

The Left in-and-of-itself is almost inconsequential in *Curva Sud*. This is because the vast majority of the Ultras and unaligned fans who consider themselves Leftists desire a non-political *Curva*. Even *Fedayn*, which is now associated with the Right, also desires a non-political *Curva*; that is, a *Curva* in which political affiliation and ideology do not factor in the act of fandom. As we have seen, though, *Fedayn's* non-political stance does not influence the political aspects of the Ultras' war against *Calcio Moderno*. The unaligned fans with whom I spoke and experienced games are far more lenient than *Fedayn*. According to Gabriele, an unaligned fan who considers himself an Ultra, 'In the *Curva* we should be able to do what we want. We have no fear of police reprisals. We can come, drink, be with friends, show our support for AS Roma, and no one should be able to tell us otherwise — the groups included. We who are not affiliated with a group,' the sixteen-year veteran of *Curva Sud* and away games continued, 'are far freer than the organized fans [Ultras]. They are just like soldiers who unthinkingly follow whatever their bosses tell them.'

The groups, by contrast, feel that the *Curva* should be a militarized zone, with Ultras standing in formation whether in supporting the team or in making statements, through song or banner, about the society of which the *Curva* and Ultras are a part. Coordination, suffering for the team and Rome, singing and clapping even when AS Roma is losing, and taking part in the ritualized traditions of *Curva Sud* are necessary for the *Curva* to represent itself in an honorable fashion. Those fans who come to games only to spectate are seen as a hindrance to a unified and disciplined *Curva*. 'If one makes complaints against [*Boys*] because we sell merchandise,' explained Fabio, one of the group's leaders in 2007, 'they should be far more concerned with the fans who enter the *Curva* unwilling to be Ultras. The *Curva* is not an anarchic utopia but a hierarchical and mechanical space. We come here with a job to do. If they want to hang around and get stoned with their friends they should do so outside this hallowed ground.' I asked Fabio if the *Curva* was ultimately a Fascist space. 'Absolutely,' he said, 'one should have the mentality of a *squadrista* when entering the *Curva*. Relax at home. Come here as a militant marching into battle.'

Interestingly, Ultras on both sides of this question talk of the Ultras as a movement. To the groups the *Curva* is a place of fraternity, bonding, becoming conscious of the world, a place to demonstrate one's political ideology and to make connections between sport and society.[3] To them, the Ultras are a movement with a particular understanding of soccer and society — even if that understanding can vary greatly depending on one's position within the phenomenon. The Ultras are a collection of young, aggressive, like-minded individuals who, for all their differences, desire a soccer that is pure and symbolic of only the communities its teams represent.[4] To the unaligned fans, the *Curva* is and should remain neutral in every way except in its devotion to AS Roma. It is a space best left devoid of politics; a place where black, red, white, and green hold no power — where instead the red and yellow of AS Roma are the only colors that matter. To them the Ultras might very well be a movement, but it should be one only at game time and in relation to the game.

For some of the smaller groups that inhabit the lower areas of the *Curva*, the anti-commercial dimension of the *mentalità* is so sacred that to join with 'merchant' groups in anything is a betrayal of being an Ultra. Even with their absence the Ultras filled the central island of the *Circo*. The distance between Ultras and non-Ultras is palpable in stadiums, but in the *Circo*, although a stadium, the distance was heightened to the point of surrealism. Along the edges of the mass of Ultras, tourists looked

---

3   Ginsborg, 2003, p. 119.

4   Ginsborg, 2003b, pp. 112–119.

on curiously with no way of knowing what they were seeing, and local Romans jogged or walked their dogs without being bothered.

To follow the second half, one of the most respected Ultras in *Curva Sud*, a longtime member of *Fedayn* named Giorgio, used a megaphone to announce to all within earshot what was happening. Giorgio is covered in tattoos ranging from the Lupa Capitolina to the AS Roma logo to a message about being an Ultra and carrying Rome in his heart. He speaks in an unmistakable gravelly voice that sounds impossible to be human. Before the Amato Decree banned megaphones in February 2007, he carried the megaphone *Fedayn* used to coordinate their singing. In December 2006, AS Roma played in Turin against Torino FC. After this somewhat memorable game Giorgio regaled the entire section of AS Roma fans with jokes and songs, one of which became instantly famous in *Curva Sud*. Titled 'Bastardo Steward', it begins with a hummed bar of the Police Academy movie's theme song.

The less-than-optimal conditions for following the game were noted with pride by all with whom I spoke. Standing in the rain and awaiting bursts of cheering or swearing from those closer to a radio was seen as far superior to watching the game on television. Many vowed that they would never watch a game on television — only at the stadium or on the radio, just as their parents and grandparents had done. As always with the Ultras, there was a longing for purity that made sense of many of their actions, from *squadristi* raids to acting as the self-proclaimed 'conscience' of soccer. In previous chapters I discussed the idea of sacrifice that is an important aspect of their worldview. Standing in the rain listening to distant voices describe a game in which one would normally play an active role certainly falls into the category of sacrifice.

Just as in the United States, radio produced 'voices' that were inseparable from one's experience of the teams. In the case of AS Roma, the voice of the team is a Roman named Carlo Zampa. Most Ultras prefer following games with Carlo because he is an obvious partisan. There is no attempt to be diplomatic, professional, or even decent when Carlo Zampa broadcasts. Zampa's job as the public-address announcer for AS Roma's home games ended in 2004–2005 because he used the PA to insult a Juventus

player who had demanded a 'transfer,' or trade, from AS Roma the previous season. Partisanship was one of the guiding principles for which the
Ultras in *Circo Massimo* were protesting.

All told, the *Circo* protest was the most important event during my
time amongst the Ultras, even as it occurred in December 2007, my last
full month in Rome. Not only did it afford me the opportunity to meet
and speak with the most important and influential Ultras in *Curva Sud*, it
also gave me credibility and a high level of acceptance amongst the Ultras.
Before the *Circo* there were Ultras whom I had seen at away games and in
Rome who were reluctant to accept my presence. Many of these barriers
were diminished that day. It was explained to me that they and I had faced
the same choice. I, with little to gain by associating myself with the hardest and most committed of Ultras, nor from actually choosing to miss an
important game, had nonetheless done so.[5]

I had stayed under the rain with no umbrella and participated in a protest that meant, in their eyes, the survival of the Ultras and of, as Stefano
of *Padroni di Casa* explained it, 'freedom in Italy.' Indeed, none of them
knew that many of my closest allies and friends beyond the Ultras had
passionately voiced their displeasure at my decision to attend the protest
instead of the game. It was made clear to me by many in Monteverde that
those at the *Circo* were not fans, that they only went there to bate and hate
the police, that they have ruined the *Curva*, once open to all fans and even
the opposition but now exclusionary, and that their silly hatred was killing
the game. In the end, I had chosen the Ultras over AS Roma.

As I mentioned in the previous chapter, in addition to giving me legitimacy and credibility amongst the Ultras, this decision also prompted
some of the leaders of *Boys* to proclaim me a Roman. This romantic move
was made with a simple but affectionate hug by Giulio of *Boys* midway
through the game's second half. In the weeks after, though, word must

---

5   I had presented myself as a fan of AS Roma, which I was, knowing that without a
     sincere devotion to what they hold most dear, I would have been seen as just another
     interloper attempting to make a name off the Ultras.

have spread because I received text messages from more than twenty Ultras wishing me well and sending me off into the world as a Roman.

From a distance, the *Circo* probably looked like a party. At the final whistle of the game which AS Roma won 2–1, it was full of song, emergency flares, bombs, and smoke candles. Members of *Ultras Romani* created a large mosh-pit, and the assembled crowd began pushing and shoving while singing. The groups who brought flags spread out along the base of the Aventine and 'put their colors in the wind.'

Figure 16. Ultras in the *Circo Massimo*, Rome, December 2, 2007.

From within the *Circo*, it was in fact a party. The flares and smoke candles blanketed the evening sky with an otherworldly red and yellow glow. Smoke was thick and so was the singing. The *Ultras Romani* mosh-pit poured forth to a song from 2002–2003: '*Siamo gli Ultras della Roma; e fieri Centurioni e cavalieri; A difendere la città; Orgoglio della nostra storia; Ave Roma, Roma vittoriosa; Comè scritto nella storia; Il vento gelido del nord; Non ci potrà fermare.*' (We are the Ultras of Roma; fierce Centurions and

Knights; we defend the city; glory of our history; Hail Roma, Victorious Roma; As history has shown; the cold northern winds; cannot stop us.)

The flags, smoke, bombs, flares, and songs were manifestations of the soccer that the Ultras are determined to save. But they are only the physical manifestations of their *mentalità*. As the words to the *Centurioni* song make clear, there was more going on in the *Circo* than partying and creating a spectacle. Just to make sure that the media and less-than-committed Ultras understood the importance of the day and how it represented the triumph of the Ultra *mentalità*, at the end of the protest, in the late-dusk light, group leaders appeared with trash-bags and the Ultras cleaned the area they had inhabited of any trash that they or others had been so careless to drop. 'The city is ours,' cried Adriano of *Ultras Romani*, 'show anyone who comes here how to care for it.'

For many Ultras, the *Circo* was the culmination of forty years of Ultra history. It was an acknowledgment of from where the Ultra had come and to where they were going. This was evident in the respect given to the older and extinct groups who attended. One of these was *CUCS*, which was represented by its founder Stefano Malfatti. After a touching ovation, he held court with an umbrella and a megaphone during the first half. Malfatti, with his gray mop of hair and slight build, looks nothing like today's hard-edged Ultras. Nor does he look like he ever could have. Courageously he urged the Ultras to change, saying that they need to end the war against the police, as it is a war they cannot win. He would never have been harmed or shouted down in that environment, but he still took a position unpopular on the day.

He said that violence had always been a part of the Ultras, but that before they made war on other Ultras, which the police were happy to accommodate. He concluded by saying that one is born Ultra and one dies Ultra, and that both of his children will be in the *Curva* when they are old enough. Malfatti affirmed the Ultras' form of life, making it clear that it is a way to live with honor, values, and dignity. He seemed to understand his role as a father figure to most of those present. For it was the *CUCS* that created the idea of a '*mentalità Ultras*' that *Curva Sud Roma* was still bound to protect and serve.

In addition to Malfatti I heard various active Ultras speak. Amongst these were members of *Padroni di Casa, Fedayn, Boys, Razza Romana, LVPI,* and *Primavalle-San Lorenzo.* By the end of the game, I had compiled a list of themes that they used to explain the current aims and attentions of the Ultras. The list became the basis for this book. I divided what had been said to me and to those near me into two categories: either affirmation or negation. The affirmations outweighed the negations, which even if unintentional, perfectly promotes the 'life affirming' nature of the Ultras. For even the 'protest' was more a celebration of being Ultra than a negation of what they do not want to be.

The Ultras in protest at *Circo Massimo* said Yes to: flags (*bandieri*), banners (*striscioni*), bombs (*petardi*), smoke candles (*fumogeni*), flares (*razzi illuminati*), love (*amore*), enemies (*nemici*), loyalty (*fedeltà*), hatred (*odio*), aggression (*aggressione*), honor (*onore*), rivalry (*rivalità*), commitment (*impegno*), sacrifice (*sacrificio*), laughter (*riso*), tears (*lacrime*), romance (*fascino*), strength (*forza*), virtue (*virtù*), brotherhood (*confraternità*), adventure (*avventura*), conquest (*conquista*), danger (*pericolo*), discrimination (*discriminazione*), passion (*passione*), tradition (*tradizione*), glory (*gloria*), war (*guerra*), and, finally, Rome.

By contrast, they said No to: egalitarian soccer (*egualitario*), standardized soccer (*standardizzato*), moralized soccer (*moraleggiarato*), soccer only for the selling of advertising (*da fare pubblicità*), soccer without particularities (*senza particolarità*), soccer without connection to place (*senza rapporto di posto*), soccer without passion (*senza passione*), soccer for consumers (*da consumatori*), and soccer for a TV audience (*dal pubblico di TV*).

Calcio Moderno and the Business of Football
Origins

Calcio Moderno is the postmodernization of fandom and commoditization of soccer. It seeks to diminish the primacy of the live audience in order to focus on the television audience, and to make of the game a marketable commodity, so as to generate advertising revenues. The concept itself began appearing in the Italian *curvas* in the late-1990s. The first organized protest against it that involved AS Roma's Ultras was in 1999. It was prompted by changes to the format of UEFA's Champions League competition that went into effect for the 1998–1999 season, giving the impression of UEFA being desirous of creating a TV based European 'super league.' Why this idea was particularly threatening to the Ultras will be explained below. First I will detail some of the recent trends that have combined to make soccer more important to many as a business than as a cultural experience.[6]

The idea that the game was becoming more overtly commercial began with the International Federation of Football Associations' (FIFA) decision to have the United States host the 1994 FIFA World Cup. Given its history as one of the few countries without a discernable 'soccer culture,' as well as its position at the forefront of the globalization of consumer culture, warnings of the game's demise, or at least corruption, are rampant in literature from the period. English tabloids decried the 'Coca-Cola-ization' and 'media-ization' sure to follow the game's grandest stage being erected in a country with 'more world renowned serial killers than footballers.'[7] The feeling was that FIFA had made a final greedy move to take the game's popularity and presentation to a new level.

This is not to suggest that soccer was not already associated with advertising, celebrity, and multinational corporations. However, even at that late date, the game was far more locally based, even given its broad international popularity, than American sports had been since the late-1950s.[8] The fears of many seemed to be realized when, with the purpose of making the 130-year-old game more charming to the uninterested US market, FIFA proposed using twenty-five minute quarters to appeal to

---

6   Although it is not part of this book's scope to describe the relationship between the English language media and the particular understanding of the game in English-speaking countries, the discussion that follows is largely based on English examples and statistics, because these issues are being explained by English language scholars.

7   Giulianotti and Williams, 1994, p. 9.

8   Markovits and Hellerman, 2001, pp. 128–161.

advertisers and, in a bid to attract American viewers, making the goal size larger to promote higher scores.[9]

Given the audacity of these proposals, which rendered the game a malleable form of entertainment rather than a deeply ingrained aspect of local cultures, it was a short slippery slope to envision its further Americanization.[10] The most extreme form of the expected transformation was a lowering of the game's topophilia (deep connection with place). From Britain and Europe, scholars and fans saw in the US experience of sport a lack of symbolic fixity. This was evident in the football, baseball, and basketball teams (not to mention players) that had moved from city to city; sometimes, as with New York's baseball Giants and Brooklyn's Dodgers, leaving behind devoted fans and historic stadiums in order to seek higher profits thousands of miles from where the teams began. With this lack of connection to their surroundings, American sports was seen as the domain of mere franchises that lacked the depth of memory that had made football clubs synonymous with the populations of which they were a part.

The Bosman Ruling

Almost fifteen years removed from the 1994 World Cup, British and European football is not the freak-show many envisioned, but neither is it the game it once was. FIFA, UEFA, and the European Union have combined to set in motion a system that many see as damaging the local particularities of the game. The first two began working together (and with member nations) in the late-1990s to amend citizenship requirements and taxation statutes in order to make transfers of players less cumbersome — in effect, to ensure their legality. They did so in order to synchronize international transfers, or player moves, with the 1995 European Court of Justice's Bosman Ruling. According to 'The Bosman Rule,' soccer transfers are subject to the same rules as Article 48 of the

---

9   Giulianotti and Williams, 1994, p. 7.

10 Sandvoss, 2003, p. 161.

European Community Treaty, which states that no European national (provided they are a citizen of an EU member state) can be prohibited from working in any member state. In other words, soccer players must be considered part of the free movement of labor between states. The ruling also declared illegal (because discriminatory) any attempts to place quotas on the number of foreign players in a given club, league, or nation.

Global Clubs

In Europe, it is the clubs that have the most to gain and lose from globalization. Although the majority of Europe's clubs remain attached to a fixed locale, relying upon the loyalty of fans and local businesses to provide enough profit to stay in business, there is a noticeable trend wherein certain clubs have gained tremendous stature and power, thus placing their connections to place in jeopardy. These are the so-called 'global clubs,' those that rely on a global, as opposed to local, fan base and globally recruited players.

There are seven truly global clubs: Manchester United and Liverpool of England, Internazionale, AC Milan, and Juventus of Italy, and Real Madrid and Barcelona of Spain.[11] These clubs formed the core of the G14, a group of the largest clubs in the world, which united with the intent of lobbying FIFA and UEFA collectively for restitution from national associations in the event of player injuries occurring on 'international duty' (when the player is playing for his national team).[12]

Soccer in this context is understood as big business. This has rendered community focus, not to mention community ownership (which had

---

11   Recent changes in the ownership and spending power of two other clubs have led to their having 'global' aspirations. These are Chelsea FC and Manchester City FC (both of England).

12   G14 disbanded in early-2008 after winning their battle against FIFA and UEFA. The fourteen were, in addition to the seven noted above, Marseilles and Paris Saint-Germain of France, Ajax and PSV Eindhoven of Netherlands, Bayern Munich and Borrusia Dortmund of Germany, and Porto of Portugal. In 2002, the G14 expanded by four: Arsenal of England, Valencia of Spain, Lyon of France, and Bayer Leverkusen of Germany.

been a part of the English experience until the second-half of the twentieth century), as counter-to-progress. Of the teams mentioned above, four are foreign owned. Indeed, foreigners owned seven of the twenty teams that played in the English Premier League (EPL) in 2007–2008; two of them, Manchester United and Liverpool, are owned by Americans (Malcolm Glazer and Tom Hicks and George Gillett, respectively) who acted through investment banks to gain sufficient funds for their purchases. Roman Abramovich, a Russian oil magnate, owns Chelsea FC. And, until September 2008, Thaksin Shinawatra, the former Prime Minister of Thailand, owned Manchester City, at which time it was bought by Abu Dhabi United Group, a private equity company of Sheikh Mansour bin Zayed Al Nahyan, a member of the royal family of the United Arab Emirates.

There were no foreign owners in Italy's *Serie A* until 2011, when American Thomas DiBenedetto led a consortium of American financiers and hedge fund managers to the purchase of AS Roma. The American takeover sent shockwaves through Curva Sud, as instead of being able to perceive of the club as a local property the Ultras had to face the reality that *Calcio Moderno* was now imbedded in the symbols and traditions that they hold so dear. No longer could AS Roma be held up as a Roman team for Romans. Instead it became the sport's most visible symbol of all that is wrong with globalization and capitalism, as the new owners quickly brought Nike and Disney onboard to help promote the 'global brand of AS Roma.' Unfortunately, I had long left Rome by the time of the takeover (which was spurred in part by the neoliberal adjustment of sovereignty from States to financial institutions that left many banks in crisis, including Unicredit, the Italian bank holding AS Roma's debt) and have been unable to precisely register the Ultras' response. From afar, however, it seems to be surprisingly complex, as some Ultras considered it the final nail in the coffin of AS Roma's centrality to their symbolic universe, while others shrugged it off as of little importance, as the club and Ultras had long been contentious of one another.

The latter reaction is the more interesting of the two, as it allows the Ultras to continue to cheer on the colors of the city without concern for the machinations of global finance that now govern the fortunes of the team. But it also puts the relationship between Ultras and clubs in starker contrast — becoming something akin to their distance from the State and the media. Keeping *Curva Sud* — and their daily lives — clean of the tentacles that attach bourgeois men and women to the debts, rationalities, and rhythms of hyper-capitalism and its Statist lackeys is still a central thrust of the Ultras. Indeed, it must be so if Italian soccer is to maintain any of the color, pageantry, and ferocity for which it became renown.

Giancarlo Abete, president of the Italian Football Federation (FIGC), has often stated that the EPL is the ideal model to move Italy's soccer into the twenty-first century. Foreign investment, in the form of ownership and players is key, but more so, according to Abete, is a 'professional-ization' of the Italian league, and a changing of Italy's 'culture of sport.' Leaving aside, for the moment, the question of culture, the English league has ascended to the top of European soccer by focusing on profits. These are made primarily through television rights, merchandise branding, and through winning the UEFA Champions League.

The English Premiere League and Television

The EPL has changed the experience of soccer for English and worldwide fans. The EPL was formed in 1991 in order to revolutionize English soccer, which at the time was seen as 'suffering' from old stadiums, dwindling attendances, and widespread hooliganism. The impetus for the EPL was the 1989 Taylor Report, a governmental investigation into the causes of a 1988 stadium riot and stampede that left ninety-six Liverpool supporters dead.[13] Lord Taylor of Gosforth concluded that the deaths resulted from poor stadium design and limited policing of fans inside the Hillsborough stadium.

---

13   Armstrong, 1998, pp. 5–9.

The 'problems' of the English game at that time are regularly cited to describe today's Italian soccer. It is not lost on the Ultras that they are the only ones at the games. Just considering AS Roma, game attendance data show significant drops in every year since 2000–2001. In that year, AS Roma averaged 59,402 spectators. By 2007–2008, AS Roma's average was 37,276. *Serie A*'s attendance from 2004–2005 to 2007–2008 fell from 9,421,549 (an average of 26,098 per game) to 8,575,314 (an average of 23,887 per game).[14] In that time, attendance figures for *Curva Sud* remained stable at 19,000 and then 17,000 in 2007–2008 per game (the maximum number of seats).[15] In other words, Curva Sud is completely full for every game.

What lies behind the decrease in soccer attendance is debated in every café, piazza, and newspaper in Italy. The reasons given range from structural to behavioral, but always include three things: Ultra violence, TV, and stadiums. For their part, the Ultras agree that the explosion in popularity of televised soccer and the horrible state of many Italian stadiums are factors contributing to diminished attendances.

The most important aspect of the EPL is that it negotiates its own television deal. Thus, it is financially separated from the five (lower) associated levels of the EFA, which are home to hundreds of local small-town teams across England. The first EPL television deal was signed in 1992 with SKY for 191 million pounds over five seasons. The latest was signed with SKY and Setanta, a Scottish broadcaster, for 1.7 billion pounds over three seasons. When combined with highlights permissions and international rights, the total television related income for the 2007–2010 EPL will be 2.7 billion pounds (an average of forty-five million pounds per team per year).[16]

In 2003, Rupert Murdoch created SKY Italia as a way to compete with Berlusconi's Mediaset for Italy's untapped television potential. Until

---

14 Overall attendance given from 2004 to 2008 because *Serie A*'s increase from 18 to 20 teams in 2004 increased the attendance figures from 2003, even as most team's per-game-average fell.

15 Statistics from an official AS Roma document in the collection of the author.

16 http://en.wikipedia.org/wiki/Premier_League.

the 2003–2004 season, RAI and Mediaset combined to televise a handful of games on free television per week. The larger teams had satellite
distribution contracts with Telepiù and Stream. It was these companies
that Murdoch purchased for 600 million British Pounds. By September
2008 SKY Italia had between five and seven million subscribers. These pay
between thirty and fifty euros per month (adding up to between 300 and
500 euros per season) to watch all of the games of their favorite team, the
Champions League, other European soccer leagues, and special program-
ming such as AS Roma Channel, which broadcasts news, training sessions,
and other activities within the club. Meanwhile, a season ticket for *Curva
Sud*, ensuring entrance (plus the right to purchase the same seat for *Coppa
Italia* and Champions League games) to nineteen *Serie A* games, cost 155
euros for the 2008–2009 season.[17]

In order to hasten the creation of EPL-style profits, in 2008 the State
agreed to the collective selling of broadcast rights beginning with the
2010–2011 season. It was estimated that such a deal would cost someone
(either Murdoch or Berlusconi) approximately 900 million euros. In fact,
the rights to televise the two seasons between 2010 and 2012 were sold to
SKY for 1.149 billion euros!

The EPL and Merchandising

American-style merchandising is another way EPL clubs are seeking to increase profits. When Tom Hicks was introduced as co-owner of Liverpool
FC, he told a Sky audience that besides the UEFA Champions League,
he would use merchandising to make Liverpool the 'richest club in the
world.' To do so, he explained, Liverpool would be made into a brand that
would produce its own line of football and sports related merchandise and
attract the highest caliber of corporate sponsorship. The model for such a
venture, he continued, was Malcolm Glazer's Manchester United, whose
superstore was selling literally thousands of Manchester United related

---

17   The cost to renew was 155 euros. For a non-renewing subscriber, the cost was 235
     euros. However, the *Curva*, as every year, sold out during the renewal phase of AS
     Roma's season ticket campaign.

items, while AIG paid 56.5 million pounds over four years for its sponsorship logo on the player's jerseys and Nike paid 302.9 million pounds over thirteen years to supply the team's uniforms. By contrast, AS Roma's income from the Turin-based Italian sportswear firm Kappa is five million euros per season — although that figure is expected to rise considerably in 2014, when Nike will begin sponsoring the team.

The EPL and Champions League

Because of their income from television and sponsorships, EPL teams have recently dominated the third avenue of revenue increase: the UEFA Champions League, whose competition runs concurrent with the domestic leagues of Southern and Western Europe. It consists of the champion of each UEFA affiliated nation's highest professional league, plus finishers from second to fourth position in the most difficult leagues (i.e. Italy, England, Spain, Germany, Netherlands and Portugal).

The EPL placed three teams (Manchester United, Chelsea, and Liverpool) in the final four of the 2006–2007 and 2007–2008 Champions Leagues. Even as Italy's AC Milan won the competition in 2006–2007, its victory did not keep Italy from falling further behind the English in terms of profiting from 'the business of soccer.' According to Deloitte's 'Football Money League,' Italy's *Serie A* is worth 40% less than the EPL based on overall club revenues. According to the 2007–2008 list, released each season with details of the previous season, six of the fourteen wealthiest clubs in the world are in the EPL. That includes Newcastle United, which finished the corresponding EPL season in thirteenth position.

There is no set prize money. Instead, a club will receive an increased share of the income generated by independent national television rights agreements, pay-per-view, and internet pay-per-view. When AS Roma reached the final-eight during the 2007–2008 competition, they received approximately thirty-five million euros. Manchester United, winner in 2007–2008, expected revenues of eighty-five million pounds. Runner-up Chelsea FC expected to receive thirty-five million pounds. The same article explained that the final, played in Moscow, was expected to be a financial boon to more than the two competing clubs. The betting industry, bars and restaurants, travel, consumer goods, and supermarkets hoped to benefit from approximately two hundred and ten million pounds in revenue (consumption increases comparable with the NFL's Super Bowl in the United States).

With this kind of money to be made, the EPL was quick to rid itself of the 'problems' it had inherited. The game experience until the Taylor Report has been described as 'chaos'.[18] Urination in the stands, pushing, shoving, drinking, smoking, and singing were ritualized behaviors one expected to encounter at soccer games. The attendance of women and young children was rare. The political voice of the working class was historically galvanized at soccer matches. Political songs and occasionally banners spoke of local identities through tales of pride and defiance.[19] Fireworks, field invasions, and fighting were also common. While many sociologists, most notably Eric Dunning, have studied the violence and general mayhem associated with English soccer fandom, and concluded that such behaviors are due to a failure in the 'civilizing process' of the English working class, others look back on the days before the Taylor Report and the EPL longingly.[20]

One of these is Dave Boyle, one-time president of the Football Supporters' Association (FSA), an organization that campaigns for fan representation on club boards as well as fans' rights such as the right to stand during a soccer match.[21] Boyle maintains that soccer has abandoned its original (and still core) supporters. He says that fans are now understood 'merely as consumers with a ceaseless thirst for all things football related.' The FSA, he explained, was against the FIFA/UEFA model of big clubs and leagues operating for the benefit of corporate sponsors and

---

18   McGill, 2001, p. 8.

19   McGill, 2001, p. 7.

20   Dunning, 1999, p. 48.

21   The FSA merged with European bodies of similar design in 2007. It is now known as the Football Supporters Federation.

spectacular television.[22] What the FSA seeks, then, is a return to a time when local fans were the driving force behind the game's popularity.

AS Roma and *Calcio Moderno*

According to SKY News, AS Roma was the tenth richest club in the world as a result of the 2006–2007 season, making 106.1 million British Pounds. 70.3 million of that came from broadcast revenues. With so little money being generated locally (the club brought in less than three million euros from the sale of *Curva Sud* season tickets during the same season), and with so much of *Calcio Moderno* focusing on the financial and business aspects of the game, it is no wonder, say the Ultras, as self-proclaimed 'protectors of the game' (by which they mean its deep connections to place), that clubs are seeking profits rather than public approval. The close relations between the Ultras and the clubs (which the 2007 Amato Decree destroyed when it went into effect) were designed to keep pressure on the clubs to keep their local constituents in mind at all times. The two most recent and damaging large-scale Ultra eruptions (before Raciti and Sandri) were not only attacks on *Calcio Moderno* (by disrupting broadcasts and making the game too risky for investment/advertisement) but also on clubs which had been seen as taking the Ultras for granted while only pursuing the commercial interests of the game.

Despite AS Roma's position amongst the wealthiest clubs in the world, and despite it regularly fielding a team that includes foreign players, the Ultras still feel that the club is an organic part of Rome's locality. As I explained above, foreign fans can be accepted into the legion of Ultras through their display of loyalty to the Ultras, Rome, and AS Roma. Likewise, foreign players who 'play for the shirt' are given a type of 'honorary Roman' status, not unlike that granted to me. In this way, the Ultras negotiate the contradiction between supporting a financially successful 'modern' club and the desire to have AS Roma all to themselves. Although the long-standing (until 2007) relationship between AS Roma and the

---

22   McGill, 2001, p. 11.

Curva provided the Ultras a way to actually influence the running of the club, thus promoting the feelings of proprietorship that guided such a relationship, it can be argued now that the war that the Ultras are fighting against *Calcio Moderno* and the destruction of localism in soccer, is over.

If so, and the Ultras have been 'culturally dispossessed' of AS Roma, then they may be entering the last phase of their history.[23] After all, there is little-to-nothing that is compromising in their make-up, and, as Andrews and Ritzer have argued, within global capitalism, cultural forms that are 'generally indigenously conceived, controlled, and comparatively rich in distinctive substantive content are a virtual impossibility'.[24] What we might see instead is the shifting of Ultra behavior to other areas of social and political life (to be examined in the concluding chapter).

Issues of Soccer and Globalization

The disconnection between long-time local fans, the business of soccer, and what some perceive as FIFA and UEFA's vision for the game is consistent with other responses to postmodernity and turbo-capitalism. In essence, what is being experienced is the deterritorialization of fandom.[25] Deterritorialization is a process first theorized by Gilles Deleuze and Felix Guattari. It occurs when an 'event' (thought or action) is detached from its original environment (of meaning or location).[26] Poststructuralist theorists use the concept most consistently to explain the radical changes to the experience of space since the onset of postmodernity. The deterritorialization of space through geographical mobility and inconsequentiality (via the internet and global capital systems), coupled with flexible labor processes and markets, not only de-territorializes the individual but also re-territorializes him or her within a structural and functional system

---

23   Creed, 2011, p. 3.

24   Andrews and Ritzer, 2007, p. 41.

25   Sandvoss, 2003, p. 12.

26   Deleuze and Guattari, 1987.

designed to accommodate radical increases in consumption.[27] Fandom is impacted similarly.

The features of deterritorialized fandom are multifarious, impacting the non-local fan, the clubs, and the local fan. For the fan who is part of the global audience, deterritorialized fandom allows him or her to actually be a fan. Indeed, the act of consuming the game demonstrates the sometimes-positive effects of deterritorialization, namely the reterritorialization of the event as a personal experience full of meaning and value. As Deleuze explains, each act of deterritorialization is concurrently destructive and constructive. While the local context is negated, such an act of negation also opens new 'conditions of possibility'.[28] The process here is entirely subjective, even as it occurs as a benefit of recent communication technologies.[29]

It is possible to explain reterritorialized fans as a 'third culture.' Mike Featherstone explains 'third cultures' as practices and knowledges that are independent of nation-states and particular locales.[30] Internet and satellite television make it possible to engage in fan activities for events occurring anywhere in the world at any moment. While this fan is not yet the norm, it is the target of EUFA's Champions League. Part of the Champions Leagues approach to transnational marketing is the use of the 'global clubs' discussed above and de-and-re-territorialized fandom.

The disconnection of clubs from their local contexts makes them ripe for the polysemic narratives so necessary to the promotion of transnational consumption.[31] The creation of identities around such consumption is a must if the game is to be experienced worldwide. For their part, fans now have an unlimited number of choices regarding which club or clubs to support. 'Third culture' fandom thus may include an expansion of knowledge, as the deterritorialized fan may possibly gain awareness

27 Castells, 1996, pp. 1–14.
28 Deleuze, 1995, pp. 30–31.
29 LaFeber, 2002.
30 Featherstone, 1995, p. 114.
31 Sandvoss, 2003, pp. 28–30.

of places and political processes otherwise unknowable.[32] 'Third culture' fans might also develop, or enhance, their appreciation of the game — its strategies and aesthetics — through ever-improved televised images of the players' skills.

While for the non-local or global fan, the processes of deterritorialization and reterritorialization, or of globalization, are experienced positively, it is clear that for others these processes can be negative and quite destructive. For many clubs, the processes damage not only their financial viability but also their cultural worth. Smaller clubs, those without the following or resources to position themselves within the global flow of capital and information, are often rendered superfluous.

If a club is unable to compete at a level that allows Champions League qualification, and their local constituents are able and willing to follow, through the television and Internet, a larger or even 'global' club, they eventually find themselves playing to empty stadiums and without the ability to support themselves financially. This has happened to numerous clubs in Italy. Most recently, in 2008, FC Messina, club of a small Sicilian city, was declared bankrupt and disbanded. The club's history began in 1900 and survived depression, migrations, and earthquakes but it was unable to compete financially in *Calcio Moderno*.

Many fans in the United Kingdom (as well as the Ultras of Italy) fear that globalization will render their clubs contentless. As they lose their symbolic connectivity to place and particular fans, clubs become the empty signifiers that are thought (and sought) to generate consumptive desires, but they lose what made them important in the first place.[33] The language of placelessness and contentlessness forms part of the discourse of deterritorialization. It argues that experiences of culture are losing their connectivity to space, time, and place, wherein the local is subsumed by global identities and processes.[34]

---

32   Featherstone, 1995, p. 117.

33   Deleuze and Guattari, 1983, p. 4.

34   Hardt and Negri, 2000, p. xiii.

The decimation of cultural worth occurs as local particularities are replaced by the new postmodern universals: consumption, multicultural identities, psychology, and increasingly, genetics. Behaviors are motivated by, and meanings are sought in, the most ecumenical and bourgeois explanations available.[35] In Europe, the most telling example is the changing relationship of the two clubs of Glasgow Scotland: Celtic FC and Glasgow Rangers FC. As Celtic has begun positioning itself as a 'global club' it has been forced to distance itself from the very thing that has made it an institution in Scotland: its identification with Catholicism; more specifically, Catholicism against the Unionism and Protestantism of its biggest rival Glasgow Rangers FC.

Since the 1880s, Celtic has been an institution amongst Catholic Scottish and Irish soccer fans. It became a symbol of these communities at an early date, after Rangers became the team of choice for Scotland's Protestant majority. Celtic has no prohibition against Protestant players, but until recently it focused on fielding a team entirely of Scottish players. For their part, Rangers enforced an un-written rule of not fielding Catholic players. The first openly Catholic player to sign, and play, for Rangers was Mo Johnston in 1989.

Both clubs, known collectively as the 'Old Firm,' are now actively engaged in fighting sectarianism amongst their fans. Sectarian songs, flag waiving, and aggressively religious support are now banned in both of the clubs' stadiums. Celtic has launched numerous campaigns aimed at calming sectarian passion amongst its fans. One, called 'Youth Against Bigotry,' was an educational initiative for the promotion of respect for 'all races, all colours, all creeds.'

Not coincidently, it is playing in the Champions League that has prompted Rangers to police its supporters. Rangers fans were accused of sectarianism by UEFA after a 2006 match against Spanish club Villareal and the club was ordered to pay a fine as well as to make public address announcements against religious or nationalist singing or display. They were specifically ordered to make announcements prohibiting the singing

---

35 Lipovetsky, 2005, pp. 29–71.

of the song 'Billy Boys,' which honors Billy Fullerton, the leader of a 1930s Protestant gang in Glasgow.

The Ultras and the Spiritual Attack on *Calcio Moderno*

The example of the Glasgow clubs brings us closer to what is driving the Ultras' critique of a globalized, modern, soccer. While the influx of money into the game has made it harder to win without money, it is more so the sterilization and standardization promoted by *Calcio Moderno* on which the Ultras have declared war. Simply put, it is the encroachment of a vision of globalized modernity on the particularities of, in this case, the Ultra (and Roman) form of life. It is, then, a spiritual, rather than economic, issue.

Figure 17. AS Roma's Ultras salute their SS Lazio counterparts, December 2006.

What is at stake for the Ultras is apparent in the shrinking of the earth by televisual technologies. It is apparent when Joseph Maguire explains that the local and the global are more interconnected and interdependent now than in the 1970s, or that the world is 'compressed' via a world economy, global technology, transnationalism, and global division of labor.[36] It is interesting to consider Anthony Giddens' proposal that social relations are now worldwide, revealing multidimensional links between local happenings and universal understandings.[37] However, theorizing such a development cannot prepare us for the force with which universals destroy particularity, nor for how this destruction is experienced.[38]

Just as Italy's economy is deemed 'structurally unsound' and 'uncompetitive' because its productivity is low and production costs are high, so too is its soccer explained by neo-liberals to be 'uncompetitive.'[39] As competitiveness has become a universally valid concept to explain and justify global capital and production flows, it has also become the mantra of the upper-echelon clubs seeking 'global' status and success in the Champions League. When it was reported that the vast majority of Italians support the imposition of some form of quota on the number of foreigners able to be fielded by sporting teams, it was suggested in the English press that this was a 'step back in time.'

The same article explained the folly of the Italian attitude, saying that 'a plan to make all clubs field at least six footballers from their own country, a cap if you like, [is] completely against the laws of the European Union. It would restrict movement, personal freedom and the currents of globalization.' The anonymous author notes that Italy's *Serie A* is still, at this juncture, composed of 64% Italian players. The Ultras think this compares favorably with England's Premier League, which is dominated by foreign players (60%) and coaches (50%). However, the author explains

---

36 Maguire, 1999, pp. 13–14.

37 Giddens, 1990, p. 64.

38 Harvey, 1990, p. 117.

39 'Addio, Dolce Vita: A Survey of Italy' in *The Economist*. Volume 377, Number 8454, Nov 26–Dec 2, 2005, p. 6.

that the predominance of Italian players in Italy is indicative of the country's backward attitude or xenophobia. Without an end to racism and a gain in foreign investment, the article concludes, the Italians will be unable to compete with the English clubs.

But this form of competitiveness is not the concern of the Ultras, except as a corruption of the game. There is no question that AS Roma's Ultras would like to see the team win all of its games in *Serie A* and in Europe. They are, after all, fans of AS Roma. However, the issues that a globalized *Calcio Moderno* celebrates, be it competitiveness due to television contracts, foreign investment, or the creation of 'third cultures' of reterritorialized fans of global clubs, are understood as too damaging to how the game is experienced as an Ultra to have any value.

Under a banner reading '*Non Omologati, Non Omologabili,*' (Unstandardized, Unstandardizable) *AS Roma Ultras* presented their manifesto against *Calcio Moderno* in 1999. It contained much of what is still argued today: that *Calcio Moderno*, as an element of globalization, seeks to render all life in its path standardized, moralized, egalitarian, multicultural, passionless, and consumerist. *AS Roma Ultras* proposed that they coordinate with other Ultras and anyone else to disrupt the televised product of soccer. They suggested that, in order to do so, the Ultras violate every limitation placed on their potential behavior by any authority.

The manifesto explained the future proposed by *Calcio Moderno*. 'Soccer fans must understand,' it begins, 'what is being established by the television industry, FIFA, UEFA, and the various national leagues: the creation of a European championship open only to the biggest clubs on the continent. This is being done for the sole purpose of creating profits for those involved. It is being done with the largest clubs in mind because these are the ones with television followings. Smaller clubs, those without large television audiences, will be sacrificed. The fight is, thus, between the television audience and the local aspects of *calcio* including those at the stadium — which are destined to disappear in the future.'

'The industry of soccer,' the manifesto continues, 'works in conjunction with local authorities, bringing in hundreds of police officers to help subdue those at the stadium. No flags, banners, or songs that may offend anyone in the worldwide audience will be permitted, nor will the voicing of criticisms of society. The future has already been promised to the moderate, standardized fan — those who watch from home and are ready to purchase what is being sold — always a multinational product and never one that is local and artisanal.' It concludes by saying that the industry promoting *Calcio Moderno* misunderstands the Ultras as a fringe that can be eliminated from soccer. 'Instead,' it says, 'the Ultras are a faith, for whom the symbols of their cities and teams are tattooed on their bodies, and for whom their cities are worth defending at all costs.'

CHAPTER NINE

Conclusion

Che importa soffrire se c'è stata nella nostra vita qualche ora immortale

(What does suffering matter if there were some immortal hours in our lives?)

Curva Sud Roma

2007 was marked by the deaths of police officer Filippo Raciti and SS Lazio Ultra Gabriele Sandri. The period between these two deaths, the first in February and the second in November, was tension-filled for the Ultras of AS Roma, as the Italian State took a 'zero tolerance' approach to the Ultras. Despite years of conflict between the Ultras and the State, it was seemingly Raciti's death that exhausted the State's patience with the Ultras and their violent and antagonistic form of life. As the State began implementing laws and policing measures that banned the Ultras' style of fandom from Italian stadiums, the Ultras turned inward, becoming more introspective about 'being Ultras.' The major groups of *Curva Sud Roma* decided to continue attending games of AS Roma in whatever forms the State would permit. If they did so without flags, flares, and bombs, at least they demonstrated that the Ultras themselves were going nowhere. However, after the death of Gabriele Sandri and the night of extreme violence that followed, those same groups began to think more critically about their involvement with the industry of soccer that was determined to rid itself of the Ultras. Thus, the Ultras began a four-week strike period with the protest at Rome's *Circo Massimo* described in the previous chapter, and thus I ended my time amongst the Ultras an exile, imbued with the same defiant *mentalità* and love of Rome that drove the Ultras.

By removing their voices and their passion from the stadium, AS Roma's Ultras were not only seeking to give the State, media, and bourgeois fans a vision of soccer without the Ultras, as was explained above, but were also self-abnegating in an attempt to preserve what is most dear to them. By withholding their performances, they were also preserving the right to be Ultras in the sense that the State was removed from any position of authority over them. In other words, the Ultras decided to remove themselves by their own accord rather than allow the State the power to have them removed. In this way, their silence preserved the integrity of the Ultras phenomenon rather than have it dispossessed by the State.

It was the State's and the Ultras' actions in this period of open hostility that I have tried to explain here. Perhaps oddly, considering the amount of discussion (on both sides) about violence, there was little physical contact between the Ultras and the State during this time. It can be said that one death on each side is a high enough price to pay. However, the lack of physical confrontation made the discourses of violence being employed by the State and the Ultras that much more important. To the greatest extent possible I sought to use statements from the Ultras as empirical data. And, because the Ultras utilize an ethic of violence purposely at odds with the hegemonic aversion to violence in the modern West, I sought to avoid a sort of paralysis in the face of their statements that would be generated by anthropology's own ethical position. An anthropologist who claims complete objectivity and detachment from their subjects is being disingenuous, given the creative act of ethnographic writing. This is especially true when the subjects of study stand outside the bounds of our comfortable notions on violence, morality, and altruistic inclusiveness.

That being said, I have let my subjects 'speak for themselves,' even going so far as to use philosophical and theoretical sources that they themselves use to understand the Ultras phenomenon. In writing this way it made for an interesting slippage between their voices and those of Nietzsche, Evola, and Sorel. Actually, the Ultras of *Boys Roma* and *Antichi Valori*, two of the most influential groups in *Curva Sud Roma*'s history, had made their use of Nietzsche and Sorel clear to me before Raciti's death in February 2007. It was only to become more evident after his death to what extent the other Ultras of *Curva Sud* acted in a way that could be called Nietzschean or Sorelian.

If I may be allowed a slight detour, I would like to provide a few examples of the power of epistemological and conceptual apparatuses to weave what might be called a 'web of morality' through what they make knowable. In the case of Far Right politics and violence, there is almost nothing in the American Academy that will allow for their being studied without condemnation. In choosing methodology and theory, then, I had to circumvent the bureaucratic conceptual and institutional structures that work to delimit intellectual freedom. I needed a way to legitimate fascism by moving it beyond bourgeois liberalism, just as I needed a way to understand violence that did not psychologize the Ultras or attempt to explain it away via socialization.

A common theme in the anthropology of violence is that its adult perpetrators tend to be violent as children.[1] Regardless of how the Ultras might have accorded with such a model, it was irrelevant to the *uses* they put to violence. That violence can also lend itself to courage, strength, and rites of passage is largely lost to current anthropology. To solve these problems, I went to sources that were not only used by the Ultras themselves, but that were also well beyond the proper legitimacy of most anthropological theory.

Indeed, without having done so it would have been impossible to convey the clash of moralities and forms of life definitive of the Ultras and the bourgeois state — a critically important addition to the study of the Ultras (and of Fascism). My political reading of Nietzsche — one that put him, as Fredrick Appel (1999) says, 'contra democracy' — was necessary because it allowed the Ultras' critique of modernity and its impingement of what

---

1   Plesset, 2006; Strathern and Stewart, 2006; Merry, 2009.

they know as their traditions, to flow forth. Similarly, I am unaware of anthropologists having used Evola as a way to understand the uses of history and tradition. Yet, his works on the destruction of valor, strength, and honor — the Roman values — by the forces of modern liberal politics, gave a true sense of what the Ultras despise about globalization and *Calcio Moderno*. Finally, Sorel's theory of 'ethics of violence' allowed me to think and explain the ways in which bourgeois morality could be highlighted as well as contradicted. Once properly embedded with the Ultras, it became difficult not to see a bourgeois fear of violence in almost every human action.

This use of 'native' philosophy and theory took me far beyond our scholarly traditions and normalized interpretative frameworks. Nietzsche and Evola were read alongside the Ultras' own words. By engaging all three together, I found similar criticisms posed to all three — they promote division, discrimination, violence, and a frightening vision of the world from a certain perspective.

Although it has been important since the late-1960s to study not only the physical act of violence but also the 'assaults on personhood, dignity, and value' (i.e. symbolic violence) that come in its wake, the anthropological study of violence is still largely indifferent to discourses and ethics of violence as subjects of study.[2] The 'value' I have given Sorel's 'ethics of anti-bourgeois violence' is inconceivable within the current focus of anthropology on (the victims of) war, terrorism, and gender violence.[3] Likewise, the Nietzschean ideal, taken up by the Ultras, of using violence (and a repudiation of the ethics of benevolence) as a way to create distance between themselves and the modern bourgeois form of life, would be dismissed as 'barbaric and unsustainable' by scholars such as Douglas Fry, recent author of *The Human Potential for Peace*.[4]

And yet, the 'meaningful world' is 'fluid and ambiguous, a mosaic of narratives,' even when those narratives are discomforting to our own bourgeois assumptions about the content of theory and the values of our

2   Scheper-Hughes and Bourgois, 2004, p. 1.

3   Strathern and Stewart, 2006, pp. 1–7.

4   Fry, 2005, p. 168.

research subjects.[5] I have placed ethnographic writing in this context as well, being forced to contend with sources and ideas that are beyond the bourgeois norms of the American Academy. Valentine Daniel explains that violence is difficult to study because it cuts to the heart of objectivity by way of creating victims with whom we readily co-identify. Violence, he explains, is, by nature, 'morally illegitimate'.[6] As an American reader, it is obvious that violence is something of negative value. Daniel himself begins his study of Sri Lankan political violence with a discussion of identity and difference, seeking to place violence within the context of an always-constructed reality. He does so in the hopes of diminishing the vitriolic arguments of essential difference between Tamils and Sinhalas. His role as an anthropologist, then, goes beyond attempting to understand native conceptions of violence, seeking instead to establish the grounds for a cease-fire of sorts.

By understanding the Ultras' justifications for violence, I was forced to acknowledge their awareness of both Sorel and the concept of revolutionary violence. Later, when mild instances of violence occurred in my presence, or in the aftermath of the 2007 killing of Gabriele Sandri, I was able to comprehend both it and the 'imaginative horizons' made knowable by their complex statements on violence.[7] While studies by Crapanzano (2004) and Strathern and Stewart (2006) point to the terror done to 'various intra-personal fields' — including the imagination — of the perpetrators of violence, the Ultras seemed instead fully aware of the implications of their actions and competent in the ways they understood them.

While this in no way is meant to dismiss or demean the victims of 'wife beaters, sexual abusers, and torturers,' it does point to a void in the acceptable subjects of research amongst anthropologists.[8] While Scheper-Hughes and Bourgois invoke Malinowski and his denunciation of the imperial legacy to remind us that we carry a heavy responsibility

---

5   Comaroff and Comaroff, 1992, p. 3.

6   Daniel, 1996, p. 8.

7   Crapanzano, 2004, p. 2.

8   Plesset, 2006; Merry, 2009.

against racism and the 'imperial gaze,' there seems to be less of a concern to unpack the equally culture-specific and epistemological tendency to create victims and be aghast at violent behavior.[9] In other words, there seems to be a lack of critical awareness of our operative bourgeois ethic against violence amongst many scholars working within the anthropology of violence.

I was similarly beyond the limits of the acceptable in my approach to the Ultras' and Romans' political approach to local particularity, having demonstrated the need to understand the native inhabitants of European places in their own terms when it comes to issues of globalization, immigration, and multiculturalism.

I am reminded of a quote attributed to Jean-Marie Le Pen in which he equated Europeans to Native Americans in the contemporary processes of demographic relocation, pointing to a shift in moral/altruistic identification in an argument that usually forces Europeans to defend themselves against charges of racism and xenophobia from those speaking on behalf of non-European immigrants. This study does not assume the Romans to be natives as much as people with something to lose in the process of globalization. Too often, the neo-liberal economic assumption that immigration is a positive force for the West creep into our anthropological studies of the situation, which argue not only that the West has a democratic responsibility to the Third World but also its own demographic opportunity to 'globalize' while maintaining marketplace stability.[10]

To compound the issue, my use of Counter-Enlightenment and radical sources of political philosophy as a challenge to the 'pure reason and enlightened self-interest' found in nineteenth century (Enlightenment) philosophy, certainly moved me beyond the realm of State-sponsored anthropological thought. Nietzsche, Sorel, Evola, and others like Carl Schmitt combined to form a useful critique of modernity and the bourgeois form of life, not only for me but also the Ultras. These thinkers questioned the value of egalitarianism, democracy, the prohibition of violence,

---

9   Scheper-Hughes et al., 2004, p. 7.

10 Vincent, 2002, p. 9.

and a life without (political) enemies. Any such vision amongst modern men and women will not only lead to castigation for noncompliance with our bourgeois multicultural ideals, but also willful incomprehension by those still ensconced within the comforts of the bourgeois form of life.

Indeed, it is in a complex intellectual environment that we must demand to understand those who, like the Ultras, are fighting to celebrate and protect local cultures and traditions. These men and women — among them the European New Right, the more radical elements of the Italian Slow Food movement, and, of course, the nationalist neo-Fascist organizations of Western and Eastern Europe — are unknowable in the terms of the dominant intellectual and conceptual apparatuses of the contemporary bourgeois world. Indeed, this points to the very dear need for a derelict anthropology — one that serves the needs of those on the most radical and critical edges of modernity instead of the States and capitalists that seek the homogenization of human diversity and eradication of extremism.

Additionally, the epistemic situation points to the need of phenomena like the Ultras to present an alternative to the becoming-universal of bourgeois human. While this can only happen in a context created by a coterminous experiential relationship between the human and forms of sociality, those in revolt against the bourgeois human must have the audacity to exist in a parallel/derelict space. For instance, against the truth and morality making functions of the liberal State and capitalist media there is a belief amongst the groups that the children being courted by the industry of soccer to consume the game without aggression will be enamored enough with the Ultras and their form of life that they will reject the bourgeois model. They believe this because the same thing happened to them; and it happened to them because others had stood against the State and the bourgeois form of life.

While we have seen the potential of AS Roma's Ultras to formulate and maintain a radical form of life — one whose violence moves it far beyond the proclivities of bourgeois conservatism — we have yet to either connect them with other Italian Ultras, or fully contemplate what actually *makes* them Ultras. With an eye toward both of these problems, I will conclude

this unique examination of one of the West's most confounding and exhilarating phenomena.

AS Roma's Ultras and Italian Ultras in General

This study is so deeply rooted in the worldview of the AS Roma Ultras
that it might not make sense to Ultras in other Italian cities. The Ultras are
much like the songs they sing. Even though various *curvas* might share the
melodies of popular Italian songs from the Fascist hymn *'Faccetta Nera'* to
Pooh's *'Chi Fermerà la Musica,'* they all change the lyrical content to match
their context. What's more, the *curvas* will also borrow liberally from the
folk songs of their city, such as *Curva Sud Roma*'s singing of popular
Roman songs *'La Società dei Mangaccioni'* and *'La Canzone di Testaccio.'*
Clearly, the content is more important than the melodies borrowed.

There are foundational and elemental characteristics that are shared
by Italian Ultras wherever they are found. Maurizio Stefanini (2009)
has identified these broadly as *identità* (identity), *politica* (politics), and
violenza (violence). Instead, using the language already established in
this study, I identify these broadly as performance or style of fandom,
agonism, and politics. It is with these three groupings that I will place AS
Roma's Ultras in the context of Italian Ultras in general.

Performance

The Ultras' in-stadium performances act as a framing device that demar-
cates the *curvas* they inhabit from the other parts of the stadium. This is
because there is no reason that the other fans do not participate in their
revelry and rivalry — other than that they are not Ultras. It is the songs,
bombs, flares, smoke candles, and flags that separate the Ultras from the
non-Ultras. As we have seen, every *curva* in Italy, at least until the death of
Raciti, was marked by incessant singing, occasional bombs, timely flares
(such as during pre-game rituals like AS Roma fans singing *'Roma Roma,'*
the club's anthem), smoke candles, and constant flag waving.

Bromberger (1993) was one of the first anthropologists to study Ultra
performances. Being a structuralist, he discerned in them an entire cultural

universe of meanings and oppositions. His most vivid case study was the dichotomy between the northern, modern, and efficient FC Juventus of Turin and the southern, pre-modern, and artistic SSC Napoli of Naples. Not only did he contrast the fans and their devotion to either modern rationality (Juventus) or pre-modern superstition and faith (Napoli), but also the playing styles of two teams were said to match the characteristics of the fans.

Figure 18. Game day in *Curva Sud*, 2007.

Instead of a structuralist reading of the Ultras' style of fandom, I probed the rationality of their choices, linking them to the context that propelled them. For the Ultras of AS Roma this meant studying banners and the content of choreographies. It meant, more occasionally, studying the content and history of songs. Armstrong and Young studied soccer chants and songs as 'a collective expression of social and cultural identity' that often takes the form of a new poetry or folklore.[11] Aside from deriding the

---

11   Armstrong et al., 2000, p. 180.

occasional 'racist' content of the songs, the Italian media is fond of refer-
ring to them as a form of folklore. Indeed, I frequently heard the same
Romans of Monteverde who chastised me for involving myself with the
Ultras humming and signing the songs of the *Curva* while they worked.
As Armstrong and Young determined, the songs from the stands become
just as integral to the experience of the game as the play on the field.

In the highly-policed stadiums of 2007–2008, songs were used to
insult or intimidate the opposing Ultras in a way that pre-game fights
or shows of aggression would have done in the past. For the big rivalry
games of AS Roma, *Curva Sud* would spend more than half of a game's
ninety minutes singing against the opponent. In special cases, like the AS
Roma-SSC Napoli game of 2007 (described in Chapter Four), the *curva*
sang against Napoli and Naples for close to the full ninety minutes. For AS
Roma-SS Lazio of that season, the *curva* debuted a new anti-Lazio song;
a reworked version of 'Old MacDonald Had a Farm' called '*O Bastadro
Bianco-Blu*.' The Ultras sang this song for a twenty-minute stretch of the
game. Afterward, Augusto, an SS Lazio Ultra who worked in a Monteverde
pizzeria, told me how incensed Lazio's *Curva Nord* had been by the song
and the length of uninterrupted singing by *Curva Sud*.

For less important games, *Curva Sud Roma*, just like other *curvas*,
might use standardized songs against their opponent. These include stating the opposing city's name and '*vaffanculo*' (go fuck yourself) or stating
'*Odio*' (I hate) and the city's name. Sometimes these became synonymous
with certain cities, like '*Odio Napoli*' or '*Roma Roma Vaffanculo*,' so that
every *curva* would sing them even when not facing SSC Napoli or AS
Roma.

The bombs used by Italian Ultras are usually homemade, or made by a
few people in each *curva* and sold amongst their peers. They take the form
of a pipe bomb although they are made with cardboard and paper. They
are long and skinny tubes filled with blasting powder and have a long
fuse. The flares used in each *curva* are quick burning emergency flares
that are purchased online or in auto supply stores. The smoke candles
are also purchased online and can be procured in a wide variety of colors

(whichever are appropriate to one's team). The point of each of these is to create a spectacle that will shock, awe, and intimidate outsiders. The bombs, flares, and smoke candles, however, were also used as weapons during fights with the police, which is why the State banned them in the wake of Raciti's death.

Each Italian *curva* will also have a measure of flags, representing individual groups, the team, the *curva*, the city, or now the region. In *Curva Sud Roma*, group, team, and city flags dominate, each one predominantly yellow and red, the colors of both AS Roma and Rome. In Milan, one sees flags of the teams (red and black for AC Milan and blue and black for Inter Milan) and the red and white cross of Saint Ambrose, the patron saint of Milan. Amongst other intra-city rivals this is not the case. Neither FC Torino nor FC Juventus display their city's flag. In Genova, only Genoa CFC displays that city's flag, which is identical to Milan's. Because the flag is incorporated into the crest of Genoa CFC, the city's other team UC Sampdoria does not display it during games. In Rome, SS Lazio's Ultras are never seen with the Rome city flag for similar reasons. In *Lega Nord* cities like Verona, Brescia, and Bergamo, that party's flag is often seen in the *curvas*.

Likewise, the materials used in Ultra choreographies are similar from *curva* to *curva*. 8.5" by 11" colored paper or cardboard squares often suffice to turn a *curva* into a backdrop for the message of a choreography, which is usually printed or painted onto large industrial rolls of paper. Designs are discussed and finalized by the group or groups paying for the choreography. Each group would then be responsible for producing their portion of the design, which is either created by the group members themselves or by neighborhood design shops. Perhaps it is an industry driven by Ultra and political activism, but each Roman neighborhood seems to have an abundance of print shops. Certainly, Monteverde has its fair share. It is rare for *curvas* to display choreographies that involve props or materials beyond paper and cardboard.

If the songs, bombs, flares, and flags are the frames by which Ultras are distinguishable from non-Ultras and these are removed, then what remains? If the Ultras are dispossessed of soccer, yet still amass in piazzas are they still Ultras? Stefanini (2009) points to Ultras' style or mode of sociality as the template for radical political actors like the anarchist Black Block and All Whites *(Tutte Bianche)*, yet these cannot be said to be Ultras. On one level this points to the importance of the *mentalità* as it allows an identifiable essence of 'being Ultra.' However, it also leads us to wonder about the future of the Ultras. If they are dispossessed of the stadiums, is remaining together in the form of a movement enough to have any relevance as Ultras?

The importance of soccer to the Ultras must not be underestimated. If the Ultras take their performances out of the stadiums do they still have the same importance or impact? If they amass at Campidoglio and sing hymns to the equestrian statue of Marcus Aurelius or to Castor and Pollex would this suffice? In fact, they have done so, most recently following AS Roma's victory over AC Parma to clinch the 2001 Italian Championship. But this merely underscores the fact that their performances beyond the stadiums are still motivated by momentous AS Roma victories and thus by soccer. It should be clear that I am arguing that the Ultras are far more than their in-stadium performances. In turning now to agonism and politics I will demonstrate why.

Agonism

Just as with performance, I believe that the form of Ultra agonism I explained in Chapter Five to be common to all of Italy's Ultras. It is the content that differs from place to place and *curva* to *curva*. Dal Lago and De Biasi studied the Ultra phenomenon as a single cultural entity, but struggled to find many unifying cultural elements. The one they did identify was a worldview centered on 'war.'[12] It was with this in mind that I identified agon and agonism as the central elements of the Ultras' form of life. Not only does agonism incorporate both the natural, territorial,

---

12   Dal Lago and De Biasi, 1994, p. 85.

soccer-based rivalries of the Ultras, but also and meta-natural rivalries made of the state and the media.

The idea that soccer is interconnected with the political and social contexts in which it is played is common to Italy's Ultras. Although the media and the bourgeois fans of the game are intent to have it be somewhat displaced from the regional and political divisions so important to Italian society and history, the Ultras make of these the very rationale for their involvement with soccer. Just as AS Roma's Ultras have a visceral hatred for the Ultras of SSC Napoli, AC Livorno, Inter and AC Milan, SS Lazio, FC Juventus, Brescia Calcio, and Atalanta BC, these clubs' Ultras return that hatred for AS Roma. Some of these rivalries are local and historical, like SSC Napoli and SS Lazio, and others are more recent and political, like AC Livorno, Brescia Calcio, and Atalanta BC. These latter teams are based in Brescia and Bergamo, two centers of support for the *Lega Nord*. The two Milan-based clubs are hated for different reasons. AC Milan is hated because their Ultras killed AS Roma Ultra Antonio De Falchi in 1989, and Inter Milan is hated because it is a sister club to SS Lazio. Each of these teams has a long-standing political rivalry with AC Milan, which is traditionally a club of the political Left. And so, it continues, until the Ultras make of soccer a web of rivalries and hatreds.

These rivalries are also marked by the current social and political topics of the day, as when UC Sampdoria Ultras wave trash bags at the SSC Napoli supporters on the other side of the stadium in reference to problems in Campania with State-enforced privatization of trash collection. Otherwise, the *'tifare contro,'* or root against, aspect of Ultra agonism will pick up on a local enemy of the team being played. For instance, when AS Roma played at FC Messina in 2006, the AS Roma Ultras sang *'Messinese Sei un Catanese'* (person of Messina you are of Catania) at the Messina crowd, not only playing on Messina's biggest soccer rivals but also Catania's status as the 'Other' of Sicily.

What is distinctive is the content of the altruistic associations with agonism. For each *curva* there will be a concordant 'propter nos,' or people on whose behalf they act. I argue that the purpose of the agonistic form of life is to promote a narrowly defined people or in-group. For *Curva Sud Roma*, that people is obviously Roman. In Brescia, by contrast, it may be limited to Brescia or it might be moving to incorporate the surrounding Lombard region or more fully 'the North.' For certain, though, it does not include Rome and the Romans. Likewise, SSC Napoli's Ultras have an extremely limited range of altruistic co-identification, being restricted to the city itself. I have been told that the other small teams of the Campania region despise SSC Napoli as do the Romans.

In Chapter Six, I explained *Romanità* as a central element of the AS Roma Ultras' worldview. That chapter also addressed the applicability of *Romanità* to *campanilismo*, the form of extreme localism that is still a powerful socializing force in Italy. From the perspective of the Ultra phenomenon in general, *Romanità* is a local Roman form of *campanilismo*. From within the concept's own history, though, it is far more compelling as a political discourse that outweighs the other forms of Italian localism. Nonetheless, the point here is that, while I identified *Romanità* as a crucial part of the experience of AS Roma's Ultras, it would be unknowable to other city's Ultras in the same terms. For instance, whereas AS Roma's Ultras use *Romanità* to attack their *Milanesi* counterparts as the former slaves of Rome, the *Milanesi* would not use their relative status under Roman rule against another *curva*, say that of Vicenza or Venice.

Identifying the media and State as rivals of the Ultras allowed me to consider the political ideologies and the political and social environment of the Ultras in relation to their conceptualization of agonism. It became clear that the Ultras had proper reasons to be hostile toward the media and Italian State, which often went beyond the treatment they themselves received by both. As I found myself deeper in the world of the Ultras I also became more closely affiliated with group leaders on the very Far Right. It was from the leaders of *Boys Roma* and *Antichi Valori*, in particular, that I became aware of the deep moral divide between them and the bourgeois press and State. In time, like them, I began to see the conflict between the Ultras and the media (especially) as a conflict between two competing moralities. This consciousness of morality came from their readings of

Friedrich Nietzsche, who understood morality as the basis not only of peoples but also of millennia.

It is impossible to say if Nietzsche is a popular theoretical influence on other Italian *curvas*, but I can say that the bourgeois modern world he describes, in complete contradistinction to the warrior-based pre-modern forms of life that preceded it, makes sense well beyond *Curva Sud Roma*. In Juventus' *Curva Sud*, for instance, the main groups are *Viking* and *Drughi*. Both groups are of the Right and, while the first is an obvious reference to the Nordic anti-Christian raiders of the Middle Ages, the second is taken from a violent gang in Anthony Burgess' *A Clockwork Orange*.

Aligned with the dominant and Ultra moralities are competing ethics of violence. In Rome, one can see with certainty how Sorel's understanding of violence as a force of change is combined with Nietzsche's understanding of violence as a way to transcend the meddling bourgeois morality of modernity. It thus acts as a tool for understanding the Ultras as a phenomenon outside or beyond the bourgeois form of life. If an American can pass time with AS Roma's Ultras and see Sorel and Nietzsche at work, then it no surprise that both the government and the Ultras believe *Curva Sud Roma* to be the most violent *curva* in Italy. That is not to say, however, that AS Roma's Ultras are the only violent Ultras in Italy: they are all violent to some degree, enough so to produce a cottage industry of books on Ultra violence. I will now turn to the issue of violence, especially as it relates to the conflict between the Ultras and the State.

Violent Politics

In the early years of the Ultra phenomenon, the 1970s and 1980s, it would have been difficult, if not impossible, to describe a single unifying political characteristic of Italian Ultras. While some groups were born of the Left and Right, either from offshoots of the student movement or the postwar Fascist parties, others were apolitical and genuinely benign.[13] Those on the political edges, though, were organized in a time of political extremism

---

13   Foot, 2006, p. 197.

and domestic terrorism perpetrated by both sides of the liberal political divide. Even as the Leftists were weary of State repression and the Fascists were weary of the State in general, neither set of Ultras was known to attack the police as became common in the mid-to-late-1990s.[14] So it is that most scholars who search for the origins of violence between the Ultras and the police begin their surveys between 1994 and 1996.[15]

Although neither Mariottini nor Roversi point to specific instances that triggered the now twenty-year war between the police and the Ultras, relying instead on Leicester School assumptions that the origins of social violence lie in the psyches of the perpetrators, Stefanini lays the blame clearly upon the police. 'Whenever there was the smallest of incidents between Ultras,' he says, 'the police would come on the scene as hard as possible, with batons crashing down upon t-shirt clad soccer fans until all movement in the danger zone ceased'.[16] He goes on to list a series of beatings into states of irreversible coma and even death by the police — deaths that became the organizing principle in Brescia and Perugia, whose *curvas* were re-named after the victims of police brutality. Amongst the victims, he lists thirty-two-year-old Alessandro Spoletini, an Ultra of AS Roma beaten into a coma by police in Bologna in 2001. The following week, he says, AS Roma's Ultras attacked the police on guard at a Champions League game between AS Roma and FC Liverpool.[17] He continues in this way, up through the G8 Summit in Genova 2001, where a *Carabinieri* officer killed Carlo Giuliani. As a result, the Ultras developed what he calls an 'ACAB (All Cops Are Bastards) syndrome,' and began to engage the police before the police engaged them.[18]

I struggled to understand the relationship between the State and the Ultras. As I said above, there was very little violence to speak of between the Ultras and none between the police and Ultras. The Ultras were, in

---

14 Stefanini, 2009, pp. 132–136.

15 Mariottini, 2006; Roversi, 1994; Stefanini, 2009.

16 Stefanini, 2009, p. 132.

17 Stefanini, 2009, p. 135.

18 Stefanini, 2009, pp. 131–134.

my estimation, well policed, in that when they arrived in opposing cities by train they were met with a large contingent of assault rifle wielding *Carabinieri*. When they arrived by car they were often stopped on highways and driven *en masse* with police escort to the stadium. In Rome, the police were visible in large numbers both inside and outside the stadium.

Because of this, I turned my attention to the ethics and discourses of violence being deployed by the Ultras and the State. What became clear is that both the State and the Ultras have a purpose behind their violence. While AS Roma's Ultras, at least at the highest levels of involvement, are committed to using violence as a way to create and maintain distance between themselves and the bourgeois form of life, they do so at the micropolitical level. As a group or *curva*, their violence is an attack on the forces protecting the industry of soccer from those who wish the game to return to its communal roots. It was thus that the Ultras invoked *Calcio Moderno* as a rationale for violence.

Calcio Moderno is the Ultras' moniker for the globalized, deterritorialized, and super-profitable soccer that now defines the game in the industrialized world. 'No al Calcio Moderno' has become a rallying cry for Ultras in all parts of Italy and it is the one example of a unified political agenda or model amongst the Ultras. In Rome, the experience of *Calcio Moderno* — of globalization as a destructive force for soccer clubs and fans — politicized Ultras in ways that moved them far beyond stadiums and the world of soccer. It was also at the core of their ethical aversion to the bourgeois form of life. Again, the details of other *curvas'* involvement with this discourse and agenda are unknown to me. I have, however, perused numerous websites and Facebook pages devoted to a rejection of *Calcio Moderno* and have read words very similar to those I heard in Rome.

Elsewhere, the extreme political actions of the Ultras, like raiding Roma camps, were witnessed in Campania. In one instance an SSC Napoli Ultra was implicated, but never convicted, for taking part in an attack. In Palermo, I saw Ultra graffiti against African immigrants and in Milan I saw Ultra graffiti proclaiming Lombardy a separate nation. Thus, I can assume that Ultra politics take the form of issues that are closest to home.

In Rome, *Calcio Moderno* meant not only a world where money and the global marketplace counted more than the interests of localized Romans, but also a world in which the morality of that marketplace was hegemonic. Multiculturalism, anti-racism, tolerance, immigration, and the American tropes of democracy and freedom were to be resisted as much as foreign ownership of soccer clubs. In Rome and in *Curva Sud Roma*'s Rightist Ultras, one also finds a long tradition of Extreme Right politics. I cannot say if *Forza Nuova, Fiamma Tricolore,* and *CasaPound Italia* are as popular elsewhere in Italy as they are in Rome — or at least amongst Rome's Ultras. But in Rome, as I was told by a Leftist *Fedayn* Ultra, 'Fascism is in the air one breathes, and in the cobblestones that we walk [upon]. Almost every building is Fascist and even the monuments to the "real Romans" are Fascist.' It was the normalcy of Fascism in Rome, at least amongst the Ultras, which I hope to have made clear in the previous chapters.

Returning to the violence of the State, above I used the work of Giorgio Agamben to explain the 'state of exception' that defines the State's interaction with the Ultras. These exceptional states, or states of emergency, are always militarized and place a high value on State security at the expense of individual liberties. I also used Max Weber's template of State monopoly of the legitimate use of violence to explain how the rather inconsequential violence of the Ultras can be construed to be a threat to the State. These theorists, combined with Schmitt, Wolf, and Gramsci, helped me see how the bourgeois ethics and morality of the State are legitimized and disseminated by the liberal press. Against all this, I described the Ultras as inhabiting what Deleuze and Guattari call a 'derelict space,' beyond the hegemony of the bourgeois form of life. Interestingly, Stefanini described the Ultras' *curvas* as 'Indian reservations, or spaces where the sovereignty of Italy does not reach'.[19]

---

19   Stefanini, 2009, p. 127.

Regardless of city or region, the relationship between the Italian State and the Ultras is the same. The Italian media makes it clear that violence amongst soccer fans in any form would not be tolerated by the State. Regardless of the fascists in Rome's *curvas*, as both AS Roma's and SS Lazio's Ultras are dominated by the Far Right, or the Communists in AC Livorno's *Curva Nord*, the State with its troops of *Carabinieri*, and the media with its ability to define, signaled after the death of Raciti that the derelict spaces or Indian reservations would no longer be allowed to exist.

The Future of the Ultras

In Chapter Four I asked the question, as I did above, what will become of the Ultras if they are dispossessed of their role in Italian soccer. Returning to AS Roma's Ultras, it is difficult to say. There are three discernable possibilities, each of which is problematic from the perspective of the Ultras.

One, the Ultras are hoping that a change of regime will loosen some of the restrictions put in place by the government of Romano Prodi and since strengthened by the Berlusconi government. This seems unlikely, as having virtually banned away-game travel and effectively banned Ultra in-stadium traditions, the State has finally rid itself of a large part of its problems with the Ultras.

Two, there is a strong enough political consciousness among the Rightist Ultras that an Ultra-based social movement might be possible. However, as I wondered above, how relevant would being an Ultra be to a social movement if soccer were removed from the equation? Fascist Ultras already mirror the earliest manifestations of the Fascist movement begun by Mussolini in 1919. The *Fasci Italiani di Combattimento* (The Italian Fighting League) was a small group of *arditi* (Italian infantry storm troopers), Futurists, and anti-communist agitators that violently engaged communist and pacifist organizers in and around Milan.[20] The Rightist Ultras share the same passion for anti-liberal politics, *squadrismo* (political action in the form of fascist bands), and a similar ethic of violence and

---

20 Farrell, 2003, pp. 97–103.

critique of modern morality. It seems unlikely in any case that the Ultras, as Ultras, would seek a role in parliamentary politics, as so much of their critique of modernity rests on a critique of the liberalism at its foundation.

Three, the Ultras have an inordinate amount of faith in their *mentalità* and form of life as a viable alternative to the bourgeois form of life and its consumerist pleasures. It is possible that they could maintain the *mentalità* outside the stadiums with little damage occurring to either its forcefulness or relevance. Similar to Slow Food, the movement for a return to Italian culinary habits and traditions in the face of the Americanization of local cuisines and eating practices, the Ultras offer a passionate critique of the changes to traditional life being demanded by globalized free-market capitalism. Resisting globalization, much as it is resisted in the developing world,[21] may be, in my view, their most productive and sustainable option. However, it presupposes a high level of commitment to the political aspects of being an Ultra that a large number of Ultras reject.

There is a fourth possibility: that the Ultras will be policed out of existence. Based on my experience, the current generation of Ultras is defiant enough that the State will be forced to kill far more Ultras than the public is willing to accept in order to make them extinct. I am convinced that in the immediate future the Ultras will continue to wait and to play a game of cat and mouse with the State. 'Think' said Federico of *Antichi Valori* and *Romulae Genti*, 'of how many governments we have seen come and go in Italy, just since I entered *Curva Sud* in 1995 [there have been ten governments since 1995]. Think of how many seasons we have seen, how many players and coaches come and go. Through it all there has been *Curva Sud Roma.*' Although Federico ignored the internal strife within the *Curva* during that same period, his point was made nonetheless. With stadiums in growing disrepair (according to the Italian Football Federation [FIGC]), attendances dwindling, the number of low-priced foreign players rising, and the hegemony of soccer as a television commodity, the Ultras are the one constant in Italian soccer.

---

21   Falk, 1999, pp. 1–27; Prempeh, 2006, pp. 14–39.

Each of these scenarios is based on the Ultras being stripped of their ability to perform in soccer stadiums. Because I propose that what is essential about the Ultras is their commitment to their *mentalità*, which entails a particular critique of modernity and the bourgeois form of life, I believe that they can continue to exist in some form after the stadiums are closed to them. As said *CUCS* founder Stefano Malfatti at the *Circo Massimo*, 'one is born an Ultra and one dies an Ultra.' Having stripped away the frame of stadium performances, Malfatti answers the question posed above. Not surprisingly, as he was one of the first to use the term, the '*mentalità Ultras*' remains when the stadium disappears. However, and it is a perhaps fitting conclusion to this project, if that occurs, and the Ultras are in fact dispossessed of their experience of soccer, what they will lose is the joy of being an Ultra. Rivalry and hostility will remain, but the unbridled thrill of an AS Roma goal or victory will be lost. In the end, if the Ultras are able to move beyond the relative safety of the stadiums and into a more active engagement with political extremism, the State may wish it had allowed them their fights, flares, bombs, songs, and flags. That the State fails to do so points instead to another of this project's conclusions, that the war against the Ultras is ultimately a war against their worldview and critique of modernity. As said Andrews and Ritzer, cultural forms that are 'generally indigenously conceived, controlled, and comparatively rich in distinctive substantive content are a virtual impossibility' in the realm of global capitalism.[22]

---

22   Andrews and Ritzer, 2007, p. 41.

AFTERWORD

Hated and Proud

17 January 2018

> Voi non potrete mai eliminarci, perché noi siamo un sogno,
> un emozione ... noi siamo la libertà![1]
>
> *Curva Sud Roma*

Ten years ago today, my wife and I left Rome at the conclusion of the fieldwork that produced this book. It was one of the darkest days of my life, preceded by weeks of dread; as well as anger and frustration at being unable to enter *Curva Sud* one last time. Although we didn't get to properly say goodbye to so many friends and *camerate*, enough of them knew of our departure to bring me to sobbing tears through their messages of gratitude and support. I remember so vividly, waiting hand-in-hand with my wife in a Fiumicino airport lounge, reading and responding to texts proclaiming me — and us — a valuable part of what, in our minds, is one of the most beautiful brotherhoods that the modern West has produced. I remember the barista who prepared us one last *caffè* for the road, the beautiful chatter of the language in which I had come to dream, and the view of the majestic pines ringing the expanse of the airport. And when one of the messages

---

1 'You will never get rid of us because we are a dream, an emotion ... we are freedom!'

spoke to me of being a 'true Roman,' I remember breaking down in one of the only true fits of despair of my life, as well as my wife's tender consoling embrace as I shuffled like a death row inmate to our departure gate.

There is something wonderfully disjointed in the toothy greeting one usually gets when boarding an America-bound plane, as if the crew has taken on the 'Wherever I stand is America' attitude of an infantryman in Afghanistan (but without his solemn and ferocious dignity), and on this day I found in the contrast between the smiling, overly helpful, overtly American stewardess and my own anguished Roman pathos an affront to whatever nobility I felt my life had acquired in our time in Rome. In my silent, expressionless response to her ebullience I only wanted to convey, 'I don't belong in such a small space with anyone so happy to be leaving Rome … for Atlanta.'

As we settled into our seats, I retreated to my noise-cancelling headphones so as to enjoy my misery in solitude. I wasn't alone for long, though, as, somehow, Thom Yorke of all people, broke through my calcifying cocoon. As 'Nude' from Radiohead's *In Rainbows* wafted into my ears, I began to relax and to embrace the moment for all the potentials it was blasting into my life. For we hadn't even backed away from our departure gate and yet the distance that now separated us from the world to which we were returning couldn't have been any starker. Just being in such close quarters with all the good people on board made me defiant, and all the anxiety that had built up to this moment surrendered to my renewed resolve to never, ever, live so happy to 'broaden my horizons through travel,' or to read 'all the news that is fit to print,' or to 'think outside the box,' or to take comfort in anything that made these people happy, justified, secure, hopeful, proud, sensical, or even sensible. Normal modern people of any shape, color, or creed, were no longer my people. I was bringing my enemies home with me. I was happy again.

I knew I had to write the dissertation and finish school, but beyond that, and even why I was doing that, I could make no one any promises. The Academy had become less an aspiration than a rebuke of my aspirations. An ascetic approach to knowledge and to life was no longer in the cards — I was far more concerned with what I could *do* than with what I could *know*. In other words, I understood as we prepared for takeoff that I could never be an 'expert' on, or even an advocate of, the Ultras, the Romans, or the *Romanità* I had come to know and love. And this was all the Academy would ever allow: me as a middle-aged talking head, explaining multicultural Rome and its 'invented traditions' to a handful of disinterested teenagers — a caged wolf fighting a losing battle against the ease of satiation when being fed on a schedule, dreaming of what I once was, and stockpiling *ressentiment* as I waited either to die a shameful death or to become a hand grenade.

Instead I wanted to continue to live as an Ultra, as one of the 'last rebels,' a derelict space in the heart of the West, a radical, unrepentant, proud, and aggressive outcast. When we reached Atlanta, I was steeled for what is normally called 'culture shock' but what is more like the revulsion an alimentary canal feels for salmonella infused chicken: I thought of Nietzsche hugging the neck of the horse in Turin, despairing and desperate in the face of so much power and vulgarity. (Encounters with rabble-strewn representatives of the State in Italy instead always seemed to inspire an image of a Viking band entering a sleeping monastery.)

When we reached our abode — after all, one never goes *home* again — my wife and I both realized that something was irretrievably left behind in Rome: namely the people we were when we arrived there in 2006. What had we done in this space back then? Dressed up to go shopping?!? Dressed up to go to fine restaurants?!? Watched TV?!? Watched AS Roma games on TV?!? How? How did this add up to a life? We were beside ourselves. How had we been so docile? How had we been so mediocre for so long and not known it? Where was the aggression, the transgression, the *squadrismo*, the dynamism? We were thinking like Ultras and Romans.

My new goal became to find like-minded people in America, even if, at the time, I was pretty-well convinced that they didn't exist. Pretty soon though, I began to get an inkling that something was afoot. I found something of which I should have long been a part: hardcore and punk music. Hardcore (and its aggressive anti-social DIY message) became the blaring, jarring soundtrack to my seemingly endless writing sessions, although for editing I turned to the abstraction of glitch-based computer music. I also found Traditionalism and neo-paganism; and after finding *Tyr* on Amazon.com, I met Josh Buckley, who introduced me to Greg Johnson and John Morgan. The pieces of a radical, dynamic, dissident life were beginning to come together.

It was through *Tyr* and the world of ideas in which it is situated that I began to make better use of Evola and his understanding of Roman paganism; although no one impacted my thinking — or life — as much as Nietzsche. To have known Nietzsche as a philosopher among other philosophers and critical theoreticians left me as he does many other students: bemused, amused, and rather unimpressed. But to have been forced to return to him in Rome, amongst an aggressive, virile, cadre of 'free spirits,' was the most momentous event of my intellectual life. With Nietzsche I had a weapon, a way to understand the 'Yes' and 'No' of the Ultras and the modern West; a way to appreciate the physiological dimension of language, truth, and political position; a way to explain degeneration and the distance between the Ultras and the normal Romans; and a way to facilitate my own becoming-Ultra: in finding happiness where others find their downfall: in harshness, in trials, in self-overcoming all of the mediocrities that had made my life so useful to our enemies.[2]

Many now know of the journey that ensued, and of my travels to and from the farthest reaches of American dissident life: from the blinding rays of the dawning Right, to the soothing traces of the setting Left, both pushed me on to attempt a true transvaluation of what I so enthusiastically and repetitively call the bourgeois form of life. The highlights of the journey have been the birth of my son — and what my wife and I have attempted to create through him — and what became of a rather innocent suggestion by Greg Johnson that I return to the philosophy of Gilles Deleuze and Félix Guattari in order to see what value they might have for the extreme dissident Right. What I learned is that Nietzschean

---

2   Nietzsche, 2005, p. 59

transvaluation cannot mean merely a transvaluation of *what* our enemies think, but also and more importantly *how* they think; I learned that the State and Capitalism must be integral to our analyses of our enemies; and I learned that counter ontology and epistemology only have limited value if they remain separated from a counter ontography and epistemography.

Just after making this leap with Deleuze and Guattari — after what amounted to attacking the overly clichéd and lazy explanatory models of the Left and the Right, as well as my own putrid, slavish, fascistic analyses and judgements — I was contacted by a man named Hugh Maguire, a veteran of America's Iraqi regime change, and the most dangerous man I've ever had the pleasure of knowing. Maguire had been impressed by my essays on physiology and violence — the ideas for which began to take shape during my time in Rome — but when we began our correspondence and friendship, I was in the first stages of becoming unable to explain anything without using Deleuzian concepts: an affliction found amongst most, if not all, 'Deleuze scholars.'

Instead of chafing at my ham-handed use of theory, though, Maguire would ask for a definition, say of the 'territorialization of desire flows' by which we become conscious, thinking, acting expressions of a form of life — each with a rhythmic and dynamic relation to apparatuses of power and counter-power. In more cases than I can remember, Maguire would then say something like, 'Oh yeah, we do that in the Army, only we call it canalizing: we restrict people's options for movement by funneling them through terrain or obstacles that we control. It's the same thing the State does with infrastructure, or that Capitalism does with marketing.'

And just like that we would be on our way to completely reterritorializing Deleuze into a new terrain that has yet to be captured or controlled. Now, instead of contemplating and thinking to create abstract, static, and formal manifesto-ready truths with which to judge and condemn life that fails to conform to our vision, we attempted to make thinking a part of a larger revolt of incessant movement, aggressive struggle, and speed against the staid, docile, and pedantic nature of the slavish men who attempted to control both our enemies and our friends. We began to move away from the Right; but instead of going back to the Left, we created and traversed as many *nec plus ultras* between us and bourgeois politics as we could. Eventually we stopped trying to explain why people do things because we no longer cared what they do. As Hugh once said to me, 'The wolf pack cares nothing about the cleanliness of the shearing shed.'

Thus, my life became the actual living of a counter-form of life: at first very Ultra, very Roman, and then more focused on what was happening right here and now: which in the end was far more Roman than most people could realize. Ken Gemes once said that Nietzsche is a 'local rather than global' thinker because what he condemns or affirms is only ever a particular case: sometimes History, for example, might seek to emasculate and enslave; at other times it might seek to strengthen and liberate: its only value is the use-value of each of its expressions.[3] What can I do with what is at hand right now?

And so, 'right now' prompted my wife and I to find strengthening and liberatory forces closer to home. Rome began to fade into memory, and mercifully I found some peace in that, as we turned north to Southern Appalachia and the enthralling frontier it still offers. Ultras gave way to mountain homesteaders, moonshiners, and bushwhackers. America gave way to the tenuous hold that the shibboleths of the State have on the violent and dangerous fringes of its subject-citizenry. And the South became home for the first time in my adult life.

Because of my extreme-liberal political positions, the South was always something I was in, but not of (or so I thought). When we moved north to Ohio and New York to attend a few graduate schools, I not only remained hostile to my roots, but was given immense approval for doing so; at least during my Black Studies years. Anthropology, to its credit, never seemed to care, but by then, we were all assumed to be very much the same liberal humanist cattle. And even in Rome, it was far easier to tell people we were from New York than to try to explain our nomadic

---

3   Gemes, 'Nietzsche on the Will to Truth, the Scientific Sprit, Free Will, and Genuine Selfhood' in Gudrun von Tevenar (ed.) *Nietzsche and Ethics* (Bern: Peter Lang, 2007), p. 27

odyssey from the South. Then in 2007 my paternal grandmother died, and because I couldn't return to America for the funeral, I wrote an open letter for someone to read on my behalf. While doing so I came to realize how closely my family had always lived to the values and ideals with which my wife and I had fallen in love in Rome — and in the name of Rome; my Nanny, especially.

For her there was no joy that was too small to be shared, no travail too burdensome to embrace, and no beauty too difficult to appreciate — as long as one's surname is Dyal. Just like our Roman friends, my grandmother had no use for a universalized conception of altruistic grace. As has become clear to many, it does not matter that one might exclude by race and another by culture — and yet another by family or behavior — the type of liberalism under which we are now living cannot tolerate *any* exclusionary logic employed by our people — unless of course, it is used to exclude us.

The principle of exclusion functioned on a local level in most non-State forms of life as a way to ensure exogamy, the proper delineation of social and religious spheres within the included group, and the maintenance of the distances required between peoples to induce warfare. But as Pierre Clastres explains, for the extremely war-like Indians of the Amazon, the necessary 'outside' of the included group is not always a mortal enemy, but nonetheless forms the crucial partner in a violent dance that envelopes the shared boundaries of a larger territory in some form of perpetual warfare; a warfare that wards off both the accumulation of an overarching and universalizing power, and also the type of acquiescence to State power that comes with final victory.[4]

In place of a principle of exclusion, though, the State mandates a *right* of exclusion that is implemented at the level of the Law and imposed on its subjects just as much as its enemies. For the sake of simplification, let's say that the ability to exclude, full stop, has been taken from the people and the local communities that the people create on a daily basis, and

---

4   Clastres, *Society Against the State*, translated by Robert Hurley, New York: Zone Books, 1987, pp. 60–64.

given to State sponsored pillars — not of our communities, but of multi-national corporations and their political and cultural lackeys; and be they in commutations, finance, retailing, or education, they all preach the same moralized logic of near universal inclusion that serves their interests as profiteers. And as this logic has hardened into totalitarianism, the only exclusion permitted is of people like the Ultras — and ourselves — who refuse to bow down to the intellectual disarmament now being demanded of all Western subjects, just so, as we will see, they can do something as innocuous as watch a game of soccer: and so a perusal of Internet articles written by good, loyal, safe, sure, secure, sound, consumers that comment on the Ultras will show a patterned logic that celebrates both the use of fabulatory community symbols — soccer teams — as corporate profit-machines, and the aggressive policing and exclusion of those who offer a radical critique of what is happening to our lives.

And what is happening is doubly problematic for the Ultras. Firstly, as this study has shown, the Ultras are actively involved in the fabulation, or active creation, of a community that is based on shared commitments to *Romanità*; an aggressive celebration of having, and being, an enemy; and a brotherhood born only of these shared commitments and experiences; so much so that they refuse to unite with other Ultras and will only tolerate other groups in their own curva. But, unlike the State, they will tolerate them. They will allow space for dissent and disorganization. It might not always be pretty, and it is often violent, but *Curva Sud Roma* will allow a person or group to bring whatever they want into the *Curva*, asking only that one be willing to fight for it, and for Rome and AS Roma. And secondly, to that end, the State demands that it be the arbiter of what a community is, thinking only in demographic and socio-economic terms, making it the abstract counterpoint to active fabulation.

The Ultras demonstrate what has long been apparent in Italy, and that which constitutes its lesson for the rest of the West: The State is an imposition by a particular type of human life and made for a particular purpose. It is the enemy of local autonomy. It is the enemy of collective, communal organization. It is the enemy of a type of strength that is smothered by the State's homogenizing economic utilitarian needs. Its enemies are to be your enemies; its need for order is to be your freedom; its need for bodies to feed as laborers to capitalism is to be your culture; and its right to violence is to be your right to obey.

But, like the Romans, my grandmother was inclined to stand defiantly opposed to any harsh judgement by outsiders. It didn't take too much effort to connect her life — and our inherited traditions — to a larger Southern context. But whereas those traditions had always been easy for me to question, — perhaps I was born either a good Anthropologist or a bad Leftist because I was never comfortable condemning that which I knew little, or nothing, about — in Rome I was a visitor, and what's more I had forgotten to pack the bag containing my trusty American academic conceptual tool box through which the world is condemned for either being racist, classist, or sexist; or more likely, all three. Whatever was going on in Rome amongst the Ultras, I was certainly not going to get to the bottom of it by focusing on race, class, or gender; although as I've said elsewhere, the Ultras made the decision for me: what I didn't say is how thankful to them I am for having done so.

I will admit to being genuinely taken aback by the lack of guilt or shame that I found amongst the Ultras, their friends, and families. In many ways, their freedom to live the joys, travails, and beauties of *Romanità* with nothing to corrupt their affects, liberated me from the confusion and self-mortification that had dominated my academic life to that point. I remember being schooled in 'political symbols as floating signifiers' by a middle-aged woman selling Ultras' gear in a shop in Rome. One item was a patch of the Confederate battle flag but stitched in the yellow and red colors of Rome. I asked her somewhat incredulously, 'What is this?' To which she explained, first, that the colors were those of Rome and AS Roma; second, that the symbol is a symbol of the South; third, that the South is the home of AS Roma's Ultras — as in *Curva Sud*; and fourth, that the South is also a term of resistance to Northern economic and social policy, just as it is in America. 'We are,' as she said, '*Sudisti:*' of the South.

Figure 19. AS Roma Ultrà at the Stadio San Siro, his scarf reads:
'I hope that God strikes you all with lightning,' Milan, 2007.

As she began speaking I immediately felt stupid for having asked, but as she continued, and connected Curva Sud to southern Italy and its struggle since the creation of the Italian State to maintain its own values and traditions, I was overjoyed that I had asked. For how could I have hoped to understand anything I encountered in Rome if I had been content to go by the prejudices that I had lived — and loved — in America? Imagine that: I first came to appreciate the Confederate battle flag in Rome, both as a minor symbol of *Curva Sud* and as a broader symbol of Southern Italy's defiance of Northern neoliberalism; and now back in Georgia I get to point reverently to a symbol that inspires so much hatred and devotion, but for reasons that would be foreign even to those who know me well.

Meanwhile, *Curva Sud Roma* continued to fight against the multicultural and neoliberal morality regime that was being imposed upon the Italian populace. The strike that was in effect when we departed in January, 2008 lasted 3 more weeks. We returned to Rome in May of that year to witness AS Roma's *Coppa Italia* triumph over Inter Milan. Although we got to visit the River Bar and to embrace some of our friends before the game, we watched the match while roving along the lower level of Tribuna Tevere: a long-standing haunt of the most violent Ultras during big rivalry games because it allows access to opposing Ultras. Because we had season tickets until the summer of 2009, we returned to Rome for several more games, unwilling and unable to give up on the life that we had begun creating there, to say nothing of the danger and dynamism that we had come to crave.

Ever since the death of Raciti, the State had become far more vociferous in its attacks on the Ultras. Many of these have been outlined in the previous chapters, but the ones that left the deepest impression in the subsequent years were those that infringed not upon the pageantry of the *Curva* but its very freedom. These had begun with the seemingly simple demand that the Ultras notify the police by fax machine of their desire to carry a banner into the stadium, so that it may either be approved or prohibited. By now, of course, the Ultras were fully aware that the battle was not against soccer-related violence but against their voices as critics of *Calcio Moderno* and the abasement of Italian life in general. The State, then, was seen as merely trying to provoke the Ultras into abandoning the curvas and leaving the business of soccer free to make its profits, and the political class and media free to force Italians to submit to the needs of neoliberalism and what the Ultras always called turbo-capitalism.

In response, however, the Ultras merely stopped bringing banners into the stadium, as much as an affront to their sense of defiant freedom as this was. There were a few, however, such as the group that consistently managed to bring in a crude banner saying only, 'No Fax;' or the other brave souls who brought in a larger one to Roma's 2007 game against AC Milan explaining that their fax machine was broken. The latter's sense of humor, panache, and defiance was applauded throughout Italy, and it felt similar to the spirit of the 'Odio Napoli' game later that year (described in Chapter Four).

An uneasy status quo eventually returned to the Curva, even after the polemics in the wake of the violence following Sandri's killing. A government minister would proclaim this or that prohibited, and yet invariably one curva or another would be seen reveling in whatever had just been outlawed. It was a merely a new terrain to traverse, some new struggle to endure for the sake of AS Roma, Rome, and the *Curva*. But then in 2009, Roberto Maroni, Minister of the Interior, announced the creation of a new identification system called the *Tessera del Tifoso*.[5]

The *Tessera* would be required by anyone wishing to buy a season ticket, but also anyone seeking to attend an away game. On the face of it, the *Tessera* is merely an identification card. In theory, this is little different from the named tickets that were required during my fieldwork period. However, as the weeks and months went by, it became clear not only that the *Tessera* was going to be implemented for the 2010–2011 season, but that it would be — and is — more than a mere identificatory device. In order to be issued one, a police background check must be passed, prohibiting anyone with a history of sports-related violence or with another arrestable anti-social offense. In effect, this amounts to a lifetime ban from soccer stadiums, regardless of the original terms of one's sentence. If one is decent enough to pass the police interrogation, they may then be issued the passport and be proclaimed an 'official' fan of one's club.

---

5   Fan's Passport.

What they must then do is link the *Tessera* to a bank account complete with an individual fiscal code (equivalent to the US's Social Security Number) and a photograph. It is the linking of the card to a bank account that raised Ultras' collective eyebrows. Why, they and many others asked, were soccer fans being forced to open or maintain bank accounts just to watch soccer games? Why were soccer fans being forced to deposit money in banks that had very recently expropriated billions of dollars and euros in austerity measures and 'misappropriation' forgiveness? The answer is unsurprising if also a bit audacious: fans that maintain good behavior records — including the buying of many tickets — receive points that may be redeemed for discounts at official club stores when the fan pays using the *Tessera*. Eradicating violence, the Italian State seemed to understand, went hand in hand with increasing personal debt through consumption. It is as if Maroni was reading Maurizio Lazzarato's works on how neoliberalism rules by increasing debt and by linking ideas of optimal individual behavior to those of financial responsibility and finding some perverted destructive power therein.[6]

To its credit, AS Roma listened to the indignant howls coming from its least favorite fans, and attempted to side step the *Tessera*, especially after the realization that the microchip implanted in the card was to share personal data between the police/surveillance apparatus and the banks. Nonetheless the government made clear that the passport was mandatory, and it remains so today, albeit in slightly modified form.

When it was implemented, *Curva Sud Roma*, of course, refused to cooperate, citing its own exalted role as a theater of freedom in Rome, Italy, Europe, and the World; although the issue, like most with the *Curva*, was contested, and some chose to accept the terms of the *Tessera* in order to attend games, while others, like *Boys Roma*, chose to stay away (if only for a short protest). Several of the groups that had been integral to the *Curva* of 2006–2008, like *Ultras Romani* and *Padroni di Casa*, disbanded as a result of the *Tessera's* implementation or soon thereafter, leaving *Fedayn* and

---

6   Lazzarato, *The Making of the Indebted Man*, Los Angeles: Semiotexte, 2012; and *Governing by Debt*, Los Angeles: Semiotexte, 2015.

Boys Roma as the only remaining large groups of the *Curva*. For their part, many of those who chose to continue attending games cited Maroni's, and by extension the State's, desire to rid the stadiums of the undesirables: 'If Maroni wants me out,' they said, 'I'm going in.' Although some went in, season ticket sales plummeted as the *Tessera* became the norm, bottoming out at 16,000 in 2011–2012.[7]

Eventually attendance stabilized, topping 27,000 for the 2014–2015 season, as the Ultras begrudgingly accepted the price of their collective ticket. Or perhaps they were all just anxious to get another chance to create a Roma-Napoli game of epic proportions. On May 3, 2014, at the end of the 2013–2014 season, Napoli played against Fiorentina in the *Coppa Italia* Final in Rome. Before that game could commence, though, there were clashes near the stadium between AS Roma Ultras and their Neapolitan counterparts.

As game time approached, word was circulating that a Napoli fan had been shot during an ambush. Napoli Ultras were understandably furious, pelting the field with anything at hand and making menacing gestures at the police who were hastily filling the stadium. Eventually, however, the Ultras calmed as Marek Hamsik, captain of the Napoli soccer team, met with one of the Ultra leaders. They came to an agreement, and the game was played. 'But wait!' the television commentators were exclaiming, 'What the hell did we just witness?!?' As I said, one of the leaders of the Napoli Ultras gave his approval for the game to be played, and it was played: not the Police Prefect, the Minister of the Interior, or even the Prime Minister, but a lowly Ultra.

This situation was not unique. In 2004, the Lazio-Roma derby had been suspended at halftime under similar circumstances. Rumors spread throughout the stadium that the police had killed a child before the game, and by halftime both curvas were boiling with rage. Francesco Totti, the venerable Roma captain, came below *Curva Sud* and met with Ultra leaders who demanded the game be suspended. He gave the message to other players and officials and the game was canceled. By then, though,

---

7   The capacity of Rome's *Stadio Olimpico* is 72,698.

the rumor had proven to be just that. So, what was actually happening? Perhaps nothing more, but the message eventually became that the Ultras stopped the game as a demonstration of fan power: that the fans are more important and powerful than the profiteering and homogenizing forces of *Calcio Moderno*.

During the Napoli-Fiorentina game, images of the Napoli Ultra were as ubiquitous as the Napoli players. Focus immediately settled on the message printed on his black t-shirt: 'Speziale Libero:' Free Speziale, in other words, Antonino Speziale, the Rightist Catania Ultra imprisoned for killing Filippo Raciti. Within hours, the police and the world knew the Ultra's name: Gennaro de Tommaso, and we were told that he had already been given a five-year ban from entering a soccer stadium — not for his role in getting the match played (much to the benefit of the advertisers) but for wearing an offensive t-shirt.

'Speziale Libero,' though, quickly became but a footnote as details of the shooting emerged. The victim was Ciro Esposito, a car washer from a poor Neapolitan neighborhood. Evidently, he and other Napoli fans riding in a bus near the stadium had been ambushed by a group of AS Roma Ultras, a fight ensued, and the Roma Ultras retreated. In doing so, however, they were overrun by the Napolitani. One of the Romans pulled a gun and fired, hitting Esposito, as he was swarmed and severely beaten. The shooter's name was Daniele De Santis and he quickly stole the show from de Tommaso and Speziale. De Santis was in fact a longtime AS Roma Ultra, and a notorious one at that.

When Francesco Totti had met with Ultra leaders during the suspended derby, one of them had been De Santis. And not only that, after having been a member of *Tradizione e Distinzione*, one of the *Curva*'s most legendary Rightist Ultra groups, he had helped Giuliano Castellino create the now disbanded *Padroni di Casa*, noteworthy for its former connections to *CasaPound Italia*. For his part, De Santis lived the life of a devoted fascist, being active in demonstrations and various punitive expeditions against Leftists.

So, as the dust was settling on the 2013–2014 soccer season, we had a Napoli fan shot by a fascist Ultra of AS Roma, and a Napoli Ultra banned for five-years for wearing a shirt asking for freedom for the Catania Ultra convicted of killing Filippo Raciti. Ciro Esposito eventually died from his wounds, and De Santis was sentenced to sixteen years of prison. But the story didn't end there. For *Curva Sud Roma*, it was just getting started.

Three days after the ill-fated *Coppa Italia* final, Roma hosted Juventus. The *Curva*, however, was in no mood to celebrate, but instead chose to begin the match with thirty minutes of silence in protest of the weeks' worth of sensational moralizing against soccer violence, hatred, regionalism, parochialism, fascism, and anything else that could be used to tarnish the Ultras. When the thirty minutes had passed, the *Curva* gave its enemies exactly what it wanted: songs and banners in defense of De Santis. It was the last home game of the season. Thoughts were already on the next season's games against Napoli.

The first of those games was in Naples and it came and went without incidence, besides the expected banners against *Curva Sud Roma* and Rome. One read, 'Every word is in vain: if the opportunity presents itself, there will be no mercy.' Romans were forbidden from traveling to the game, as the Napolitani would be later in the season for the game in Rome. In the meantime, however, another chapter to the *Coppa Italia* story had been written, literally. Antonella Leardi, the mother of Ciro Esposito, had written a book about her son, and had become a minor celebrity appearing on talk shows to promote her book and vilify the Ultras. The *Curva* reacted as one would expect: with derisive horror that a mother would seek to profit from the death of her son. Banners were unfurled throughout the *Curva* during the long-awaited home game against Napoli: 'How sad. You make money off the funeral from books and interviews;' 'There is one who mourns a son with pain and morals, and one who makes of it a business without dignity. Honor to you Mrs. De Falchi;'[8] and 'After the book, the film.'

---

8   Antonio De Falchi was an AS Roma Ultra killed by AC Milan Ultras in 1989.

After the Roma-Juventus game the previous May James Pallota, chairman of the AS Roma board, had condemned the *Curva*'s support of De Santis as a 'defeat for civil society,' but chose to make the issue one of security rather than immorality, as he was in the process of organizing financial and political support for a new, state of the art multipurpose stadium through which to maximize his profits.

As I previously mentioned, AS Roma was purchased by a group of American investors in 2011. Whereas *Calcio Moderno* had always been a guiding, ethical narrative for the Ultras, its effects were largely felt as abstractions in Rome. It was seen in the general trends pushing soccer to become a televisual advertising-based event, with little regard for local communities of supporters, but it was always possible to see AS Roma, at the very least, as an unwilling partner in the process — paying its star players as well as comparable players in other, wealthier, teams and leagues — but always teetering on the edge of bankruptcy to do so. When Bologna FC faced being purchased by Americans in 2008, none of the Ultras seemed to care as Bologna's Ultras are amongst the most bitter enemies of *Curva Sud*. (The animosity stems from 1996, when the Bolognese named members of Boys Roma to the police after the Romans were seen attacking North African drug dealers after a game in Bologna. Henceforth the Bolognese have been considered by *Curva Sud* to be spies and servants of the State.) But now AS Roma was to be in the hands of men who admitted to buying the club only to profit from its fans, players, colors, and emblems.

At first the takeover seemed tolerable enough given the unstable situation of the club. After all, a Roma in American hands is better than no Roma at all.[9] Thomas DiBenedetto, the head of the consortium that bought the club, was a likable enough man. He was part of the group of American finance capitalists that owns England's Liverpool FC, and had been vocal in explaining the need to understand and utilize world

---

9   In the past decade alone, financial insolvency has forced several teams, such as Parma, Verona, Venezia, Messina, and Bologna to restructure and restart from the lowest divisions of Italian soccer.

renowned soccer clubs as multinational brands at the time of that club's takeover. But he seemed genuinely impressed, and perhaps overwhelmed, by the emotional nature of the Roman support for AS Roma; and oversaw very little change with the club, as its finances had to be sorted out after the takeover. Once all was in line, however, DiBenedetto handed the club's chairmanship to billionaire James Pallotta, part of the group ownership of the NBA's Boston Celtics; but where DiBenedetto had been grandfatherly, Pallotta was downright rapacious in his quest to turn AS Roma into a cash machine. He quickly announced a series of deals with Disney and Nike to begin in 2014 that were designed to increase the 'brand's' visibility in America and the world. To that end, he oversaw the redesigning of the club's beloved shield/crest, simplifying its image so that it would better reproduce on merchandise.

And now Pallotta was watching helplessly as his plans of plunder in the name of Roma were being held ransom by perhaps the only entity that saw itself worthy of such a fight. It must be said that *Curva Sud Roma* is extremely savvy in its use of the media to spread as well as facilitate its agenda. In Rome from 2006 to 2008, I got a very good sense of how the Ultras used the press to spread awareness of themselves, but perhaps I overlooked how well the Ultras actively manipulated their enemies through the press. The 2007 'Odio Napoli' game is a perfect example. Given the climate at the time, and the incessant baying of the media for a soccer without Ultras, the *Curva* could have silenced itself as a portent of what that would mean (much as they did after Sandri's killing). Instead of giving the media what it said it wanted, however, the Ultras gave it what it *really* wanted: another week's worth of denigrating the racist, violent, fascist Ultras. Looking back, singing 'Odio Napoli' for ninety-minutes was exactly what the Ultras had wanted to do, and certainly even more so because of how much it disturbed the media — which then, from the Ultras' perspective, got to show itself an active agent in the spreading he- gemony of neoliberal multiculturalism. It was, then, a double win, as they stood against the moral force of the strongest nations and corporations on Earth, and then got to be excoriated by the very people — and *types* of people — they despised.

Likewise, the cheers and banners in support of De Santis, which had at once been a chance to support one their own — and at any rate a Roman being castigated in all of Italy at the expense of Naples — but had also outed the temper of James Pallotta. For his part, Pallotta seemed to know and to enjoy his notoriety amongst the Ultras. From America it was hard to watch, seeing the arrogant billionaire talking about AS Roma as if it were just numbers on an account balance. From Rome it must have looked the same, especially as Pallotta became more and more adamant that Roma be highly profitable as a leader in Calcio Moderno.

Perhaps just as the Ultras expected, Pallotta lost his cool after the banners were displayed criticizing Antonella Leardi as a hypocritical profiteer. On the radio following the game, Pallotta railed against the Ultras:

> We are incredibly frustrated and disappointed in some of the actions. We just don't really have the power in the stadium to stop all of this. We did take away some of the banners — whatever banners that we did see outside before the game, our stewards did — but at the end of the day, the security inside have to choose to take action and we don't control that security inside. But in spite of that, it's just not fair for all of our fans to be tarnished by a few fucking idiots and assholes that hang out in the *Curva Sud*. And I'm sure that the vast majority of Roma supporters are sick and tired of these fools, and it's up to all of us together — not just in Rome but in Italy — to put an end to their antics. It's time we put an end to their antics. We are doing a lot of good things with "Roma Cares" against bullying and violence and racism, and we'll continue to do that and we're working very hard at this, sometimes fairly quietly. I am pledging right now $1 million to "Roma Cares" to continue to combat this bullshit that's going on in Rome by a few, and in Italy by a few. And I'm hoping that we get others to contribute for educational programs to stop all of this crap.

A morning later, those entering AS Roma's headquarters in Trigoria were greeted to a banner written in English: 'This fucking idiot gonna pay you mother fucker.' The Ultras had accepted the challenge. How much they were prepared to fight became apparent later in the day, when the *Curva* released a response to Pallotta's moralistic rant:

When your father was just born, we were at Campo Testaccio for any random Roma-Dominante game, and when there was still no trace of you in your father's balls, we were in Turin for a Roma-Milan that sealed our only relegation. At the time that you were excited by your Boston Celtics, we were drawing 2–2 against Atalanta thanks to Pruzzo, while later — as you cheered for a tip-in — we were celebrating *our* Roma-Torino and crying for *our* Roma-Liverpool. At the age of fifty-three you became owner of *our* Roma and the first thing you did was modify the 1927 club shield, making many wonderful promises that we believed, albeit with the wary eye of a Roman.

Meanwhile, in every stadium, we Roma fans were insulted with chants and banners that we never complained about, because it's part of soccer, which is not a sport with a basket and a Jumbotron telling the audience when and how to applaud. Yet you allowed yourself to call 14,000 fans "fucking idiots" and refused to look after those who paid you in advance, instead playing the game of the New Millennium Moralists (journalists, impartial observers, and various types of Leagues) who have only ever criticized Roma and its supporters. This is why we are angry with you, James, and this is why out of solidarity with the *Curva Sud* we too will stay outside the stadium for Roma-Atalanta. We invite all the real Giallorossi fans to do the same. It's better to be fucking idiots than fucked idiots.

— Fucking Idiots ASR

In this statement, the Ultras expressed the most important things that I had come to know of them. They inserted themselves into the history of Rome and AS Roma and claimed stewardship of the latter by virtue of their embodying the virtues of the former: by having had the courage and thirst not only to celebrate the great victories but also to suffer the most painful defeats as Romans; and they identified the forces aligned against them as having been brought together by a particular form of morality attached to multiculturalism and general modern slavishness. What's more, they understood that, while their season tickets had already contributed to Pallotta's ever-present balance sheet, the potential walk-up sales for the game had not. If one wants to hurt a greedy billionaire, the way to do so is through his wallet.

As if on cue Pallotta responded to the *Curva*'s statement and attempted to wrap a bow on the whole affair. He did so in the most slavish and cowardly way available to modern man: he went on Facebook and announced that 'True fans don't make racist comments and they don't make violent situations.' Throughout Italy a deafening yawn was heard all the way from Piazza San Sepolcro to Magna Graecia, while in the middle schools of America teachers demanded that some children stand with a defiant fist in the air, while others were forced instead to bow their heads in shame.

When the 2015–2016 season began, the Ultras entered *Curva Sud* to find an eight-foot tall barrier splitting the section into two smaller sections. It had been erected over the summer by Franco Gabrielli, Rome's Police Prefect, after a revelation he had while watching one of the previous season's derbies: the curvas are overcrowded and thus dangerous. Although there was no data offered that supported his fears of danger, the barriers remained. During the first home game of the season, the Ultras seemed to be in shock, but soon recovered to announce a strike that would last until the barriers came down.

One of the first statements made by the Ultras explained that they did not want to be away from their *Curva*, but that they would not enter until it was no longer a captive space, and until they could do so 'freely, and not like trained puppies.' It was a telling simile for fans used to identifying with wolves, and one that, once again, pointed to the domesticated, docile, emasculated, scared, and obedient nature of modern men. And it was one that pointed to the importance of understanding the *Curva*, and all Italian *curvas*, as derelict spaces: largely outside the domain of popular morality and dominant (State) power. If the curvas only seem to be derelict to the Ultras, then so be it, for these spaces only have use-value and are created on the spot and through a gathering of the specific forces at hand. In this light, the barriers were a line of State power cut straight into the heart of the *Curva*. In turn, the Ultras took the imposition and eventually flipped its power in their favor—forcing Pallotta's hand by refusing to enter the stadium.

When pressed on the issue of the barriers, which even seemed to confuse the media, Gabrielli stated that they had been erected so as to ease the stadium's surveillance apparatus in identifying perpetrators of illegality in the stadium. For his part Pallotta said very little, except that, as he did not own the stadium, it was not up to him what security measures were installed. His tune would change, however, but not until after a full season of empty seats began to affect his bottom line. High profile game after high profile game passed by, with AS Roma playing in a near empty stadium in almost total silence.

The Ultras refused to budge, but continually chafed at the situation. It didn't take long for them to stop attacking Gabrielli and to start attacking Pallotta: the occasion was the season's first derby, and both curvas (*Curva Sud Roma* and *Curva Nord Lazio*) united to strengthen the strike against the barriers. Roma's Ultras addressed Pallotta with another press release, saying that they 'had abandoned the stands due to the absurd impositions' that they would never accept. Addressing Pallotta, they said, 'You will never take away our dignity in cheering on our team freely and with the honesty of saying how things really are. Now it's up to you, the club, and whoever else is complicit in this travesty, to prove to everyone your good faith, and above all that you don't want to cancel forever the word passion from what has always been the fulcrum of the AS Roma support: the Curva Sud.' 'No one can buy us,' they concluded, 'because we are not for sale!'

The freedom that the Ultras so often trumpet stems from the idea that they are the conscience of the club. They've earned both their freedom and that conscience through the different types of struggle outlined in this study. It is the Ultras who brave enemy attacks in order to support Rome and AS Roma, and it is the Ultras who do so with no restitution beyond the glory, honor, and respect that their actions command. If the rest of Italy and the world are indifferent or hostile to their form of life and fandom, then so be it, but, as an Ultra said in a recent Espresso expose on the power of the Far Right in *Curva Sud Roma*, this is only a confirmation that glory, honor, and respect have been outlawed in the contemporary West, and therefore only exist in the *curvas*.[10]

---

10 http://espresso.repubblica.it/attualita/2015/05/04/news/la-marcia-sulla-roma-degli-ultra-neofascisti-1.210470, accessed January 2018.

Beyond the empty stadium, the Ultras continued to act as Ultras, and protested the poor form of the team by dumping over 100 pounds of carrots outside the team's Trigoria training center with the message, 'Enjoy your meal, rabbits.' They took the occasion to call for wider numbers of Roma fans to boycott the team's games, so as to force Pallotta's hand on the barriers. 'Pallotta,' they said, 'comes to Rome to pick up the checks generated by the club's participation in the Champions League [the emblem of *Calcio Moderno*] and then leaves.' The players and coaches continue to get paid their salaries even as they perform 'without dignity, without fighting, without sweating, and without love' for the team and city.' The Ultras were done.

The barriers stayed up until April, 2017. The Ultras stayed away for an entire season, except for one game: the final home game of the club's greatest captain and icon: Francesco Totti. But the walls hadn't come down on Totti's behalf, nor the Ultras'; for just as the Ultras understood, it was never to be an issue of respect for the city, its people, its traditions, or its heroes, but instead, of desire for the only thing that unites all of the States of the West: profits. Finally, Pallotta had had enough of the barriers because the empty stadium looked bad on television, and thus, were bad for AS Roma and its financial sponsors. He spoke up, and the barriers came down.

The Ultras of both AS Roma and SS Lazio returned to the stadium for the 2017–2018 season. And while things have been relatively quiet in Curva Sud Roma, with the new norm being the running attack on James Pallotta, *Curva Nord Lazio* must have decided that they were tired of their *Stadio Olimpico* counterparts hogging all of the glory. Because their own *curva* was closed due to 'racist chants' during their October 2017 match against Sassuolo, they were allowed to attend the team's subsequent home game against Cagliari, but only in *Curva Sud*. After that game it was discovered that the Lazio Ultras had left a few gifts in *Curva Sud* for their longtime rivals: a plethora of stickers of Anne Frank proudly wearing an AS Roma jersey. The prank referred to *Curva Nord Lazio*'s contention that

Roma is a Jewish, and thus, Leftist team, given the common narrative of its origins as the people's team during the Fascist years.

As much as one could say about the situation, everything that need be said has already been said by ESPN:

> Anne Frank's diary will be read aloud at all matches in Italy this week, the Italian football federation announced on Tuesday after shocking displays of anti-Semitism by fans of Lazio. Lazio supporters on Sunday littered the *Stadio Olimpico* in Rome with images of Anne Frank — the young diarist who died in the Holocaust — wearing a jersey of city rival Roma. A faction of Lazio ultras associates their Roma counterparts with being Left-wing and Jewish, and had hoped to incite Roma fans, since the teams share the same stadium.

> Stadium cleaners found the anti-Semitic stickers on Monday and Italian police have opened a criminal inquiry into the case. The Anne Frank diary passage reading will be combined with a minute of silence observed before *Serie A*, *B* and *C* matches in Italy this week, plus amateur and youth games over the weekend, to promote Holocaust remembrance, the federation said. The chosen Anne Frank diary passage reads: "I see the world being slowly transformed into a wilderness, I hear the approaching thunder that, one day, will destroy us too, I feel the suffering of millions. And yet, when I look up at the sky, I somehow feel that everything will change for the better, that this cruelty too shall end, that peace and tranquility will return once more." Racism has been widespread for years in many Italian and European stadiums — targeting both players and fans — and measures such as banning fans and forcing teams to play behind closed doors have not solved the problem.

> Outrage over the stickers came from a wide variety of officials and rights groups across Europe, from both inside and outside the world of sports. "Anne Frank doesn't represent a people or an ethnic group. We are all Anne Frank when faced with the unthinkable," Italian Foreign Minister Angelino Alfano said. "What has happened is inconceivable." Italian Premier Paolo Gentiloni called the stickers "unbelievable, unacceptable and not to be minimized." Antonio Tajani, the head of the European Parliament who is Italian, also denounced those responsible, saying in Brussels that anti-Semitism has no place in Europe, which must remain a place of religious tolerance. "Using the image of Anne Frank as an insult against others is a very grave matter," Tajani said.

> The Italian Football Federation will also likely open an investigation, which could result in a complete stadium ban for Lazio or force the team to play on neutral ground. "There are no justifications. These incidents must be met with

disapproval, without any ifs, ands or buts," Sports Minister Luca Lotti said. "I'm sure that the responsible authorities will shed light on what happened and that those responsible will quickly be identified and punished." Lazio's Ultra group expressed surprise at the widespread outrage. "There are other cases that we feel should lead the newscasts and fill newspaper pages," the group said in a statement on Facebook.

Lazio president Claudio Lotito sought on Tuesday to disassociate the club from its Ultras by visiting Rome's main synagogue. He said the club would intensify its efforts to combat racism and anti-Semitism and organize an annual trip to the Auschwitz concentration camp with some 200 young Lazio fans to "educate them not to forget."

Speaking at a synagogue in Rome, Lotito told reporters: "Lazio have always launched initiatives against any form of racism, which is why we disassociate ourselves from all of this. The absolute majority of Lazio fans are anti-racist and against any form of anti-Semitism. I am here to express out total disassociation to any form of xenophobia, racism and anti-Semitism. The majority of our fans share our position. Lazio will promote, annually, an initiative which will see 200 children make a trip to Auschwitz to allow these children to see and understand what we are talking about."

Still, the club's relations with Rome's Jewish community remained strained. "We are outraged by what happened in the stadium a few days ago. But we are also outraged by what happens every week in the stadiums," Ruth Dureghello, the president of Rome's Jewish community, told The Associated Press. "Stadiums cannot be places that are beyond the law and places where anti-Semitist, racist and homophobic people can find a place to show themselves," Dureghello said. "We need to sit down around a table and talk to the institutions, the teams and the federation, to enforce actions and establish a common line for the future."

The northern end of the stadium where Lazio's ultras usually sit was already closed on Sunday for the match against Cagliari, because of racist chanting during a match against Sassuolo earlier this month. As a result, Lazio decided to open the southern end and let the Ultras sit where Roma's hardcore fans usually sit for their home matches.

Lazio fans have a long history of racism and anti-Semitism. The latest partial stadium ban for the team stemmed from derogatory chants directed at Sassuolo players Claud Adjapong and Alfred Duncan. Adjapong was born in Italy to Ghanaian parents and has represented Italy under-19s. Duncan is from Ghana. Lazio will also be without fans in the northern end when Udinese visits on Nov. 5 — for racist chanting during the Rome derby in April. Also this season, Lazio beat Belgian team Zulte Waregem in a Europa League match behind closed doors because of punishment from UEFA for racist chants aimed at a Sparta Prague player two seasons ago.

A Lazio banner nearly twenty years ago aimed at Roma supporters read: "Auschwitz Is Your Homeland; The Ovens Are Your Homes." Another message honored the slain Serbian paramilitary leader, Arkan, who was notorious for alleged war crimes in the 1990s Balkans wars.

But racism and anti-Semitism have also been seen at other European clubs, highlighting the ineffectiveness of campaigns by bodies all the way up to UEFA and FIFA.

Last season, Ghana's Sulley Muntari was initially banned for protesting against racism in Italy. Muntari said he was treated like a "criminal" after being shown two yellow cards when he walked off the field during a Serie A game in response to racial abuse while with Pescara.

Four years ago, six fans of Italian lower-division club Pro Patria were issued jail sentences for inciting racial hatred during a friendly against AC Milan.[11]

With that I conclude a project that has been in the making since Daniele De Santis had the 2004 Lazio-Roma game suspended at halftime. It was at that moment that I was truly introduced to *Curva Sud Roma* and given an inkling that it was a radical counter to the type of deterritorialized fan-as-consumer culture of sport through which I had come to know of AS Roma. To my credit, I can honestly say that, while I found AS Roma as a consumer and good liberal subject of the neoliberal West, I found Rome as a becoming-Ultra, armed with a few very good friends, a few very powerful books, and a companion that knows nothing of stasis or debilitating fear. This is my story of a unique moment in the history of *Curva Sud Roma*. It is not intended to be THE story of *Curva Sud Roma*, for even when I was there, this story could have been told a thousand different ways. It just so happened that I lucked into a chance meeting with an Ultra who suggested that, to really appreciate that for which I was looking, I needed to read Nietzsche. I did, and the rest is … up to you.

---

11   http://www.espn.com/soccer/italian-serie-a/story/3241732/anne-franks-diary-to-be-read-at-italian-matches-after-lazio-fans-anti-semitic-display, accessed January 2018.

P.S. 'Peace is just a name. The truth is that every city-state is, by natural law, engaged in perpetual undeclared war with every other city-state.' — Plato[12]

P.S.S. 'The warlike capacity of each community is the condition of its autonomy.' — Pierre Clastres[13]

---

12   Plato quoted in Bernard Knox's Introduction to the Robert Fagles translation of *The Iliad*, New York: Viking, 1990, p. 24.

13   Clastres, *Archeology of Violence*, Los Angeles: Semiotexte, 2010, p. 273.

Bibliography

Agamben, Giorgio, 1998, *Homo Sacer: Sovereign Power and Bare Life.* Translated by Daniel Heller-Roazen. Stanford University Press.

Allum, Percy, and Diamanti, Ilvo, 1996, 'The Antonymous Leagues in the Veneto,' in *Italian Regionalism: History, Identity, and Politics.* Edited by Carl Levy. Oxford: Berg Press.

Allum, Percy, 2000, 'Italian Society Transformed,' In *Italy Since 1945 (Short Oxford History of Italy).* Edited by Patrick McCarthy. Oxford: Oxford University Press.

Andrews, David, L. and Ritzer, George, 2007, 'The Grobal in the Sporting Glocal,' in *Globalization and Sport.* Edited by Giulianotti and Robertson. Malden, MA: Blackwell.

Appel, Fredrick, 1999, *Nietzsche Contra Democracy.* Ithaca, NY: Cornell University Press.

Armstrong, Gary, 1998, *Football Hooligans: Knowing the Score.* Oxford: Berg Press.

Armstrong, Gary, and Young, Malcolm, 1997, 'Legislators and Interpreters: The Law and "Football Hooligans,"' in *Entering the Field: New Perspectives on World Football.* Edited by Gary Armstrong and Richard Giulianotti. Oxford: Berg Press.

Armstrong, Gary, and Young, Malcolm, 2000, 'Fanatical Football Chants: Creating and Controlling the Carnival,' in *Football Cultures: Local Contests, Global Visions.* Edited by Gerry P. T. Finn and Richard Giulianotti. London: Frank Cass.

Bar-On, Tamir, 2007, *Where Have All the Fascists Gone?* Burlington, VT: Ashgate Press.

Barzini, Luigi, 1996, *The Italians: A Full-Length Portrait Featuring Their Manners and Morals.* New York, NY: Touchstone/Simon and Schuster.

Bataille, Georges, 1997, 'The Festival, Or the Transgression of Prohibitions,' in *The Bataille Reader.* Edited by Fred Botting and Scott Wilson. Malden, MA: Blackwell.

Baudrillard, Jean, 1994, *The Illusion of the End.* Translated by Chris Turner. Stanford, CA: Stanford University Press.

Baudrillard, Jean, 2008. *Fatal Strategies.* Translated by Beitchman and Neisluchowski. Los Angeles, CA: Semiotexte.

Berezin, Mabel, 2009, *Illiberal Politics in Neoliberal Times: Culture, Security and Populism in the New Europe.* Cambridge: Cambridge University Press.

Berger, Peter, 1967, *The Sacred Canopy: Elements of a Sociological Theory of Religion.* London: Doubleday.

Bosworth, Richard, 2002, *Mussolini.* London: Bloomsbury.

Bosworth, Richard, 2005, *Mussolini's Italy: Life Under the Fascist Dictatorship, 1915-1945.* New York, NY: Penguin.

Bromberger, Christian, et al, 1993, 'Fireworks and the Ass,' in *The Passion and the Fashion: Football Fandom in the New Europe.* Edited by Steve Redhead. Aldershot: Avesbury.

Brownell, Susan, 1995, *Training the Body for China: Sports in the Moral Order of the People's Republic.* Chicago, IL: University of Chicago Press.

Buckley, Joshua, Cleary, Collin, and Moynihan, Michael, 2002, 'Editorial Preface,' in *TYR: Myth, Culture, Tradition. Volume One.* Atlanta, GA: Ultra Publishing.

Bull, Anna Cento, 2007, *Italian Neofascism: The Strategy of Tension and the Politics of Nonreconciliation.* New York, NY: Berghahn Books.

Cacciari, Patrizio, 2004, *Sud: La Curva Magica.* Rome: Libreria Sportiva Eraclea.

Campbell, John, K., 1964, *Honour, Family, and Patronage: A Study of Institutions and Moral Values in a Greek Mountain Community.* Oxford: Clarendon Press.

Castells, Manuel, 1996, *The Rise of the Network Society, The Information Age: Economy, Society, and Culture, Vol. I.* Cambridge, MA: Blackwell.

Cate, Curtis, 2002, *Friedrich Nietzsche.* Woodstock, NY: The Overlook Press.

Chambers, Samuel, 2001, *Language and Politics: Agonistic Discourse in The West Wing.* Available at: www.ctheory.net/articles.aspx?id=317.

Clastres, Pierre, 1987, *Society Against the State.* Translated by Robert Hurley. New York, NY: Zone Books.

Clastres, Pierre, 2010, *Archeology of Violence.* Los Angeles, CA: Semiotexte.

Cole, Jeffrey, 1997, *The New Racism in Europe: A Sicilian Ethnography.* Cambridge: Cambridge University Press.

Comaroff, John and Jean, 1992, *Ethnography and the Historical Imagination.* Boulder, CO: Westview.

Connolly, William E., 1993, *Political Theory and Modernity.* Ithaca, NY: Cornell University Press.

Cox, Christoph, 1999, *Nietzsche, Naturalism, and Interpretation.* Berkley, CA: University of California Press.

Crapanzano, Vincent, 2004, *Imaginative Horizons: An Essay in Literary-Philosophical Anthropology.* Chicago, IL: University of Chicago Press.

Creed, Gerald, 2011, *Masquerade and Postsocialism.* Bloomington, IN: Indiana University Press.

Crehan, Kate, 2002, *Gramsci, Culture, and Anthropology.* Berkley, CA: University of California Press.

Dal Lago, Alessandro, 1990, *Descizione di Una Battaglia.* Bologna: Il Mullino.

Dal Lago, Alessandro, and De Biasi, Rocco, 1994, 'Italian Football Fans: Culture and Organization,' in *Football, Violence, and Social Identity.* Edited by Giulianotti, Bonney, and Hepworth. London: Routledge.

Danielli, James F., 1980, 'Altruism and the Internal Reward System or The Opium of the People' in *Journal of Social and Biological Sciences.* Vol. 3 No. 2.

Das, Veena, 2007, *Life and Words: Violence and the Descent into the Ordinary.* Berkley, CA: University of California Press.

Davis, John A., 1996, 'Changing Perspectives on Italy's Southern Problem,' In *Italian Regionalism: History, Identity, and Politics.* Edited by Carl Levy. Oxford: Berg Press.

De Benoist, Alain, and Champetier, Charles, 2000, *Manifesto for a European Renaissance*. Translated by Martin Bandelow and Francis Green. Smithville, TX: Runa Raven Press.

De Biasi, Rocco and Lanfranchi, Pierre, 1997, 'The Importance of Difference: Football Identities in Italy,' in *Entering the Field: New Perspectives on World Football*. Edited by Gary Armstrong and Richard Giulianotti. Oxford: Berg Press.

de Certeau, Michel, 1984, *The Practice of Everyday Life*. Translated by Steven Rendall. Berkley, CA: University of California Press.

De Martino, Ernesto, 2005, *The Land of Remorse: A Study of Southern Italian Tarantism*. Translated by Dorothy L. Zinn. London: Free Association.

Deleuze, Gilles and Guattari, Felix, 1983, *Anti-Oedipus: Capitalism and Schizophrenia*. Translated by Hurley, Seem, and Lane. Minneapolis, MN: University of Minnesota Press.

Deleuze, Gilles and Guattari, Felix, 1987, *A Thousand Plateaus: Capitalism and Schizophrenia*. Translated by Brian Massumi. Minneapolis, MN: University of Minnesota Press.

Deleuze, Gilles, 1995, *Negotiations*. Columbia University Press.

Gilles Deleuze, 2006, *Nietzsche and Philosophy*. Translated by Hugh Tomlinson. New York, NY: Columbia University Press.

Duggan, Christopher, 2007, *The Force of Destiny: A History of Italy Since 1796*. New York, NY: Houghton Mifflin.

Dunning, Eric, 1994. 'The Social Roots of Football Hooliganism: A Reply to the Critics of the "Leicester School,"' in *Football, Violence, and Social Identity*. Edited by Richard Giulianotti, Norman Bonney, and Mike Hepworth. London: Routledge.

Dunning, Eric, 1999, *Sport Matters: Sociological Studies of Sport, Violence, and Civilization*. London: Routledge.

Durkheim, Emile, 2001, *The Elementary Forms of Religious Life*. Translated by Carol Cosman. Oxford: Oxford University Press.

Elias, Norbert, 1971, 'The Genesis of Sport as a Sociological Problem,' in *The Sociology of Sport: A Selection of Readings*. Edited by Eric Dunning. London: Frank Cass.

Evans-Pritchard, E.E., 1976, *Witchcraft Oracles, and Magic Among the Azande*. Abridged by Eva Gillies. Oxford: Claredon Paperbacks.

Evola, Julius, 1995, *Revolt Against The Modern World*. Rochester, VT: Inner Traditions.

Evola, Julius, 2002, *Men Among the Ruins: Post-War Reflections of a Radical Traditionalist*. Translated by Guido Stucco. Rochester, VT: Inner Traditions.

Evola, Julius, 2003, *Ride the Tiger: A Survival Manual for the Aristocrats of the Soul*. Translated by Joscelyn Godwin and Constance Fontana. Rochester, VT: Inner Traditions.

Evola, Julius, 2004, 'The Traditional Doctrine of Battle and Victory,' in *TYR: Myth, Culture, Tradition*. Vol. 2, 2003–4. Translated by Annabel Lee. Atlanta, GA: Ultra Press.

Evola, Julius, 2004b, *Imperialismo Pagano, nelle edizioni Italiana e Tedesca*. Rome: Mediterranee.

Evola, Julius, 2007, *Heathen Imperialism*. Translated by Rowan Berkeley. Paris, FR: Thompkins and Cariou.

Evola, Julius, 2008, *Metaphysics of War: Battle, Victory, and Death in the World of Tradition*. Aarhus, Denmark: Integral Tradition Publishing.

Falasca-Zamponi, Simonetta, 1997. *Fascist Spectacle: The Aesthetics of Power in Mussolini's Italy*. Berkley, CA: University of California Press.

Falk, Richard, 1999, *Predatory Globalization: A Critique*. Malden, MA: Blackwell.

Fanon, Frantz, 1967, *Black Skin, White Masks*. Translated by Charles Lee Markmann. New York, NY: Grove Press.

Farrell, Nicholas, 2003, *Mussolini: A New Life*. London: Weidenfeld and Nicolson.

Featherstone, Mike, 1995, *Undoing Culture: Globalization, Postmodernity, and Identity*. London: Sage.

Ferraresi, Franco, 1996, *Threats to Democracy: The Radical Right in Italy After the War*. Princeton, NJ: Princeton University Press.

Finn, Gerry P. T., 1994. 'Football Violence: A Societal Psychological Perspective,' in *Football, Violence, and Social Identity*. Edited by Richard Giulianotti, Norman Bonney, and Mike Hepworth. London: Routledge.

Foot, John, 2006, *Calcio: A History of Italian Football*. London: Fourth Estate Press.

Forsythe, Gary, 2005, *A Critical History of Early Rome: From Prehistory to the First Punic War*. Berkley, CA: University of California Press.

Foucault, Michel, 1970, *The Order of Things: An Archaeology of the Human Sciences*. London: Routledge.

Foucault, Michael, 2000, *Power: Essential Works of Foucault 1954–1984, Volume 3*. Edited by James D. Faubion. New York, NY: The New Press.

Francesio, Giovanni, 2008, *Tifare Contro: Una Storia degli Ultras Italiani*. Milan: Sperling and Kupfer.

Frantzen, Allen, 2004, *Bloody Good: Chivalry, Sacrifice, and the Great War*. Chicago, IL: University of Chicago Press.

Fry, Douglass P., 2005, *The Human Potential for Peace: An Anthropological Challenge to Assumptions about War and Violence*. Oxford: Oxford University Press.

Fugo, Claudio, 2003, *The Historic Imaginary: Politics of History in Fascist Italy*. Toronto: University of Toronto Press.

Garsia, Vincenzo Patanè, 2004, *La Guardia di Una Fede: gli Ultras della Roma Siamo Noi*. Rome: Castelvecchi Editore.

Geertz, Clifford, 1973, *The Interpretation of Cultures*. New York, NY: Basic Books.

Geertz, Clifford, 1983, *Local Knowledge: Further Essays in Interpretive Anthropology*. New York, NY: Basic Books.

Gemes, Ken, 2007, 'Nietzsche on the Will to Truth, the Scientific Sprit, Free Will, and Genuine Selfhood' in Gudrun von Tevenar (ed.) *Nietzsche and Ethics*. Bern: Peter Lang.

Gentile, Emilio, 1996, *The Sacralization of Politics in Fascist Italy*. Translated by Keith Botsford. Cambridge, MA: Harvard University Press.

Gentile, Emilio, 2003, *The Struggle For Modernity: Nationalism, Futurism, and Fascism*. London: Praeger.

Giddens, Anthony, 1990, *The Consequences of Modernity*. Cambridge, MA: Polity Press.

Ginsborg, Paul, 2003a, *A History of Contemporary Italy: Society and Politics 1943–1988*. New York, NY: Palgrave Macmillan.

Ginsborg, Paul, 2003b, *Italy and Its Discontents: Family, Civil Society, State: 1980–2001*. New York, NY: Palgrave.

Ginzburg, Carlo, 1980, *The Cheese and the Worms*. Translated by John and Anne Tedeschi. Baltimore, MD: Johns Hopkins University Press.

Ginzburg, Carlo, and Poni, Carlo, 1991, 'The Name of the Game: Unequal Exchange and the Historical Marketplace' in *Microhistory and the Lost Peoples of Europe: Selections from Quaderni Storici*. Baltimore, MD: Johns Hopkins University Press.

Giulianotti, Richard, and Williams, John, 1994, 'Introduction: Stillborn in the USA?' in *Game Without Frontiers: Football, Identity, and Modernity*. Edited by Giulianotti and Williams. Aldershot: Arena.

Giulianotti, Richard, and Armstrong, Gary, 1997, 'Introduction: Reclaiming the Game — An Introduction to the Anthropology of Football,' in *Entering the Field: New Perspectives on World Football*. Edited by Gary Armstrong and Richard Giulianotti. Oxford: Berg Press.

Gregor, A. James, 1999, *Phoenix: Fascism in Our Time*. New Brunswick, NJ: Transaction Publishers.

Gregor, A. James, 2001, *Giovanni Gentile: Philosopher of Fascism*. New Brunswick, NJ: Transaction Publishers.

Gregor, A. James, 2005, *Mussolini's Intellectuals: Fascist Social and Political Thought*. Princeton, NJ: Princeton University Press.

Griffin, Roger, 2007, *Modernism and Fascism: The Sense of Beginning Under Mussolini and Hitler*. New York, NY: Palgrave Macmillan.

Guttman, Allen, 1981, 'Sports Spectators from Antiquity to the Renaissance,' in *Journal of Sport History*, vol. 8 no. 2 (Summer, 1981), pp. 5–23.

Guttmann, Allen, 1986, *Sports Spectators*. New York, NY: Columbia University Press.

Hallyn, Fernand, 1990, *The Poetic Structure of the World: Copernicus and Kepler*. Translated by Donald M. Leslie. New York, NY: Zone Books.

Hansen, H.T., 2002, 'Julius Evola's Political Endeavors,' in *Men Among the Ruins: Post-War Reflections of a Radical Traditionalist*. Translated by Guido Stucco. Rochester, VT: Inner Traditions.

Hardt, Michael, and Negri, Antonio, 2000, *Empire*. Cambridge, MA: Harvard University Press.

Hastrup, Kirsten, 1995, 'The Inarticulate Mind: The Place of Awareness in Social Action' in *Questions of Consciousness*. Edited by Cohen and Rapport. London: Routledge.

Heidegger, Martin, 1977, *The Question Concerning Technology and Other Essays*. Trans. W. Lovitt. New York, NY: Harper and Row.

Herzfeld, Michael, 1982, *Ours Once More: Folklore, Ideology, and the Making of Modern Greece*. Austin, TX: University of Texas Press.

Herzfeld, Michael, 1985, *The Poetics of Manhood: Contest and Identity in a Cretan Mountain Village*. Princeton, NJ: Princeton University Press.

Herzfeld, Michael, 1987, *Anthropology Through the Looking-Glass: Critical Ethnography in the Margins of Europe*. Cambridge: Cambridge University Press.

Herzfeld, Michael, 2009, *Evicted from Eternity: The Restructuring of Modern Rome*. Chicago, IL: University of Chicago Press.

Hoberman, John M, 1984, *Sport and Political Ideology*. Austin, TX: University of Texas Press.

Hobsbawm, Eric and Ranger, Terence, eds., 1992, *The Invention of Tradition*. Cambridge: Canto.

Holmes, Douglas R., 2000, *Integral Europe: Fast-Capitalism, Multiculturalism, Neofascism*. Princeton, NJ: Princeton University Press.

Honig, Bonnie, 1993, *Political Theory and the Displacement of Politics*. Ithaca, NY: Cornell University Press.

Inserto Polizia Moderna n.9, 2002, Centro Nazionale di Informazione sulle Manifestazioni Sportive.

Johnson, Dirk R., 2010, *Nietzsche's Anti-Darwinism*. Cambridge: Cambridge University Press.

Kertzer, David I. 1988, *Ritual, Politics, and Power*. New Haven, CT: Yale University Press.

Kertzer, David I, 1996, *Politics and Symbols: The Italian Communist Party and the Fall of Communism*. New Haven, CT: Yale University Press.

Knudson, Are, 2009, *Violence and Belonging: Land, Love, and Lethal Conflict in the North-West Frontier Province in Pakistan*. Copenhagen: NIAS.

Koon, Tracy H., 1985, *Believe, Obey, Fight: Political Socialization of Youth in Fascist Italy, 1922–1945*. Chapel Hill, NC: University of North Carolina Press.

Kroskrity, Paul V., 2000, *Regimes of Language: Ideologies, Politics, and Identities*. Edited by Paul Kroskrity. Santa Fe, NM: School of American Research Press.

LaFeber, Walter, 2002, *Michael Jordan and the New Global Capitalism*. New York, NY: WW Norton.

Lazzarato, Maurizio, 2012, *The Making of the Indebted Man*. Los Angeles, CA: Semiotexte.

Lazzarato, Maurizio, 2015, *Governing by Debt*. Los Angeles, CA: Semiotexte.

Leed, Eric J, 1979, *No Man's Land: Combat and Identity in World War I*. Cambridge: Cambridge University Press.

Levi-Strauss, Claude, 1990, *The Naked Man: Mythologiques Vol 4*. Translated by Weightman and Weightman. Chicago, IL: University of Chicago Press.

Lieberman, Philip, 1991, *Uniquely Human: The Evolution of Speech, Thought, and Selfless Behavior*. Cambridge, MA: Harvard University Press.

Lipovetsky, Gilles, 2005, *Hypermodern Times*. Translated by Andrew Brown. Cambridge: Polity Press.

Livy, Titus, 2002, *The Early History of Rome: Books I-V of The History of Rome from its Foundations*. Translated by Aubrey De Selincourt. New York, NY: Penguin Classics.

Lofland, John, 2005, *Analyzing Social Settings: A Guide to Qualitative Observation and Analysis*. New York, NY: Wadsworth.

Lyttleton, Adrian, 2004, *The Seizure of Power: Fascism in Italy 1919–1929* (Third Edition). London: Routledge.

Lyotard, Jean-Francois, 1999, *The Postmodern Condition: A Report on Knowledge*. Translated by Bennington and Massumi. Minneapolis, MN: University of Minnesota Press.

MacDonald, Kevin, 2002, *The Culture of Critique: An Evolutionary Analysis of Jewish Involvement in Twentieth-Century Intellectual and Political Movements*. Bloomington, IN: First Books Library.

Maguire, Joseph, 1999, *Global Sport: Identities, Societies, Civilizations*. Cambridge: Polity.

Malinowski, Bronislaw, 1992, *Magic, Science, and Religion, and Other Essays*. New York, NY: Waveland Press.

Mariottini, Diego, 2006, *Ultraviolenza: Storie del Sangue del Tifo Italiano*. Turin: Bradipo Libri.

Markovits, Andrei S., and Hellerman, Steven L., 2001, *Offside: Soccer and American Exceptionalism*. Princeton, NJ: Princeton University Press.

Martin, Simon, 2004, *Football and Fascism: The National Game Under Mussolini*. Oxford: Berg Press.

Massumi, Brian, 1992, *A User's Guide to Capitalism and Schizophrenia: Deviations from Deleuze and Guattari*. Cambridge, MA: The MIT Press.

McGill, Craig, 2001, *Football Inc.: How Soccer Fans are Losing the Game*. London: Vision.

Merry, Sally E., 2009, *Gender Violence: A Cultural Perspective*. Malden, MA: Wiley-Blackwell.

Moe, Nelson, 2002, *The View from Vesuvius: Italian Culture and the Southern Question*. Berkley, CA: University of California Press.

Mouffe, Chantal, 2005, *On The Political*. New York, NY: Routledge.

Murphy, Patrick, Williams, John, Dunning, Eric, 1990, 'Why Are There No Equivalents of Soccer Hooliganism in the United States?' in *Football on Trial: Spectator Violence and Development in the Football World*. New York, NY: Routledge.

Mussolini, Benito, 1976, *The Political and Social Doctrine of Fascism*. Translated by Jane Soames. New York, NY: Gordon Press.

Naylor, Thomas, 2007, 'Cipherspace,' in *TYR: Myth, Culture, Tradition*. Vol. 3, 2007. Atlanta, GA: Ultra.

Nietzsche, Friedrich, 1977, *La Gaia Scienza e Idilli di Messina*. Milan: Adelphi.

Nietzsche, Friedrich, 1995, *Thus Spoke Zarathustra*. Translated by Walter Kaufmann. New York, NY: The Modern Library.

Nietzsche, Friedrich, 1997a, *Daybreak: Thoughts on the Prejudices of Morality*. Translated by RJ Hollingdale. Cambridge: Cambridge University Press.

Nietzsche, Friedrich, 1997b, *Untimely Meditations*. Translated by RJ Hollingdale. Cambridge: Cambridge University Press.

Nietzsche, Friedrich, 2001, *The Gay Science*. Translated by Josefine Nauckhoff. Cambridge: Cambridge University Press.

Nietzsche, Friedrich, 2002, *Beyond Good and Evil*. Translated by Judith Norman. Cambridge: Cambridge University Press.

Nietzsche, Friedrich, 2003, *Writings from the Late Notebooks*. Translated by Kate Sturge. Cambridge: Cambridge University Press.

Nietzsche, Friedrich, 2003a, *Cosi` Parlo` Zarathustra*. Translated by Mazzino Montinari. Milan: Adelphi.

Nietzsche, Friedrich, 2004, *On the Future of Our Educational Institutions*. Translated by Michael Grenke. South Bend, IN: St. Augustine's Press.

Nietzsche, Friedrich, 2005, *The Anti-Christ, Ecce Homo, Twilight of the Idols, And Other Writings*. Translated by Judith Norman. Cambridge: Cambridge University Press.

Nietzsche, Friedrich, 2006, *Thus Spoke Zarathustra*. Translated by Adrian Del Caro. Cambridge: Cambridge University Press.

Nietzsche, Friedrich, 2007, *On The Genealogy of Morality*. Edited by Keith Ansell-Pearson. Translated by Carol Diethe. Cambridge: Cambridge University Press.

Nini, Alessandro, 2007, *Una Questione di Cuore*. Published by the Author.

Nugent, David, ed., 2002, *Locating Capitalism in Time and Place*. Stanford, CA: Stanford University Press.

O'Meara, Michael, 2004, *New Culture, New Right: Anti-Liberalism in Postmodern Europe*. Bloomington, IN: First Books.

Painter, Jr., Borden W., 2005, *Mussolini's Rome: Rebuilding the Eternal City*. New York, NY: Palgrave MacMillan.

Parks, Tim, 2002, *A Season With Verona: Travels Around Italy in Search of Illusion, National Character, and Goals*. London: Secker and Warburg.

Pedregal, Antonio Miguel Nogues, 1996, 'Tourism and Self-Consciousness in a South Spanish Coastal Community,' in *Coping with Tourists: European Reactions to Mass Tourism*. Edited by Jeremy Boissevain. Providence, RI: Berghahn Books.

Peristiany, John G., ed., 1965, *Honour and Shame: The Values of Mediterranean Society*. Chicago, IL: University of Chicago Press.

Peristiany, John G. and Pitt-Rivers, Julian, eds., 1992, *Honor and Grace in Anthropology*. Cambridge: Cambridge University Press.

Petrini, Carlo, 2007, *Slow Food Nation: Why Our Food Should Be Good, Clean, and Fair*. New York, NY: Rizzoli Ex Libris.

Pitt-Rivers, Julian, ed., 1963, *Mediterranean Countrymen: Essays in the Social Anthropology of the Mediterranean*, Paris: Mouton.

Pivato, Stefano, 2000, 'Sport,' in *Italy Since 1945*. Edited by Patrick McCarthy. Oxford: Oxford University Press.

Plato, 1990, *The Iliad*. Translated by Robert Fagles. New York, NY: Viking.

Plesset, Sonja, 2006, *Sheltered Women: Negotiating Gender and Violence in Northern Italy*. Stanford, CA: Stanford University Press.

Podaliri, Carlo, and Balestri, Carlo, 1998, 'The Ultras, Racism, and Football Culture in Italy,' in *Fanatics! Power, Identity, and Fandom in Football*. Edited by Adam Brown. London: Routledge.

Polanyi, Michael, 1974, *Personal Knowledge: Towards a Post-Critical Philosophy*. Chicago, IL: University of Chicago Press.

Poppi, Cesare, 1992, 'Building Difference: The Political Economy of Tradition in the Ladin Carnival of the Val di Fasso,' in *Revitalizing European Rituals*. Edited by Jeremy Boissevain. London: Routledge.

Prempeh, Osei, K., 2006, *Against Global Capitalism: African Social Movements Confront Neoliberal Globalization*. Burlington, VT: Ashgate.

Pronger, Brian, 2002, *Body Fascism: Salvation in the Technology of Physical Fitness*. Toronto: University of Toronto Press.

Putnam, Robert D., 1993. *Making Democracy Work*. Princeton, NJ: University of Princeton Press.

Rapport, Nigel J., 1998, 'Problem-solving and Contradiction: Playing Darts and Becoming Human' in *Self, Agency, and Society*. No. 2 vol. 1.

Rocco, Alfredo, 2000, 'The Political Doctrine of Fascism (1925),' in Jeffrey T. Schnapp, ed. *A Primer of Italian Fascism*. Lincoln, NE: University of Nebraska Press.

Romanucci-Ross, Lola, 1991, *One Hundred Towers: An Italian Odyssey of Cultural Survival*. New York, NY: Bergin and Garvey.

Rose, Nikolas, 1997, 'Assembling the Modern Self' in *Rewriting the Self: Histories from the Renaissance to the Present*. Edited by Roy Porter. London: Routledge.

Roversi, Antonio, 1990, 'Calcio e Violenza in Italia,' in *Calcio e Violenza in Europa*. Edited by Antonio Roversi. Bologna: Il Mulino.

Roversi, Antonio, 1994, 'The Birth of the "Ultras": The Rise of Football Hooliganism in Italy,' in *Game Without Frontiers: Football, Identity, and Modernity*. Edited by Giulianotti and Williams. Aldershot: Arena.

Roversi, Antonio, and Balestri, Carlo, 2002. 'Italian Ultras Today: Change or Decline?' in *Fighting Fans: Football Hooliganism as a World Phenomenon*. Edited by Eric Dunning, Patrick Murphy, Ivan Waddington, and Antonios E. Astrinakis. Dublin: University College Dublin Press.

Roversi, Antonio, 2006, *L'odio in Rete: Siti Ultras, Nazifascisti online.* Bologna: Il Mulino.

Said, Edward, 1993, *Culture and Imperialism.* New York, NY: Alfred Knopf.

Saint Augustine, 1961, *Confessions.* Translated by R.S. Pine-Coffin. New York, NY: Penguin.

Sandvoss, Cornel, 2003, *A Game of Two Halves: Football, Television, and Globalization.* London: Routledge.

Schatz, Edward, 2009, 'Ethnographic Immersion and the Study of Politics,' in *Political Ethnography: What Immersion Contributes to the Study of Power.* Edited by Edward Schatz. Chicago, IL: University of Chicago Press.

Schechner, Richard, 2005, *Performance Theory.* London: Routledge.

Scheper-Hughes, Nancy, and Bourgois, Philippe, 2004, 'Introduction: Making Sense of Violence,' in *Violence in War and Peace: An Anthology.* Edited by Scheper-Hughes and Bourgois. Malden, MA: Blackwell.

Schmitt, Carl, 1976, *The Concept of the Political.* Translated by George Schwab. New Brunswick, NJ: Rutgers University Press.

Schnapp, Jeffrey T, 1998, 'Fascism After Fascism,' in *Fascism's Return: Scandal, Revision, and Ideology Since 1980.* Edited by Richard J. Golsan. Lincoln, NE: University of Nebraska Press.

Schnapp, Jeffrey T, 2000, *A Primer of Italian Fascism.* Edited and Translated by Jeffrey T. Schnapp. Lincoln, NE: University of Nebraska Press.

Schneider, Jane, Ed., 1998, *Italy's 'Southern Question': Orientalism in One Country.* New York, NY: Berg Press.

Sedgwick, Mark, 2004, *Against the Modern World: Traditionalism and the Secret Intellectual History of the Twentieth Century.* Oxford: Oxford University Press.

Silverman, Sydel, 1975, *Three Bells of Civilization: The Life of an Italian Hill Town.* New York, NY: Columbia University Press.

Sniderman, Paul, Peri, Pierangelo, et al, 2000, *The Outsider: Prejudice and Politics in Italy.* Princeton, NJ: Princeton University Press.

Sorel, Georges, 1999, *Reflections on Violence.* Cambridge: Cambridge University Press.

Southgate, Troy, 2010, *Tradition and Revolution: Collected Writings of Troy Southgate.* London: Arktos Media.

Spanos, William V., 1993, *The End of Education: Toward Posthumanism*. Minneapolis, MN: University of Minnesota Press.

Spencer, Jonathon, 2007, *Anthropology, Politics, and the State: Democracy and Violence in South Asia*. Cambridge: Cambridge University Press.

Stefanini, Maurizio, 2009, *Ultras: Identità, Politica, e Violenza nel Tifo Sportivo da Pompei a Raciti e Sandri*. Milan: Boroli Editore.

Sternhell, Zeev, 1994, *The Birth of Fascist Ideology: From Cultural Rebellion to Political Revolution*. Translated by David Maisel. Princeton, NJ: Princeton University Press.

Stone, Dan, 2002, *Breeding Superman: Nietzsche, Race, and Eugenics in Edwardian and Interwar Britain*. Liverpool: University of Liverpool Press.

Strathern, Andrew, and Stewart, Pamela J., 2006, 'Introduction: Terror, the Imagination, and Cosmology,' in *Terror and Violence: Imagination and the Unimaginable*. Edited by Strathern, Stewart, and Whitehead. London: Pluto Press.

Sunic, Tomislav, 2004, *Against Democracy and Equality: The European New Right*. Newport Beach, CA: Noontide Press.

Sunic, Tomislav, 2007, *Homo Americanus: Child of the Postmodern Age*. Self-Published via Booksurge/Amazon. http://www.booksurge.com.

Tarrow, Sidney, 1998, *Power in Movement: Social Movements and Contentious Politics*. Cambridge: Cambridge University Press.

Thornton, Phil, 2003, *Casuals: Football, Fighting, and Fashion — The Story of a Terrace Cult*. Lytham: Milo Books.

Tilly, Charles, 2003, *The Politics of Collective Violence*. Cambridge: Cambridge University Press.

Turner, Victor, 1979, *Dramas, Fields, and Metaphors: Symbolic Action in Human Society*. Ithaca, NY: Cornell University Press.

Turner, Victor, 1982, *From Ritual to Theatre: the Human Seriousness of Play*. New York, NY: PAJ Publications.

Turner, Victor, 1995, *The Ritual Process: Structure and Anti-Structure*. Piscataway, NJ: Aldine Transaction.

Van Boxel, Lise, 2005, 'Contest as Context,' in *Friedrich Nietzsche: Prefaces to Unwritten Works*. Translated and edited by Michael W. Grenke. South Bend, IN: St. Augustine's Press.

Vattimo, Gianni, 2011, 'From Dialogue to Conflict,' in *Telos*, no. 154, Spring 2011, pp. 170–179.

Vincent, Joan, 1990, *Anthropology and Politics: Visions, Traditions, and Trends*. Tucson, AZ: The University of Arizona Press.

Vincent, Joan, 2002, 'Introduction,' in *The Anthropology of Politics: A Reader in Ethnography, Theory, and Critique*. Edited by Joan Vincent. Malden, MA: Blackwell.

Wann, Daniel L, Melnick, Merrill J, Russell, Gordon W, Pease, Dale G, 2001, *Sport Fans: The Psychology and Social Impact of Spectators*. New York, NY: Routledge.

Weaver, Richard, M., 1984, *Ideas Have Consequences*. Chicago, IL: University of Chicago Press.

Weber, Max, 1958, *From Max Weber: Essays in Sociology*. Edited and translated by Gerth and Mills. Oxford: Oxford University Press.

Williams, John, and Giulianotti, Richard, 1994, 'Introduction: Stillborn in the USA?' in *Game Without Frontiers: Football, Identity, and Modernity*. Edited by Richard Giulianotti and John Williams. Aldershot: Arena.

Williams, Richard, 2006, *The Perfect Ten: Football's Dreamers, Schemers, Playmakers, and Playboys*. London: Faber and Faber.

Winner, David, 2000, *Brilliant Orange: The Neurotic Genius of Dutch Football*. London: Bloomsbury.

Wolf, Eric R., 1999, *Envisioning Power: Ideologies of Dominance and Crisis*. Berkley, CA: University of California Press.

Wolin, Richard, 2004, *The Seduction of Unreason: The Intellectual Romance with Fascism from Nietzsche to Postmodernism*. Princeton, NJ: Princeton University Press.

Wynter, Sylvia, 1995, '1492 A New World View' in *Race, Discourse, and the Origin of the Americas: A New World View*. Edited by Hyatt and Nettleford. Washington, WA: : Smithsonian Institution Press.

Wynter, Sylvia, 1997, 'Columbus, The Ocean Blue, and Fables That Stir the Mind: To Reinvent the Study of Letters' in *Poetics of the Americas: Race, Founding, and Textuality*. Edited by Bainard Cowan and Jefferson Humphries. Baton Rouge, LA: Louisiana State University Press.

Young, Allan, 1995, *The Harmony of Illusions: Inventing Post-Traumatic Stress Disorder*. Princeton, NJ: Princeton University Press.

Zamagni, Vera, 2000, 'Evolution of the Economy,' in *Italy Since 1945*. Edited by Patrick McCarthy. Oxford: Oxford University Press.

Zarkia, Cornelia, 1996, '*Philoxenia* Receiving Tourists — but not Guests — on a Greek Island,' in *Coping with Tourists: European Reactions to Mass Tourism*. Edited by Jeremy Boissevain. Providence, RI: Berghahn Books.

Zirakzadeh, Cyrus E., 2009, 'When Nationalists Are Not Separatists: Discarding and Recovering Academic Theories while Doing Fieldwork in the Basque Region of Spain,' in *Political Ethnography: What Immersion Contributes to the Study of Power*. Edited by Edward Schatz. Chicago, IL: University of Chicago Press.

Index

OTHER BOOKS PUBLISHED BY ARKTOS

OTHER BOOKS PUBLISHED BY ARKTOS